"FATS" WALLER AND HIS GREAT BAND

APOLLO 125th ST. NEAR 8½ AV. Continuous 10 A.M. to MIDNITE 20¢ to 55¢

APUS & ESTRELITA • MYRA JOHNSON

CAST OF 40

ONE WEEK ONLY *Beginning* FRIDAY, SEPTEMBER 26th

A New Band with an Old Favorite —
YOU'LL BE SURPRISED AND DELIGHTED —

Lucky MILLINDER and His BAND

with SISTER THARPE

and a Great Revue Cast

COMING SOON - ANOTHER GREAT BAND WHICH IS
HEADING RAPIDLY FOR THE VERY TOP

ANDY KIRK and His BAND

★ WORLD-FAMOUS ★

APOLLO

IN THE HEART OF FRIENDLY HARLEM!

125th St. near 8th Ave. • Tel. RI 9-1800

ONE WEEK ONLY **BEGINS FRI. OCT. 22nd**

The Absolutely Incomparable

PEARL BAILEY

AND HER REVUE FEATURING

BUNNY BRIGGS & MARTIN BROS.

3 PERFORMANCES DAILY | WED NIGHT AMATEURS

Bill Robinson

AND A CAST OF 100
Including the Fast-Stepping Chorus and Lindy Hoppers
in the Sensational Musical Comedy
Based on the GILBERT AND SULLIVAN CLASSIC

HOT MIKADO

Presented 4 Times Daily

IN CONJUNCTION WITH A SPLENDID
TALKING PICTURE PROGRAM

No Increase in Prices

FEBRUARY FESTIVAL OF SHOWS
AT THE

APOLLO

AMERICA'S FINEST COLORED STAGE SHOWS!

125th ST. NEAR 8th AVE. TELEPHONE UNIVERSITY 4 4409

ONE WEEK ONLY Begin. FRIDAY FEB. 14

Ivy ANDERSON Isabel BROWN "PIGMEAT" 4 STEP Bros.

DUKE ELLINGTON

AND HIS FAMOUS ORCHESTRA

HARLEM'S HIGH SPOT

SAT. MIDNITE SHOW

APOLLO

125th ST. near 8th Ave. - Tel. UNiversity 4-4490

WED. NIGHT AMATEURS

ONE WEEK ONLY! Beginning **FRI. DEC. 4th**

YOU WON'T BELIEVE YOUR EYES AS YOU WATCH THE MOST AMAZING, MOST GLAMOROUS, MOST EXCITING DECEPTION IN THE WORLD!!!

25 MEN AND 1 GIRL

JEWEL BOX REVUE

GLAMOROUS GORGEOUS COSTUMES | The MOST UNUSUAL REVUE

APOLLO ONE BIG WEEK BEG. FRI. APRIL 26th

"THANKS FOR SAVING MY LIFE"

BILLY PAUL "ME & MRS. JONES"

MAIN INGREDIENT "DON'T WANT TO BE LONELY"

125th STREET **APOLLO** AMERICA'S SMARTEST COLORED SHOWS!!

THEATRE 125th STREET NEAR 8th AV. TELEPHONE UN 4-4490

1937

ONE WEEK ONLY BEGINNING FRIDAY, APRIL 9th

CLARENCE ROBINSON
Producer of the New
COTTON CLUB REVUE
Presents

CHICK WEBB AND HIS BAND

with the greatest of all Sepia crooners and Swing Singers

ELLA FITZGERALD

AND A FINE SUPPORTING REVUE CAST:

MORTON & MARGO *Favorites* — COOK & BROWN *Eccentric Dancers* — WOLFORD'S PE *Sensational Dog Act*

"PIGMEAT" — JOHN MASON — JIMMIE BASKETTE

WHITE'S LINDYMANIACS — HILDA PERLENO — 16 DANCING DAMSE

also "MIDNIGHT COURT" A STIRRING DRAMA OF CROOKS AND THE

MIDNIGHT SHOW SATURDAY ADDED ACTS Reserved Seats now on Sale	WED. — AMATEUR NIGHT BROADCAST FROM STAGE

— ONE WEEK — BEGINNING FRIDAY, APRIL 16th —

DON REDMAN AND HIS ORCHESTRA with LOUISE McCARROLL	3 BERRY BROS.	CHUCK & CHUCKL

125th STREET **APOLLO** AMERICA'S SMARTEST COLORED SHOWS!!

THEATRE 125th STREET NEAR 8th AV. TELEPHONE UN 4-4490

ONE WEEK ONLY — BEGINNING FRIDAY, JUNE 12th

AMERICA'S FOREMOST AND MOST
DYNAMIC WOMAN ORCHESTRA LEADER!

Blanche CALLOWAY

And Her SENSATIONAL BAND

with RHYTHM WILL VELMA MIDDLETON RED & CURLEE And A Great Leonard Harp Revue Cast of

Three KADETS *Western Dancing Sensations* | PERRY TWINS *Sensational Dancing Fighters*

5 TOP HATS *Singing, Playing Prides of Philadelphia* | ALYCE SERI *The Year's Acrobatic Marvel*

PIGMEAT JOHN MASON JIMMIE BASKETTE And the SIXTEEN LOVELY HARPERETTES

Also The STIRRING ROMANTIC DRAMA **"The First Baby"**

MIDNIGHT SHOW SATURDAY ADDED ACTS RESERVED SEATS	WEDNESDAY AMATEUR NITE BROADCAST FROM STAGE

ONE WEEK ONLY BEGINNING FRI. JUNE 19th **CHICK WEBB** AND HIS N. B. ORCHESTRA

125th **APOLLO** AMERICA'S SMARTEST

THEATRE STREET

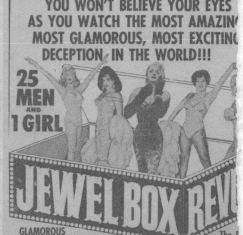

Ain't Nothing Like the Real Thing

Ain't Nothing Like the Real Thing

How the Apollo Theater Shaped American Entertainment

Edited by Richard Carlin and Kinshasha Holman Conwill

NATIONAL MUSEUM OF
AFRICAN AMERICAN HISTORY AND CULTURE
THROUGH SMITHSONIAN BOOKS
WASHINGTON, DC

To John Hope Franklin,

who taught us the

importance of remembering,

and to Percy Ellis Sutton,

whose foresight helped preserve

our cultural institutions

Ain't Nothing Like the Real Thing: How the Apollo Theater Shaped American Entertainment is the companion publication to the exhibition of the same name produced by the National Museum of African American History and Culture in collaboration with the Apollo Theater Foundation.

Published by the National Museum of African American History and Culture through Smithsonian Books.

This book may be purchased for educational, business, or sales promotional use. For information please write:
Special Markets Department
Smithsonian Books
P.O. Box 37012, MRC 513
Washington, DC 20013

Library of Congress Cataloging-in-Publication Data
Ain't nothing like the real thing : how the Apollo Theater shaped American entertainment / [prepared by] Smithsonian Books.
    p. cm.
Includes bibliographical references and index.
ISBN 978-1-58834-269-0 (hardcover)
1. Apollo Theater (New York, N.Y. : 125th Street) 2. African Americans–New York (State)–New York–Music–History and criticism. 3. Popular music–New York (State)–New York–History and criticism.
I. Smithsonian Books (Publisher)

ML3479.A36 2010
792.09747'1–dc22   2009049054

Printed in Canada by Friesens
15 14 13 12 11 10   5 4 3 2 1

Prepared by Smithsonian Books
Director: Carolyn Gleason
Executive Editor: Caroline Newman
Project Editor: Christina Wiginton
Editorial Assistant: Michelle Lecuyer
Editorial Consultant: Marie Brown
Copy Editor: Duke Johns
Captions: Richard Carlin
Timeline author through 1980s: Ted Fox
Timeline author post–1980s: Shirley Taylor and the
    Apollo Theater Foundation, Inc.
Photo Research: Heather Hart and Laura Kreiss
Book Design: Service Station | Dennis Favello

CONTENTS

Ain't Nothing Like the Real Thing: How the Apollo
Theater Shaped American Entertainment is the companion book to the exhibition of
the same name, both produced by the Smithsonian's National Museum of African
American History and Culture in collaboration with the Apollo Theater Foundation on
the occasion of the Apollo's seventy-fifth anniversary.

What makes this theater in Harlem a singular proving ground for performers
like no other? When we set out to answer this question, we called upon a diverse
group of historians, critics, journalists, and experts in dance, comedy, and music who
analyzed and synthesized the impact of this inimitable theater. We also drew on
performers and eyewitnesses who were there.

Given the complexity and nuance of the subject and the variety of narratives
it embodies, we eschewed a strictly linear or encyclopedic approach. Rather, we
chose to focus on and illuminate the stories of pivotal individuals and key moments
that together would reveal a place that is part national and international stage
and part community anchor, and would provide insight into how the Apollo, as
an incubator of reinvention, has remained at the epicenter of American culture for
seven decades.

The writers reveal the Apollo to be both the setting for soaring achievement
and an emblem of unvanquished African American creativity in the face of
enormous challenges. They also provide the reader with an experience akin to that of
the acclaimed theater's highly discerning live audiences, making vivid the Apollo's
compelling allure and abiding influence.

This extraordinary collection of essays and images is thus more than the sum
of its parts. On the one hand it paints a vibrant portrait of one of this country's
premier entertainment stages. On the other hand, much like the Apollo's vintage bills
of top-flight performers of comedy, dance, and especially music, it is a variety show
of world-class essayists. Each writer brings to life the vaunted history, the unparalleled
legacy, the unforgettable moments, and the incomparable performances that continue
to make the Apollo an iconic venue and that have garnered this historic theater its
hard-won world renown—a renown that endures into the twenty-first century.

Kinshasha Holman Conwill
Deputy Director, National Museum of African American History and Culture

Forewords

Chaka Khan performs at the Apollo, 1970s.

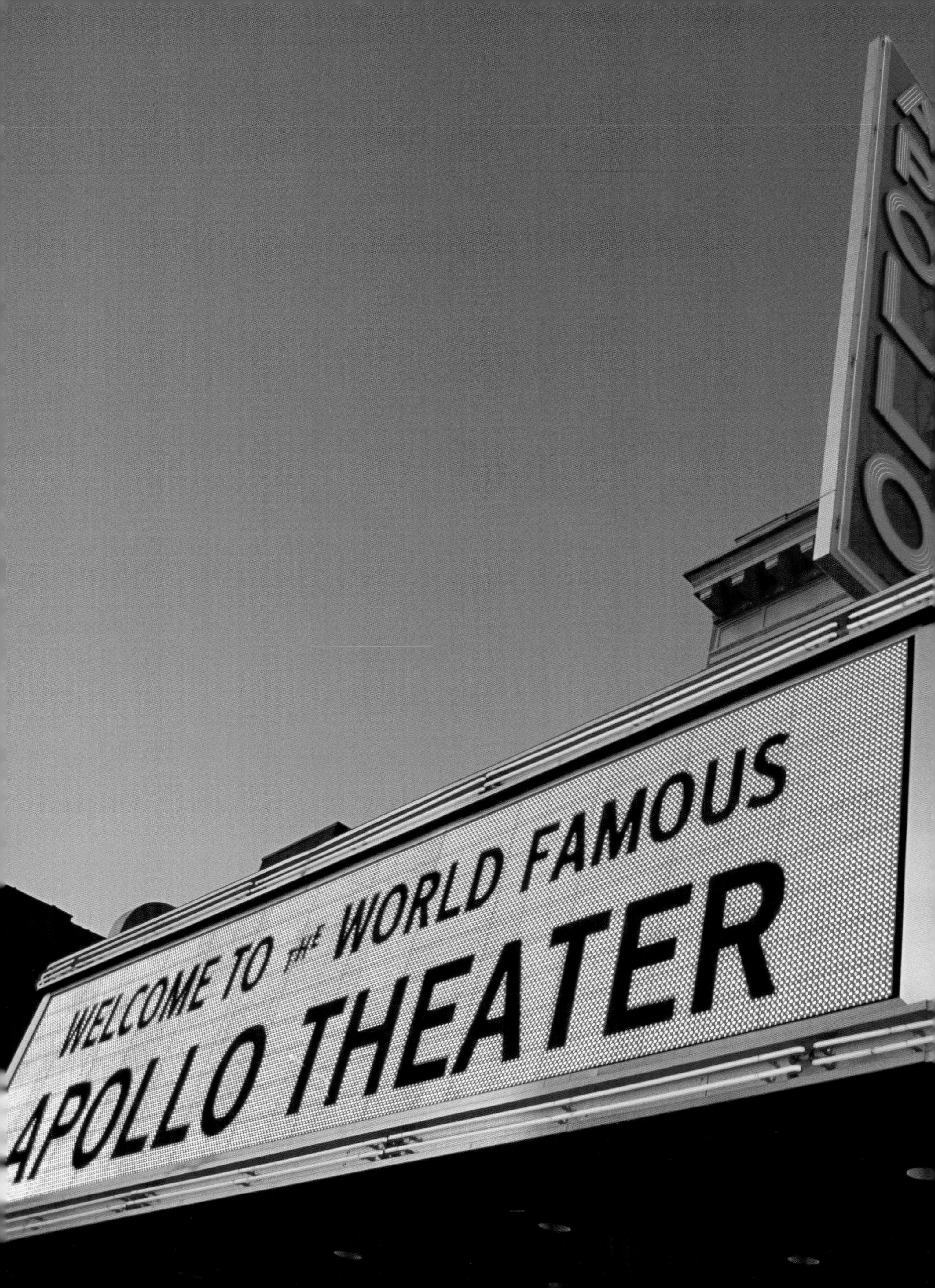
APOLLO
WELCOME TO THE WORLD FAMOUS
APOLLO THEATER

The Apollo Theater is one of America's most enduring

cultural icons. Since 1934 it has been both a source of hope and pride and a symbol of the brilliance of African American artistic achievement. It is the place where so many historic moments and dreams have been realized. The Apollo is where future stars have been discovered and time and again returned to its stage as headliners.

For seventy-five years, the Apollo has served as a theatrical home to artists across genres and generations. Many have referred to the theater as "Apollo University," often citing the close community of stagehands, staff, and performers who have shared their professional knowledge and helped beginners shape their careers, polish their acts, and learn how to engage the Apollo's daunting and uncompromising audience.

The Apollo stands virtually peerless in its tradition of hosting emerging talent as well as established artists. Long before shows such as *American Idol* and *Star Search*, Amateur Night at the Apollo helped to catapult unknown performers to superstardom. That tradition is still going strong today. Every Wednesday evening, audiences participate in determining the outcome of the same kind of show that helped launch the careers of such performers as Ella Fitzgerald, Sarah Vaughan, James Brown, Dionne Warwick, the Jackson Five, and countless others. Just as those stars did, today's contestants rub the famous "Tree of Hope" before facing the Apollo audience—a discerning yet wildly enthusiastic crowd widely known and recognized for its ability to spot talent and discover a rising star.

Over the years, the Apollo has journeyed from milestone to milestone; from memorial services for Apollo legends James Brown and Michael Jackson, to Barack Obama's rally in 2007, to the reunion of Labelle in December 2008 and, most recently, the revival of *Dreamgirls*, a musical that reflects the essence of the Apollo story. There are countless stories to share of cheers and challenges and perseverance and loss, but at its core the legacy of the Apollo is one of triumph. The bright blade of the Apollo hanging high above Harlem's vibrant 125th Street still beckons to all who dare to dream.

In this, our seventy-fifth year, we are honored to partner with the Smithsonian Institution's National Museum of African American History and Culture to present the story of the Apollo Theater. The landmark exhibition, *Ain't Nothing Like the Real Thing: How the Apollo Theater Shaped American Entertainment*, and this accompanying book will bring back treasured memories for some and introduce others to the compelling history of how and why the Apollo Theater has endured and continues to be the place "where stars are born and legends are made."

Richard D. Parsons Chairman, Apollo Theater Foundation, Inc.
Jonelle Procope President and CEO, Apollo Theater Foundation, Inc.

The Apollo:
A Place of Possibility

Lonnie G. Bunch III

I first heard of the Apollo Theater as a teenager at one of the many family barbecues that my parents forced me to attend. At these gatherings, ripe with strangers somehow related by blood, marriage, or "down south" connections, different groups would settle throughout the house and the yard. Often the aunts were in the kitchen, the children in the basement, and the adult men in the back of the house tending the grill and telling stories. For years I wanted to escape the children's quarter and join the men, whose laughter belied secrets that I wanted to understand. Finally, at thirteen, I was allowed to enter their world. I remember hearing them swap stories about the ways of white folks in North Carolina, the women who broke their hearts, or whether life was harder working for the railroad or toiling in the factories in Newark, New Jersey. Soon they told tales about baseball and debated whether or not Jackie Robinson could ever hit Satchel Paige's fastball or whether Willie Mays would hit more home runs than Babe Ruth. And then, during a lull in the conversation that allowed them to catch their breath, Uncle Johnnie began to sing—badly—and someone asked, "What is this, amateur night at the Apollo?"

I had no idea what the Apollo was, but it sure stimulated a lively conversation. One after another, these old men talked about how they were moved by the music that emanated from the Apollo, be it Duke Ellington, Lionel Hampton, Billie Holiday, or Newark's own Sarah Vaughan. They laughed as they shared lines that they had heard from the routines of Moms Mabley, Timmie Rogers, or Pigmeat Markham, lines that were exciting and risqué to a teenager on the verge of adulthood. These comic riffs allowed them to find relief from the realities of race, even if it lasted only as long as the joke being told. Since I had never heard of any of these people, I asked, just what is the Apollo? Someone answered, "It is a place where we got to be who we are and maybe who we want to be." Just when I wanted to hear more, the need to eat trumped the opportunity to remember.

While it took me years to understand the full meaning of the Apollo to those men, I never forgot the joy, enthusiasm, and laughter of that late afternoon conversation. There are many ways to look at the Apollo Theater: as a premier entertainment venue, as a site of cultural authenticity, or as a location that reflected the changing racial dynamic in America's urban centers. Yet, based on that afternoon in the mid-1960s, I have come to view the Apollo as a place of possibility: a place of possibility that reflected and mediated the tensions between aspiration and reality, between those who owned the means of production and accessibility and those who produced the culture, and between cultural innovation and the celebration of tradition.

It was a place of possibility where Amateur Night offered the chance of lasting fame or limited notoriety to anyone with the talent to impress and the courage to face an audience whose candor could produce either cheers or catcalls. Winning at Amateur Night could transform a life in ways that hitting the number or awaiting the intervention of Father Divine could not. Bobby Schiffman, one of the owners of the Apollo, claimed in 1975 that 30 to 40 percent of all "the major black attractions working today" received their start at Apollo's Amateur Night. And the impressive list of those who first triumphed at Amateur Night—such as Sarah Vaughan, Pearl Bailey, Frankie Lymon, King Curtis, and Gladys Knight— spoke volumes about the ability of the Apollo to transform hope into careers. Not everyone who performed there was a success. Many a talented performer failed to excite the audience and found themselves booed or pulled off the stage. Yet, even for those who failed, the opportunity presented was often in stark contrast to the opportunities that waited once one exited the Apollo.

Lines gather in the Apollo Theater lobby, 1965. The murals on the wall depict many of the famous stars who performed at the theater.

Comedians, musicians, dancers, and other performers mixed freely both on- and offstage at the Apollo. Here comic Eddie "Rochester" Anderson poses with comedian Red Skelton and jazz master Duke Ellington, 1943.

The Apollo was a place of possibility because it often revealed glimpses of a better day. Though owned by the Schiffman family through much of its existence, once the doors were closed and the performances began, it was no longer controlled by its white ownership. At a minimum, the black audiences found a respite, an oasis that allowed them to escape the realities of segregation and limited economic opportunities. Yet the Apollo audiences also experienced glimpses of a brave new world where the racial norms of the day were punctured by the beauty of a Billie Holiday song, challenged by the sharp comic wit of Moms Mabley or Dick Gregory, and overcome by the rhythmic movement of dancers like Cholly Atkins and Honi Coles. Once the doors closed, as my relatives claimed, "we got to be who we are and maybe who we want to be."

The other reason why the Apollo was a place of possibility was because of the cultural creativity that was spawned at the theater. The Apollo was a cauldron of innovation and vitality that enabled performers to see their peers (or competitors) at their best. This friendly (or unfriendly) competition encouraged a sense of artistic invention that could only happen at the Apollo. Each act wanted desperately to outdo the earlier act, and yet the acts often shared tips and techniques that made each other better. Gladys Knight recalled that at the Apollo "you can always learn. It was a school." And "Little Anthony" Gourdine remembered that, during the '50s, groups such as the Dells and the Flamingos would always help the younger performers. The Apollo encouraged creativity because of the great diversity of talent that performed on its stage. Singers would learn comic timing from Redd Foxx or Pigmeat Markham, and comedians would learn from Ella Fitzgerald and Sammy Davis Jr. how to command and control the stage.

Part of the importance and luster of the Apollo Theater comes from its place as a beacon of possibility. Yet there were other venues that rose above the chitlin circuit and featured an array of excellent African American performers. In Washington, D.C., talented artists played at the Howard Theatre. In Los Angeles, the Lincoln Theatre along Central Avenue was a West Coast venue that hosted the best black talent. In Newark, Symphony Hall catered to a discerning African American audience. In fact, almost every major U.S. city had sites that hosted wonderfully talented performers and catered to the burgeoning black urban audience. So what set the Apollo Theater apart from so many other important and legitimate venues?

Much of its impact has been tied to its location in New York City. As David Levering Lewis's essay in this volume depicts, for many Harlem became the capital of the black world beginning in the 1920s. Harlem was the emblem and the symbol of many of the changes that America underwent as a result of war, migration, heightened expectations, unfulfilled promises, and a long and continuing struggle for racial justice. The culturally creative period known as the Harlem Renaissance drew many of the most talented artists, writers, and performers from black communities throughout the nation to New York. This led to a large, diverse black community that gave Harlem a unique style and place in American culture. Coupled with the cultural possibilities of the musical and theatrical centers located in Manhattan, the Apollo was able to draw the most innovative and impressive African American talent available. Other essays in this volume build this portrait of the Apollo as a singular place of possibility, where the mix of cultural creativity, the discerning audience, and the power of place combined to create an unparalleled blend of American entertainment.

The complex African American community that called Harlem home was well served by the Apollo Theater. It included those striving for middle-class respectability, working-class migrants, a small but influential elite class, and members that reflected the African diaspora. The Apollo served that varied audience by creating an acceptable middle-class cultural ethos that was firmly grounded in African American culture but that also softened the roughest edges of cultural expression. Thus the musical performers were more polished than hardscrabble; down-home blues rarely had a home at the Apollo. The theater helped to create a venue for cultural expression that pushed for a better future rather than being held captive by the past. The Apollo enhanced the artist in ways that no other venue could.

Ultimately, the Apollo's strength is its imprimatur that identifies cultural excellence. Performing successfully at the Apollo meant that an act was both firmly ground in African American culture and was very, very good. After performing at the Apollo, the credibility of an artist was enhanced in ways that no other venue could. Thus the Apollo is both a beacon of possibility and a site of excellence, creativity, and pride.

Growing Up with the Apollo

Smokey Robinson

Smokey Robinison and the Miracles, ca. 1967. Left to right: Bobby Rogers, Pete Moore, Robinson, and Ronnie White. The Miracles' many major hits included "The Tracks of My Tears" and "You've Really Got a Hold on Me."

I was six or seven years old when I heard about the Apollo for the first time. I had two older sisters, and between my sisters and my mom I got a great dose of music, everything from gospel to classical, to gutbucket blues, to my sisters playing some music they called bebop. The first voice I ever remember hearing in my life was Sarah Vaughan, because my sisters loved Sarah Vaughan and Billy Eckstine. My mother played Louis Armstrong, the Five Blind Boys, and Mantovani. This was my indoctrination to music, and most of these people had played the Apollo Theater.

The Miracles and I were at the Apollo for the first time in 1958 on a Ray Charles show. It was a frightening experience. First of all, I don't think any of us had ever been out of Detroit before, other than going to Ypsilanti or Ann Arbor or somewhere close by in Michigan. But we were on the way to New York City, which in itself was "Ooh, man!" We had heard plenty about the Apollo Theater, and we thought there was this guy there waiting backstage with his hook, and if you weren't good enough, he'd pull you offstage. Not only that, one of my singing idols was the headliner, Ray Charles.

Rehearsals for the show were at the beginning of the week. At seven o'clock in the morning, you had to be at the Apollo. The rehearsals were in the basement. Honi Coles ran the Apollo at that time. Honi and a guy named Cholly Atkins had had a dance team, Coles and Atkins. They were tap dancers in vaudeville, and they were great.

We got to the Apollo that morning. We didn't know from Adam about being on a professional show, so we came there with what you call onionskins—chord sheets of our records. (We had a hit record at the time called "Bad Girl.") The sheets would tell you what the chords were, but we had no arrangements for saxophones or for a big band like the Ray Charles band that would accompany us that week.

Our time came to go over our music with the band, but we only had these onionskins. Honi Coles hit the ceiling: "What do you mean by coming here with these? What are you doing? How dare Berry Gordy send you here?" He was just raising hell because we didn't have arrangements.

For some reason or another, Ray came in that morning. He said, "What's going on, Honi?"

Ray Charles leads his big band, 1966. Charles, who admired the big bands led by Duke Ellington, Count Basie, and Artie Shaw, re-created their sound as part of his '60s R & B shows.

"These kids come in from Detroit, Berry Gordy sent them here, and they don't have arrangements."

Ray said, "That's okay, man. Don't worry about it." I was in awe because I was looking at Ray Charles. He asked, "Any of you kids know how to play your music?"

I stuttered, "Yes, Mr. Charles. I can play it on the piano."

He said, "Come over here and sit down beside me and play it." So I started playing and singing "She's not a bad girl." After I'd sung about one verse of the song, Ray said, "Okay, baby, I got it," and he started playing it. He just started playing it like he knew it already and he had written it, and I'm singing and he's playing.

He said, "Okay, saxophones, write this down. Write that down." "Trumpets, I want you to play…. Write that down." So they wrote that down. "Bass player, play…." He sat there and did all the arrangements for both of our songs that morning.

From that moment on, I could have been in Timbuktu, and if they called me and said, "Okay, Smoke, you got one day off, but we're giving something for Ray Charles in New York, we want you to come," I would have come. Because he was the kind of man who would sit down and do something like that for us, when we were just teenagers.

At that time at the Apollo Theater, you had to work your way down over time to the first floor as a leading artist in order to rate a dressing room. So we were up on the seventh floor, and there were no elevators. There was a guy named William Spayne, who was the backstage manager at the time, and I can still hear him now in my ear: "Okay, half hour." So you got ready and came down all those steps, but we would stay down to watch everybody else and see what they were doing. We wanted to see the professionalism and try to learn what was going to be our craft, because we didn't want it to be the last time. That's why we went home and got ourselves together. The next time we came back to the Apollo, we were ready.

Smokey Robinson (foreground left, in striped shirt) and Bobby Rogers (holding music) rehearse at the Apollo, 1964. In 1958 they played the Apollo in their first professional appearance at a nationally renowned theater.

Preludes

James Brown backstage
at the Apollo, 1966

James Brown Live at the Apollo

Greg Tate

Every show **James** Brown performed at the Apollo
was likely extraordinary in some way; he didn't acquire that "Mr. Dynamite" moniker
by being a wallflower. However, the three shows recorded in 1962, 1967, and 1971
represented a watershed moment for Brown and for black American music. No other
artist is more identified with the Apollo than Brown, and these recordings reveal why.
As his own performances set the bar for stage presentation and excitement in rhythm
and blues, every aspirant who took the stage in the wake of Brown had to shoulder
the burden of audience expectations he'd engendered. To this day, Brown's Apollo
recordings are the template for many performers who hope to hold an audience rapt
for two hours or more.

Throughout his career, Brown was attuned to the mercurial shifts in public
taste and musical innovation that continue to make rhythm and blues the seedbed
of American pop radicalism. When Brown was a fledgling organ and piano player
in 1930s Depression-era Georgia, he spent hours trying to cop boogie-woogie
licks and swing standards such as Count Basie's "Three O'Clock Jump" (he felt he
never developed the technique to play it). In the '40s he became enthralled by Louis
Jordan's music, especially "Caldonia"—a song whose rollicking big band blues
and outrageous lyrics may have later inspired Brown's own fearless way with jazz
quotation and the King's English. Brown was also a devotee of gospel music, and
before his plunge into the sinful world of '50s R & B was known to be a melodious
and charismatic church singer well-respected in the Toccoa, Georgia, area where
he came to reside after being released from juvenile prison at age nineteen.

It's no surprise that Brown's first hit, 1956's "Please, Please, Please,"
was a torch ballad rather than an up-tempo, juke joint number. From singing gospel
in his local church, Brown had learned how to milk a single line until the church
members said "Amen." Perhaps only an artist who'd already learned to respect the
hypnotic power of repetition would have heard a pop hit in a song that repeated
one word seventeen times as verse and chorus. By the time Brown and his band, the
Famous Flames, brought the song into Cincinnati's King Records studio, they knew
well its frenzying impact on R & B audiences. A radio station demo of the song had

James Brown works the microphone on the Apollo stage, 1968. Brown's electrifying stage shows were major draws at the theater from the late '50s through the early '70s.

brought the tune to the attention of King's A & R honcho, Ralph Bass. King's owner was the race-record industry magnate Syd Nathan, a fireplug of a cantankerous entrepreneur whom Brown remembered as a squat, stogie-puffing "Edward G. Robinson type." Brown was to find his business acumen frequently undermined by Nathan's lack of musical taste and vision. When Nathan heard Brown and his band rehearsing "Please" in his studio, he flew into a rage, fired Bass on the spot, and shut the session down. Nathan not only objected to the song's incessant pleading—as its only reason for being—but even the tune's chord changes, which Nathan's own house arranger had convinced him were "wrong" and too dissonant for the marketplace. After some cajoling and conniving by various parties, the "Please" session resumed— though Brown left the studio wondering whether the song would ever be translated from tape to vinyl. In fact he would not know until weeks later, when it begin to ascend the national charts and became his first million-selling single.

ONE

"Please" established what would become a tradition

in Brown's career of achieving his greatest success by flaunting orthodoxy, pushing against the grain, and liberating his own avant-garde instincts as a composer, arranger, bandleader, and businessman. It was his combination of artistic and entrepreneurial savvy that compelled him to record his first live album at the Apollo in 1962. As had occurred five years earlier, Nathan thought the idea was among the dumbest he'd ever heard. Brown disagreed; certain that a live Apollo album would provide the jolt his career needed, he put up the money himself for a week's worth of

Brown at his 1962 Apollo performance, when he recorded *Live at the Apollo,* a groundbreaking album that introduced a dynamic new sound to American music.

recording at the venue at the not inconsiderable cost (for the time) of $5,700—a sum roughly equivalent to about $70,000 in today's money.

The show Brown brought into the Apollo contained many of the stagy conceits that were to become his staples: the ringmaster introductions, the knee drops, the royal adorning of his cape by the Famous Flames, the shivering walk offstage, and the quickstepping, fervent return to form, action, and hysterical applause. The repertoire contained a few other chestnuts: "Please" among them, but also his minor then-current hit "Try Me," which would remain a staple of his shows well into the '60s. It also contained Brown's rendition of tenor saxophonist Jimmy Forrest's 1952 soul-jazz hit "Night Train."

By this time, Brown was already performing nearly 300 nights a year; Apollo audiences heard the fruits of those Herculean road show labors. Brown's schedule had certainly prepared him to perform a weeklong engagement with the then-requisite six shows a day. (By the mid-'60s, he would be among the first to have that chain-gang, galley-slave labor stipulation struck from his Apollo contracts.) The band Brown brought to the Apollo in 1962 was as stupefyingly tight as any he would helm in his fifty-plus years in show business. On the album, the horns stab, blast, and blurt with the precision their legendary reputation for tightness would be built on, while the rhythm section follows Brown's cues for manic stop-time breaks and restarts to the absolute letter, though with an edgy spontaneity and velocity that belies the number of times they'd rehearsed and performed the show under his whiplash guidance in the months leading up to the gig. You can hear in utero the concatenation of elements from cool jazz, gospel, and mambo that would see him in only a few short years create a wholly new genre of music—funk— prefigured in the release of 1965's "Papa's Got a Brand New Bag" and fully formed and thrust upon an unsuspecting world by 1967's "Cold Sweat." An unprecedented level of influence, acclaim, and number-one chart hits followed in the wake of Brown's alchemical funk invention.

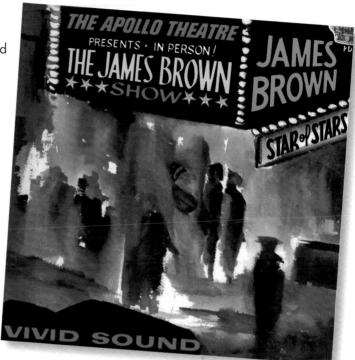

The legendary first *Live at the Apollo* album, released in 1963. Brown bankrolled the taping of his October 24, 1962, show after his record label declined. The album successfully captured the fever-pitch interplay between Brown, his band, and his audience.

What's also indisputable—even before Brown had created the repertoire that would ensure his ability to secure lucrative gigs well into his seventh decade— is his ability to control his audience's emotional pitch at American entertainment's most demanding venue with as much confidence as he controlled his fast-moving neck, torso, and feet when he danced. Some of the screams the crowd's female members unleashed on the 1962 recording are so intense you can't help believing they could only be followed by fainting spells, oxygen masks, and stretchers. Those who encounter the 1962 Apollo recording not knowing this moment in Brown's career will likely be surprised by how slow and mid-tempo-heavy the set is, but Brown's major male competitors at the time—Sam Cooke and Jackie Wilson especially— were all masters of the torch song, and doo-wop's secular take on gospel group harmony was still the dominant sound in R & B.

We now know that the 1962 moment set on the precipice of Motown's rise as well as the music soon to be loosed upon the world by Brown's fellow southern soul brethren and sistren—notably Joe Tex, Otis Redding, Rufus and Carla Thomas, and Wilson Pickett—from studios based in Memphis, Macon, Georgia, and Muscle

Shoals, Alabama. Because of the way Motown and southern soul came to dominate and define '60s R & B, few singers of Brown's '50s generation would even make the transition (and the upgrades) that surviving the '60s would require. Only Brown would see his music being as relevant to the sound and staging of modern pop music in the '80s, '90s, and into the twenty-first century as it was in the '60s.

What Brown's first Apollo recording makes clear is that he was already working in his own creative and self-produced realm outside the trendy dictates of major labels, studio arrangers, and blander, more cosmetic notions of teenybopper sex appeal. It signals that he had devised his own sui generis ways of connecting to his people and of subverting, assimilating, and overcoming the threat of any competing style that would come down the pike to confront him: from Motown to Beatlemania to disco to punk rock to hip-hop. His loyalty to the Apollo and its audiences, however, would even extend to his booking a week's worth of shows in the 1,500-seat room well into the late '70s, when he was quite capable of landing sellout headliner gigs at Madison Square Garden and drawing more than twice as many folk.

TWO

The James Brown who recorded the engagement

resulting in his *Live at the Apollo Volume II* album five years later in 1967 was no longer struggling to maintain a toehold in the kaleidoscopic, fast-changing world of '60s rhythm and blues and pop. Despite all the organized rivalry coming from all sides of the pop spectrum, he was more than holding his own as a one-man entertainment and musical innovator. Between 1965 and 1967 came the release of some of his most enduring and definitive hits—"It's a Man's Man's Man's World," "Papa's Got a Brand New Bag," and 1967's "Cold Sweat," a song that elevated funk into an actual genre and not just as a desirable musical attribute. 1967's James Brown had also begun to process the daily seismic events of the 1960s—the March on Washington, the assassination of JFK, the escalation of the Vietnam War, the murders of Medgar Evers and Malcolm X, the death of John Coltrane, and the Watts Riots. Thanks to Martin Luther King and the civil rights movement, President Lyndon Baines Johnson had been arm-wrestled into signing the 1964 Civil Rights Act and the 1965 Voting Rights Act—the most revolutionary pieces of legislation to become American law since the Depression and the most significant to deal with America's antidemocratic race pathologies since Reconstruction 100 years before. By 1967 Brown had also made appearances at benefits for Dr. King and the NAACP, taking himself off the road to do so. He had released his first official song of social relevance—1966's "Don't Be a Drop-Out"—and flown to the White House in his private Lear Jet to discuss government education initiatives with LBJ.

Brown during his 1968 Apollo show. He was admired for his ability to move smoothly from full-scale funk to soulful ballads within seconds.

Brown in the early '70s, wearing a jumpsuit emblazoned with "GFOS" (Godfather of Soul). His stage costumes reflected the funky chic of such groups as Sly and the Family Stone.

The string of freak incidents, accidents, and acts of self-immolation that would gradually decimate so many of Brown's fellow male soul singers had already begun mowing down quite a few by 1967: Sam Cooke and Otis Redding most notably, with Frankie Lyman and Brown's vocal idol, Little Willie John, soon to follow. The Temptations' David Ruffin was headed into the tailspin that would soon get him booted from the group, and in less than a decade Jackie Wilson would suffer a heart attack onstage that would lead to a coma and his eventual death. Jimi Hendrix and Sly Stone, the only two who transformed the sound of popular music as masterfully as Brown, had only begun to make noise in rock, pop, and R & B. Yet their own careers would come crashing down—Jimi's in 1970 with his death by asphyxiation, Sly's by his coke-addled determination to slide into oblivion somewhere around 1973.

That Brown would have another four decades of relevancy awaiting him in 1967 can be attributed to the fact that, as the rest of world was coming apart at the seams, he was building an empire brick by brick. His comrades, older and younger, were succumbing to the varied temptations of the age and becoming victims of all sorts of dependencies, despondency, and waste, turning high castles into sand. Brown, by contrast, who remained self-managed and self-controlled, was becoming an American entertainment institution—one who became instrumental to the development of every paradigmatic musical style that followed after him: funk, fusion, disco, reggae, Afrobeat, house, punk, new wave, hip-hop, grunge, crunk, reggaeton, you just about name it, buddy.

Brown's smash hit "Sex Machine" inspired these three jumpsuits, sported by him and his backup musicians while touring in the '70s.

The road-tested band Brown brought to the Apollo this time around is for many knowledgeable Brown devotees his best ever. This disciplined ensemble features the musical direction and horn arranging of Pee Wee Ellis, the double drum team of Clyde Stubblefield (inventor of the "Funky Drummer" shuffle that would launch a zillion hip-hop hits) and John "Jabo" Starks, saxophonist Maceo Parker, and guitarist Bobby Bennett.

A female violinist was also present to add sweetening, and unseen on the album version but quite present at the show were the tightly clad James Brown dancers. The audible and voluble changes in Brown's music since the 1962 show are nothing short of remarkable. At a time when everyone else's R & B music was becoming more orchestrated, studio-enhanced, and psychedelic, Brown's music, already pared to the bone, was stripping back even more, cutting away everything that didn't serve the purpose of percussive propulsion and polyrhythmic combustion.

While the hyperkinetic and indefatigable James Brown show made a point of requiring the stamina of two very funky drummers, the James Brown sound of 1967 had remade every musical element into a drum or percussive instrument. Every instrument had to pop and percolate and unlike 1962, when ballads were still the bailiwick of the show, the tempos of '67, befitting the explosive and incendiary times, had climbed higher than ever before, matching for fervor and intensity those favored by traveling evangelical tent preachers. The funk and black rock bands that would enter the chitlin circuit frame in the early '70s, such as Funkadelic, Rufus, Mandrill, and Earth, Wind & Fire can almost be seen on the sidelines furiously taking notes.

Because he camel-walked his way into Vegas by 1966 and because Ray Charles had made Broadway show tunes cool for soul treatment, Brown took to sprinkling jazz and Vegas fare into his sets, too. So *Apollo Volume II* opens with a gem plucked out of Sinatra's set list, "That's Life," then segues to a rocking blues guitar version of Lieber and Stoller's "Kansas City." When Brown returned from his first costume change (which occurred after "Kansas City"—Bobby Byrd reprised Arthur Conley's "Sweet Soul Music" to fill the gap), he launched into a 19:12 version of "It's a Man's, Man's, Man's World"—a rendition in which you can hear Brown tease and prod his audience with a series of come-ons, grunts, and screams that elicit near-pornographic responses from the ladies in the house—after which he let the band swing out with Ellington man Juan Tizol's "Caravan."

What's striking is that the show isn't even at the halfway point, and Brown has already churned up so much energy that even a listener forty years removed from the moment is left breathless and exhausted. (Maybe he was a little too, since his two up-tempo hits of the season, "Money Won't Change You" and "Out of Sight," are both dispensed with in under forty-three seconds.) The shape of all things to come, however, is firmly revealed in the twenty-two-minute jam-medley of "There Comes a Time" / "I Feel All Right" / "Cold Sweat," as the band and Brown lay in the one-chord groove and ad-lib with the flavor and ferocity that will establish the principle of how to properly juice a groove for all the JB disciples who will follow: from Stevie Wonder to George Clinton to Bob Marley to Prince to Fela Kuti. By this time even "Please, Please, Please" has been given a triple-time makeover that has that warhorse sound as if Brown is doing his own protopunk rock remix. By the time of the gig that produced *Live at the Apollo Volume II*, Brown had appeared on the Apollo stage over 200 times.

THREE

Recorded in 1971, the third of the Apollo albums

doesn't even mention that it is a live recording on the cover. It is instead called *Revolution of the Mind* and possesses the most memorable and artistic album cover photograph Brown would ever sit for. On it, Soul Brother Number One is pictured behind bars, in a stylish denim jacket and pants ensemble, sporting the craggy outcrop of a mountainous Afro. At this moment in American history, Brown had become as much a political figure in the African American community as a musical one. He had taken his band to perform for troops in Vietnam; he had met at the

White House with Johnson and Nixon; he had quelled unrest in Boston the night after Martin Luther King's assassination; he had powwowed with H. Rap Brown and other members of the Black Panther Party over their philosophical differences (perhaps best described as "Burn, Baby, Burn" vs. "Learn, Baby, Learn"). He had also against all logic once again concocted a Top 10 hit out of a song that completely broke the mold—musically and politically—with 1969's "Say It Loud, I'm Black and I'm Proud," a venture and act of courage to which he later came to attribute his troubles with the Panthers, the IRS, and the FBI.

At the same time Brown also expanded his media entrepreneurship from music publishing and indie record labels to ownership of two radio stations and, within a year, his own nationally syndicated TV dance show, *Future Shock,* modeled after Don Cornelius's *Soul Train.* (There were also food chain enterprises in the works, and why not?) When he had signed with the huge international music conglomerate Polygram the year before, it was for one of the largest signing bonuses in industry history. Other highlights of the period included the first of many tours to Africa, where Brown would discover he was already a cultural idol on that continent, too.

However, between his 1967 and 1971 Apollo appearances, Brown had lost arguably his two best bands. In 1970 the band heard on *Volume II* mutinied over money issues while on tour in Florida and threatened not to perform the next night in Georgia. Nonplussed, Brown let his grizzled and disgruntled veterans walk off the job, promptly asking Bobby Byrd to send him his protégé band from Cincinnati led by a young phenom of a bassist by the name of Bootsy Collins, who would become a key element in the mid-'70s mega-stadium success of Parliament-Funkadelic. This supercharged unit would, in less than a year, inspire a rejuvenated Brown to create

Brown was one of the few rock or R & B stars to entertain troops in Vietnam at the height of the conflict. Despite the unpopularity of the war, he felt strongly about supporting the soldiers.

Brown with Bootsy Collins on bass and Bobby Byrd at microphone, 1971. Although this version of Brown's band, the Original J.B.s, only lasted from 1970 to 1971, it was among the most celebrated of his long career.

a whole new slew of generationally ripe, ready, and innovative hits—"Sex Machine," "Super Bad," "Give It Up or Turn It Loose," "Talkin' Loud and Sayin' Nothing," "Get Up, Get into It, Get Involved," and "Soul Power." The Bootsy-driven version of the James Brown band can be heard on the first album Brown release on Polydor, *Love Power Peace,* recorded live at Paris's Olympia music hall.

Brown and Bootsy's crew came to a mutually agreed upon separation within a year, and Brown re-formed his band with veterans St. Clair Pinckney, Jabo Starks, and Clyde Stubblefield under the leadership of trombonist Fred Wesley. That group, soon to be known as the JBs, would serve to help Brown quickly bring to the fore yet another set of new Brown '70s classics, notably "Hot Pants," "Escape-ism," Bobby Byrd's "I Know You Got Soul," and, just a wee bit later, "The Payback." Between 1971 and 1972 Brown produced ten Top 10 singles in a row. The historic, inspirational moment as well as the collective joie de vivre of the day is represented in the magnanimous and, yes, *intentionally* hilarious, goofy style on *Revolution of the Mind.*

It isn't the tightest of the James Brown bands (though tight enough), nor the most innovative—even though it would account for easily half of the most sampled Brown records in hip-hop—but *Revolution* offers us Brown's most congenial and easygoing group—one perfectly aligned with its gregarious and good-natured music director, Fred Wesley. The band introduction segment on the album has on its own become a cherished feature to Brown aficionados—especially the bit where Brown chides Wesley for being from "L.A.," until Wesley reveals that stands for "Lower Alabama." Brown then suggests Wesley may have once visited the City of Angels on a Greyhound bus and come back on a "stray dog." And even though he doesn't do "Say It Loud," Brown's lyrics and ad-libs on the album are also the most politically charged of his career—as when he makes a distinction between "The Man" down south, whose intentions toward black folk Brown claims are transparent, as opposed to "The Man" up north, whose designs Brown finds to be more devious and obfuscated.

CODA

James Brown's last appearance on the Apollo

stage was not live. It was for his own wake. That event, three days after his death on Christmas Day 2006, found his body resting in state after being driven there in his coffin in a gold and glass horse-driven carriage, operated by drivers in tails and top hats. And it was there on the stage that he claimed as his own after nearly six decades of working there that Harlemites and others got to say their last good-byes to the Godfather of Soul. An estimated 8,000 fans gathered to attempt to view his body from early morning until late evening, braving the biting December cold for six hours or more, this writer among them.

The Godfather of Soul, Finally at Rest

Herb Boyd

Mourners wait in line to pay
their respects to James Brown.
Thousands filed past the gold-plated
coffin while Brown's landmark
Live at the Apollo album played
through loudspeakers.

REST IN PEACE APOLLO LEGEND
THE GODFATHER OF SOUL
JAMES BROWN
1933 - 2006

Hours before the doors of the Apollo Theater opened

Thursday afternoon, December 28, 2006, a line stretched down 125th Street and around the corner. Word that the Godfather of Soul would lie in state on the world-famous stage drew as many fans as one of his unforgettable live performances. Many of those in line were part of the procession through the streets of Harlem, where his coffin in a white carriage was drawn by two white horses. For a moment the procession resembled the customary "second line" segment of a New Orleans funeral, with boom boxes blasting "Say It Loud, I'm Black and I'm Proud."

When at last the throng was allowed to file into the lobby, the crowd was as diverse as it was eager to pay their final respects and to see "the hardest working man in show business," peacefully at rest. Dignitaries mingled with ordinary folks, each with his or her special memory of the dynamic entertainer. Maple Jalil, a Harlem resident, said: "My sisters and I were at the Apollo when he first came here, and we stayed for show after show and got in a lot of trouble when we got home."

Among those waiting to walk across the stage where Rev. Al Sharpton stood like a sentinel near the gold coffin was Rev. Herbert Daughtry, pastor of the

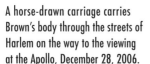

A horse-drawn carriage carries Brown's body through the streets of Harlem on the way to the viewing at the Apollo, December 28, 2006.

House of the Lord Church in Brooklyn. "We were homeboys, we came right off the red clay of Augusta, Georgia," the minister recalled. "We shined shoes together. My father started his church, the House of Prayer, at Perry and Tenth Street; I am the fourth generation of ministers in our family. Years later Ninth Street and Campbell Avenue would be named after JB."

Rev. Daughtry continued: "JB brought to the world stage the energy, the rhythm and soul. Soul means the ability to survive the worst kind of cruelty, it means compassion and reaching out and touching, and JB touched people throughout the world."

Bracketed by large floral wreaths and underneath a brightly lit Apollo sign, James Brown lay in repose, his white gloves and white shoes embellishing a dark lavender suit that seemed almost iridescent, especially in the glow of the flashing cameras from passersby. "It's hard to believe that he won't get up and glide across the stage," said one spectator, who remembered standing in frigid weather for hours to see him perform. "There was simply nothing comparable to James Brown at the Apollo, absolutely nothing."

No, "Mr. Excitement" was not about to ease out of the coffin, as Screamin' Jay Hawkins had done many times during his routine on this stage. But his most devoted fans had enough memories to sustain them, enough of his own screams and patented moves to keep his legacy forever new.

After viewing Brown's body, Clarence Parker, an international talent scout and a protégé of Ralph Cooper, the founder and emcee of Amateur Night, recounted those halcyon days: "Mr. Cooper and I organized at least fifty amateurs for Amateur night. When James Brown competed in Amateur Night, he won first prize five times, singing 'Please, Please, Please.'"

The potency of the Godfather's musical legacy shows no signs of ever diminishing, as long as there are musicians such as trumpeter Joe Dupars, who performed with Brown from 1964 to 1970, when such top hits as "I Feel Good" and "Papa's Got a Brand New Bag" were recorded. "I remember when he wrote 'Say It Loud, I'm Black and I'm Proud,'" Dupars reflected before mounting the stage to say farewell to his mentor. "A stagehand was hurrying the band on the stage, and JB came out saying 'We're hurrying, man,' so the stagehand said, 'All you black, you know what,' and JB said, 'I may be black, but I'm proud.' I love JB and I'll miss him."

So will Billy Mitchell. "I used to run errands and do chores for him," said Mitchell, affectionately known as "Mr. Apollo" because of his long association with the theater. "He was always very grateful, and most memorable for me was the generous tips. Yes, he was one of a kind, and I'm sure his kindness extended well beyond what he meant to me."

Brown lies in state on the Apollo stage. Brown's body was on view from 1 to 8 p.m. on December 28, 2006. Rev. Al Sharpton, a longtime friend of Brown's, led the mourners.

1

Black Metropolis: New York City's Harlem, 1914 to 1934

ca. 1914

Lincoln and Crescent Theatres begin presenting black entertainment to black audiences.

Hurtig and Seamon's **Burlesque**, owned by Sidney Cohen, operates at the future Apollo's location until 1933. Hurtig presents white singers and light entertainment at the theater.

1922

Frank Schiffman and Leo Brecher take over the Harlem Opera House. They already control the Lincoln and other Harlem theaters.

1925

May

Schiffman and Brecher take over the **Lafayette Theatre**; begin presenting black entertainment to black audiences.

1933

Mayor LaGuardia's campaign against burlesque closes many theaters, including Hurtig and Seamon's.

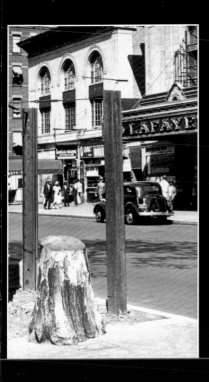

1934

Tree of Hope is cut down from in front of the Lafayette Theatre.

April
Ralph Cooper starts the original Harlem Amateur Hour at Schiffman's Lafayette Theatre.

January 26
Hurtig and Seamon's Theatre reopens as the **125th Street Apollo Theatre**. Owned by Sidney Cohen and managed by Morris Sussman. Opening show is called *Jazz a la Carte* and is headlined by Benny Carter and His Orchestra.

Early 1934
Ralph Cooper begins Wednesday Amateur Night at Cohen and Sussman's Apollo; regular radio broadcasts of the show begin shortly thereafter.

June 9
Schiffman and Brecher move operations to the Harlem Opera House and close the Lafayette.

November 21
Ella Fitzgerald is discovered at Schiffman's Harlem Opera House Amateur Night, the same week as Pearl Bailey is discovered at the Apollo's Wednesday Amateur Night.

City of Refuge

Early Harlem

David Levering Lewis

In 1905 the *New York Herald* announced the beginning of the end of white Harlem. "An untoward circumstance has been injected into the private dwelling market in the vicinity of 133rd and 134th streets," the paper noted in its edition for Christmas Eve. At 31 West 133rd Street, tenants were leaving: there had been a murder in one of the apartments.

Philip A. Payton Jr. (left), a real estate entrepreneur, lived in a fine Harlem home with his wife (right). As vice president of the Afro-American Realty Company, Payton exemplified the accomplishments of the educated, cultured "New Negro."

The apartment house manager's problems could hardly have come at a worse time. The Lenox Avenue subway was a year old, but it had failed to improve the housing market north of Central Park as expected, because of the 1904–5 depression. Desperate, the manager agreed to meet with Philip A. Payton Jr., a high-rolling young African American realtor who had been on the alert for just such an opportunity. Payton filled the 133rd Street building with reliable tenants of his own race who were happy to pay a five-dollar premium per apartment. (Fifteen years before, Jacob Riis, the photographer and journalist of the down-and-outs, had discovered that landlords frequently preferred African Americans as cleaner, more stable tenants than "lower grades of foreign white people"— and, Riis added, because they could charge the African Americans much more.)

Hundreds, then thousands, of clean, stable, high-rent-paying families poured into the new corridor extending through the mid-130s between Fifth and Seventh avenues, despite the furious opposition of the white Property Owners' Protective Association of Harlem. Unfortunately for them, the property owners were divided. Most resident owners deplored the incursion, while many nonresident owners found the lure of higher rents so attractive that they encouraged their tenants to move out.

The richest African American businessman in New York, undertaker James C. Thomas, stood behind Payton's company. When the Pennsylvania Railroad bought Thomas's property at 493 Seventh Avenue for $103,000 in cash, Payton guided Thomas into Harlem real estate speculation. Over the next fifteen years, the former waiter and the mortician invested a quarter of a million dollars in Harlem apartment buildings at prices that usually assuaged the bitterness of panicky white property owners. When Thomas died in 1922, his fortune had greatly increased. Unfortunately, Phil Payton spent money faster than he made it. "It is all gone," he told a friend a few days after a dazzling deal. Payton's company folded in 1908, but the new firm of Nail and Parker stepped into the breach. By 1920 African American expansion in Harlem no longer depended entirely upon sharp realtors and their mulatto and white front men.

Harlem was by no means all black by the early 1920s, however, and much of the 125th Street area would hold out until the end of the decade. No one knew just how many African Americans there were in New York. An Urban League study cited 1923 federal census estimates of 183,428 for the entire city. A more likely figure of 300,000 was provided by the Information Bureau of the United Hospital Fund. Whatever the exact number, most—perhaps two-thirds of them—were in Harlem, but they still represented no more than 30 percent of the total Harlem population. Whites evacuated Harlem as reluctantly as African Americans flocked to it. Slicing almost the full length of the district, Eighth Avenue cleanly severed black from white. From Eighth to the Hudson River, few African Americans were to be found. East of Eighth to the

Girls jump rope in front of a Harlem tenement on 133rd Street, 1939. By this time, approximately 200,000 African Americans had settled in the area.

Harlem River, from 130th to 145th streets, lay black Harlem, the largest, most exciting urban community in Afro-America—or anywhere else, for that matter.

Harlem had seemed to flash into being like a nova. The First World War ended, and there it was, with its amalgam of money and misery, values and vices, hope and futility. The development of black Harlem was, nevertheless, not really so swift and unheralded as it seemed. Its existence had been anticipated by the faithful of Manhattan, the sixty-odd thousand African Americans who lived in midtown's vastly overcrowded Tenderloin and San Juan Hill districts. The Tenderloin, stretching roughly from West Twentieth to Fifty-third streets in Manhattan, had first become the city's home for nonwhites during the early nineteenth century. By the 1890s African Americans had pushed above Fifty-third Street into the congested area of San Juan Hill, where they fought the Irish for a portion of that pitiable turf.

The thousands of new New Yorkers from Georgia, the Carolinas, Virginia, and elsewhere gave the area a decidedly southern overlay. Of Manhattan's 60,534 African Americans in 1910, only 14,300 had been born in New York. Problems of overcrowding, assimilation, and friction within the group and with the Irish racked the Tenderloin (a bloody riot in 1900 had been one result), but on the positive side was the *New York Age* reminder that "the great influx of African Americans into New York City from all parts of the South made…possible a great number and variety of business enterprises." Just as the Lower East Side Jews had accumulated money through hard work and group unity and had then stampeded to Lower Harlem in the 1890s, African American families in mid-Manhattan with a prayer of meeting Payton's rents signed up with the Afro-American Realty Company.

For two varieties of African American enterprises— churches and cabarets—money was especially abundant. St. Philip's Episcopal Church disposed of its Tenderloin property on West Twenty-fifth Street for $140,000 in 1909 and liquidated its cemetery two years later for $450,000. Unable to buy a white church in Harlem, the congregation hired African American architect Vertner Tandy and erected an admirably restrained early Gothic building on West 134th Street. St. Philip's also astounded the New York real estate market by purchasing $640,000 worth of apartment buildings, one of the largest exclusively African American transactions of the era. An African Methodist Episcopal congregation followed three years later, purchasing the Church of the Redeemer through a ruse and renaming it "Mother Zion." The Mighty Abyssinian Baptist Church, founded shortly after the turn of the century along with St. Philip's, also sold its holdings for a fortune and migrated to

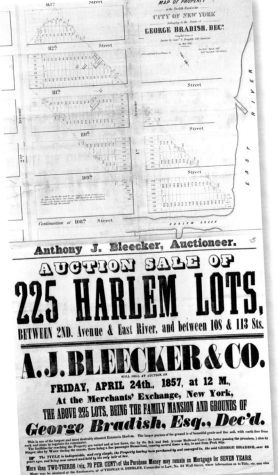

This mid-nineteenth-century auction notice for East Harlem lots was an early sign of development coming to the area. The Bleecker family were prominent landowners and real estate brokers for whom Greenwich Village's Bleecker Street is named.

Harlem, as did the 100-year-old Bethel African Methodist Church. Little Salem Methodist, a basement operation organized in 1902 by the Reverend Frederick Asbury Cullen, Countee Cullen's adoptive father, began in Harlem, quickly enriched itself, and expanded into grander quarters.

Of the several cabarets in the Tenderloin destined to play a notorious Harlem role, three—Banks's, Barren's, and Edmond's—were particularly outstanding. Banks's Club was raunchy, boozy, ragtimey honky-tonk, slightly dangerous, and too raw for successful musicians and Tenderloin dignitaries but beloved of the masses. Barren's Little Savoy was high-toned, racially integrated, a place where James P. Johnson, "Jelly Roll" Morton, Willie "the Lion" Smith, or even occasionally Scott Joplin came to dazzle patrons. Edmond's (officially the Douglass Club) was run by an ex-prizefighter named Edmond Johnson, whose one-legged pianist, Willie Joseph, was a midtown institution. Banks's, Barren's, and Edmond's decamped for Harlem well before the country went to war. Barren Wilkins's brother Leroy also moved to Harlem and went into the cabaret business.

The board of directors of the Afro-American Realty Company, organized in 1892. Philip Payton Jr. is seated fourth from left. He spent money faster than he made it, and his company closed in 1908. Other entrepreneurs, however, quickly rose to fill the void.

Farther uptown, along Fifty-third Street, was Jimmie Marshall's hotel (127–129 West Fifty-third). Here was the heart of what was called "Black Bohemia," the artistic cradle of the future, the nursery of talent and tradition without which the muses of Harlem would have had to study much harder. As blighted as the Tenderloin unquestionably was, there was at least this one block, plus a row or two of dwellings nearby, whose elegance and excitement dimmed from view and banished from memory the hovels, prostitutes, gin-soaked derelicts, and tubercular children. "It was an alluring world, a tempting world," James Weldon Johnson recalled. Marshall's was two large brownstones, gas-lit, red-plushy overfurnished in the style of the day. It was an elegant boarding house, with just a touch of refined bordello, where regulars Rosamond and James Weldon Johnson whiled away late evenings with the likes of Harry T. Burleigh, "Diamond Jim" Brady, Bob Cole, Will Marion Cook, and Paul Laurence Dunbar. Jim Europe was a Marshall's fixture, and singers, musicians, vaudeville stars, and theater entrepreneurs such as Lillian Russell, Noble Sissle, Bert Williams, George Walker and his wife Ada Overton, and Florenz Ziegfeld and his wife Anna Held were also faithful to the place. In addition to its unbuttoned professional congeniality, the hotel also served as forum for serious racial palaver. "Our room, particularly at night, was the scene of many discussions," James Weldon Johnson recalled. "The main question talked about and wrangled over being the status of the Negro as writer, composer, and performer in the New York theater and world of music." They were to carry that preoccupation to Harlem, where it gained a potency and direction few of them could have anticipated.

Almost everything seemed possible above 125th Street in the early '20s for these Americans who were determined to thrive separately to better proclaim the ideals of integration. You could be black and proud, politically assertive and economically independent, creative and disciplined—or so it seemed. Arna Bontemps and fellow literary migrants made a wonderful discovery. They found that, under certain conditions, it was "fun to be a Negro." "In some places the autumn of 1924 may have been an unremarkable season," Bontemps wrote. "In Harlem, it was like a foretaste of paradise. A blue haze descended at night and with it strings of fairy lights on the broad avenues." Harlem's air seemed to induce a high from which no one was immune. Standing on "the Campus" (the intersection of 135th Street and Seventh Avenue), which was where English major Arthur Davis was more regularly found than on the campus of Columbia University, "one of the pleasures...was seeing celebrities. Just around the corner at 185 West 135th Street lived James Weldon Johnson. Next door to him lived Fats Waller." Florence Mills was two blocks away. "If we strolled down the Avenue to the Lafayette Theatre at 132nd Street, we often found under the famous Tree of Hope such artists as Ethel Waters, Sissle and Blake, Fletcher Henderson, and Miller and Lyles. It was truly bliss to be alive then."

There was almost too much to do and see. Columbia's John Dewey might be speaking at the 135th Street YMCA, at the invitation of W. E. B. Du Bois. More likely, though, it would be Hubert H. Harrison, the omniscient Danish West Indian socialist. There were plays at the "Y," ambitious productions drawing on heavyweight selections from the Anglo-Saxon repertoire, with Du Bois's Krigwa Players valiantly stretching themselves into their parts. Attendance was excellent, and an undertow of extra excitement flowed because of the probable presence of whites from the theater world. Harlem remembered how, in 1920, when Paul Robeson had been a reluctant recruit for a part in the first revival of Ridgely Torrence's *Simon the Cyrenian* at the "Y," Torrence, Robert Edmond Jones, and Kenneth Macgowan, founders of the experimental Provincetown Playhouse, had dashed backstage to offer him the lead in something called *The Emperor Jones*.

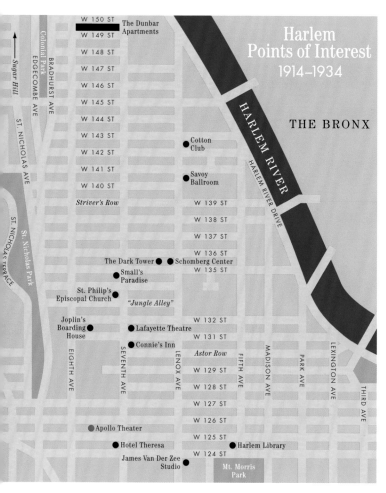

Modern map shows various locations prominent during the Harlem Renaissance. Walking tours of Renaissance landmarks have become major tourist attractions for Harlem.

"I went home," Robeson recalled, "forgot about the theater, and went back next morning to the law school as if nothing had happened." But Harlem's hungry young actors remembered the story.

The "Y" and the library were but two of the evening choices for a cultured Harlemite. Classical music concerts by the Harlem Symphony were well attended, with performers such as Fletcher Henderson, Hall Johnson, James P. Johnson, and William Grant Still contributing to its mastery of Mendelssohn and Brahms. For rarer tastes, there was the Harlem String Quartet. As Bontemps's "blue haze descended at night," invitations to the Charles Johnsons or James Weldon Johnsons, the Walter Whites, or the wealthy Enrique Cachemailles or far wealthier A'Lelia Walkers were honored, anywhere from one to two hours late. There was likely to be a good deal of affectation and posturing at these evenings, the mode shifting from poetry to politics at the drop of a name or event. At the Reverend Frederick A. Cullen's fourteen-room Seventh Avenue brownstone, soirees were notably elevated. Who you were was important to Countee Cullen's adoptive father.

Whatever their affectations, though, most Harlemites had spent an evening at Arthur "Happy" Rhone's, an establishment that virtually invented the Harlem nightclub. Happy Rhone's was at 143rd and Lenox Avenue. The decor was black and white; it was the first upstairs club; and it was plush—the "millionaires' club." Rhone was the first to hire waitresses and the first to offer floor shows. Noble Sissle himself often served as impromptu master of ceremonies to a well-liquored clientele that frequently included John and Ethel Barrymore, Charlie Chaplin, Jeanne Eagels, W. C. Handy, Ted Lewis, and Ethel Waters. What "Texas" Guinan—the lady credited with originating the American nightspot—had not learned in Parisian *boîtes de nuit*, she probably lifted from Happy Rhone's, or else from Pod's & Jerry's (the Catagonia Club) in what was called "the Jungle" of 133rd Street. Banks's, "Basement Brownie's," "The Bucket of Blood," and Leroy's (where vaudevillian Bert Williams sometimes drank at a corner table) were usually beyond the pale for the literati. Barron's posh retreat for the sporting crowd was almost exclusively reserved for whites, apart from Jack Johnson, the prizefighter who had just sold his 131st Street club to Connie Immerman. Connie's Inn and the new Cotton Club barred African Americans and were beyond the pocketbooks of most, anyway. But there was Hayne's Oriental (a favorite of physician-writer Rudolph Fisher, Fritz Pollard, the All-American halfback, and Paul Robeson) and the haughty but fading Lybia, of which it was said that "people you saw at church in the morning you met at the Lybia at night." Even Alain Locke was known to end a hard day at the newly opened Smalls' (owned by a descendant of ex-slave Robert Smalls, a Union navy captain and South Carolina congressman), where the clients, about equally divided between black and white, were served by roller-skating waiters.

Sociologist, writer, and activist W. E. B. Du Bois came to Harlem from Atlanta in 1910 and became the influential editor of *The Crisis,* the house journal of the NAACP.

And when they were not too busy being starchy symbols of the New Negro, they were known to dance, too. Mamie Smith's open-air Garden of Joy cabaret was no more, its corner lot at 138th Street having recently become the site for the Reverend Adam Clayton Powell Sr.'s Abyssinian Baptist Church, a garden of spiritual joy. But at the Renaissance Ballroom and sometimes to Fletcher Henderson's polished jazz at the aging but still majestic Rockland Palace (the old Manhattan Casino), the cream of Harlem would unlimber with the Charleston and black bottom. Annual galas sponsored by alumni of prestigious colleges like Fisk, Howard, and Lincoln; fraternity bashes hosted by Alphas, Kappas, and Omegas; fashion shows; club nights; and, at the pinnacle of posh, the yearly NAACP ball drew even such dyspeptic types as George Schuyler.

"Everybody," say the lyrics to a West African high life, "likes Saturday night." Saturday nights were terrific in Harlem, but rent parties every night were the special passion of the community. Their very existence was avoided or barely acknowledged by most Harlem writers, like that other rare and intriguing institution, the buffet flat, where varied and often perverse sexual pleasures were offered cafeteria-style. With the exception of Langston Hughes and Wallace Thurman, almost no one admitted attending a rent party. These were times, Willie "the Lion" Smith recalls, when "the average Negro family did not allow the blues, or even raggedy music, played in their homes." In fact, though, after a sedate parlor gathering and after the cabarets closed, poets and writers (and even an NAACP official) would frequently follow musicians to one of these nightly rent-paying rites.

Rent parties began anytime after midnight, howling and stomping sometimes well into dawn in a miasma of smoke, booze, collard greens, and hot music. Willie the Lion called them "jumps," "shouts," or "struts," where, for a quarter, "you would see all kinds of people making the party scene; formally dressed society folks from downtown, policemen, carpenters, mechanics, truckmen in their workingmen's clothes, gamblers, lesbians, and entertainers of all kinds. The parties were recommended to newly arrived single gals as the place to go to get acquainted." At the more elaborate struts, along about 3 a.m., the tempo would quicken when Willie the Lion, James P. Johnson, Claude Hopkins, Fats Waller, or "Corky" Williams—and even Edward Kennedy "Duke" Ellington—arrived, palm slapping and tuning up. Some musicians hired booking agents to handle this after-hours volume.

Looking back through a prism of census tracts, medical data, and socioeconomic studies, the evidence is persuasive that Harlem was becoming a slum, even as Charles Johnson and Alain Locke arranged the African American coming-out party of the arts, sponsored by the Urban League and the NAACP. Rent parties were a function first of economics, whatever their overlay of camaraderie, sex, and music.

Alain Locke, the leading intellectual of the Harlem Renaissance, asserted that African Americans should adopt the values of the dominant culture while drawing on their own rich heritage, especially the legacy derived from Africa.

In its 1927 report on 2,326 Harlem apartments, the Urban League found that 48 percent of the renters spent more than twice as much of their income on rent as did comparable white New Yorkers. For a four-room apartment (more than half the Urban League's sample), the average monthly rent was $55.70; average family income was about $1,300. The New York white equivalent was $32.43 in rent on a family income of $1,570. That a fourth of Harlem's families had at least one lodger (twice the white rate) and that an unknown number of householders practiced a "hot bed" policy— the same mattress for two or more lodgers on different work shifts—was as inevitable as the existence of rent parties to relieve the fear and trembling of the first of the month.

Floor show at Connie's Inn in the '30s. Along with the Cotton Club, Connie's was among the most celebrated of whites-only Harlem nightspots, established by notorious bootlegger Connie Immerman in 1923.

It was also true that Harlemites lived in cramped conditions. Many lived deplorably, in tenements so "unspeakable" and "incredible," the chairman of a 1927 city housing commission reported, "the State would not allow cows to live in some of these apartments." Harlem's statistics were dire.

What the statistics obscured was the mood of the universe north of Central Park. Whatever its contradictions, disparities between its reality and *Amsterdam News* fantasy, the one certainty almost all who lived there shared was that Harlem was no slum. Ghetto, maybe. Slum, never. Publications overflowed with Horatio Alger successes: frugal custodians who amassed hefty savings, invested in real estate, and sent their children to Lincoln or Syracuse universities; laundresses and barbers who parlayed modest revenues into service industry empires; graduates of Howard or Harvard who won brilliant recognition in their fields, despite repeated racist rebuffs; show people and racketeers whose unorthodox careers were capped by exemplary fortune and philanthropy. Not only newspapers like *Amsterdam News* and *New York Age* but also critical organs like *The Crisis* and *Opportunity* joyously catalogued every known triumph over adversity as particular manifestations of universal African American progress.

Jobs and rent money might be hard to come by, and whites might own more than 80 percent of the community's wealth, but the ordinary people of Harlem— not just civil rights grandees and exhilarated talents from the provinces—exuded a proud self-confidence. It was the unlikely true success story of "Pig Foot Mary" rather than the fictional but more typical tale of Rudolph Fisher's cruelly abused Solomon Gillis that gripped Harlemites. "Early in the fall of 1901 a huge Goliath of a woman," Lillian Harris, reached New York, a Federal Writers' Project monograph relates. Appropriating a segment of Sixtieth Street sidewalk over which she reigned with a baby carriage provisioned with chitterlings, corn, hog maw, and pig's feet, and persuading the proprietor of nearby Rudolph's saloon to share his stove, Pig Foot Mary plied a brisk trade. "A month passed and her pig's feet business boomed." Pig Foot Mary now presided "over a specially constructed portable steam table which she had designed herself." Moving to 135th Street and Lenox Avenue in 1917, at which corner she acquired both a husband and his thriving newsstand, Mrs. John Dean soon invested in Harlem real estate: a $44,000 Seventh Avenue apartment building, more buildings at 69–71 West 138th Street, still more at 2324 Seventh Avenue, and houses in Pasadena, California, until, by 1925, her holdings were conservatively valued at $375,000. It was said that when renters fell behind, she enjoined them by post, "Send it, and send it damn quick."

Pushcart vendors on a Harlem street, 1930s. A few lucky vendors, such as "Pig Foot Mary," rose from working the streets to become major players on the Harlem scene, buying real estate and supporting social causes.

But Pig Foot Mary was by no means Harlem's greatest success story. That distinction went to Madame C. J. Walker, the richest self-made woman in America. Born of sharecropper parents in Delta, Louisiana, in 1869, Sarah Breedlove was married at fourteen and widowed at twenty when Charles J. Walker crossed into Mississippi one day and was never seen again; he was presumed dead. Taking her daughter, A'Lelia, Mrs. Walker headed north. For five hard years, from 1905 to 1910, she wandered from St. Louis to Denver, Pittsburgh, and then Indianapolis, winning markets for her product, a secret formula for hair strengthener. Shortly thereafter, as Madame C. J. Walker, she settled in New York. Now fabulously rich, she built a Harlem town house and an adjacent school of beauty culture on 136th Street. Within hailing distance of Jay Gould's Irvington-on-Hudson estate, she also built a $250,000 Italianate palace designed by Vertner Tandy, Harlem's most distinguished architect. She dabbled in politics and gave lavishly to charities. Indignant over the War Department's segregationist policies, Madame Walker led a delegation of women to see President Wilson. Proud of her African roots, she quietly encouraged some of the more intellectual Garveyite sympathizers.

Madame Walker died, much lamented, in May 1919. She left sums to civil rights and missionary organizations, a million dollars to her daughter, a mighty hair-strengthening empire, and two-thirds of her net corporate profits to charity. A'Lelia Walker Robinson, her headstrong daughter, who was known not to pray much for others, dazzled black and white Manhattan by her lavish lifestyle. Her mother's Hudson River retreat, known as Villa Lewaro (an appellation devised by houseguest

Enrico Caruso from the first syllables of A'Lelia's names), became the Xanadu of Harlem's artistic and intellectual elite.

Harlem had so many successful bootleggers and racketeers, and so many political, religious, and other characters, that it took most of them for granted: the barefoot seer, "Prophet Martin"; the mysterious herbalist-publisher, "Black Herman"; the Senegalese world boxing champion, "Battling Siki," and his lion mascot (both of whom died violently after wandering into an Irish neighborhood in 1924); "Black Jews"; and on and on. Of course, it could never take Marcus Garvey for granted, but his Harlem days were numbered. With the African American establishment against him, the federal authorities prosecuting him for mail fraud, and the Liberian government denouncing him and impounding fifty thousand dollars' worth of his organization's construction equipment, Garvey made a last-ditch stand with a spectacular 1924 international convention—and then entered Atlanta federal penitentiary. With or without Garvey, Harlemites had good reason to believe that their ghetto was truly a vibrant microcosm of America, and that successes— even shady successes—were the rule rather than the exception.

With Bill "Bojangles" Robinson tapping up and down Lenox Avenue and every actor and musician worth knowing palavering, at one time or another, in the shadow of the Tree of Hope, Harlem's outdoor labor exchange at 142nd and Lenox, the notion that they lived in a slum would have been received by most

Madame C. J. Walker and her daughter, A'Lelia, take their new Model T out for a ride on Indianapolis's streets, 1912. The Walker family fortune was built on a line of hair-care products aimed at the African American market.

Harlemites with puzzlement. Even in the trough of the Great Depression, sociologist Myrtle Pollard would find the people generally well dressed and happy. She saw the fatalists, Harlem's "third class," too abused by circumstances to hope, but they were overshadowed by the "strivers" and the professionals. Harlem was far from a "slum or a fringe," James Weldon Johnson maintained in 1925. It occupied "one of the most beautiful and healthful sections of the city," and there were three good reasons why it would maintain its mainstream character: "First, the language of Harlem is not alien; it is not Italian or Yiddish; it is English. Harlem talks American, reads American, thinks American. Second, Harlem is not physically a 'quarter.' It is not a section cut off....Third, the fact that there is little or no gang labor gives Harlem Negroes the opportunity for individual contacts with the life and spirit of New York."

Anthropologist Melville Herskovits agreed after a few investigative visits: "It occurred to me that I was seeing a community just like any other American community. The same pattern, only a different shade!" Yet in certain respects the distinguished anthropologist's "community just like any other" was significantly unlike most others.

New York City Mayor Fiorello La Guardia (middle) looks on while dancer Bill "Bojangles" Robinson kisses the relocated Tree of Hope, 1941. The original tree had stood in front of the Lafayette Theatre for decades before it was cut down in 1933.

The men and women of color north of Central Park defined the very meaning of success in the performing arts. The music of New Orleans and Chicago found its East Coast niche at the Savoy Ballroom on Lenox Avenue and at the Apollo Theater on 125th Street. The Savoy came first. On a memorable opening night in March 1926, the Savoy shook New York as profoundly in its own way as the 1913 Armory Show had turned the world of mainstream art inside out. With its spacious lobby framing a huge, cut-glass chandelier and marble staircase, an orange and blue dance hall with heavy carpeting covering half its area, the remainder a burnished dance floor 250 feet by 50 feet with two bandstands and a disappearing stage at the end, the Savoy could entertain four thousand people at one showing. Neither the Alhambra nor the Renaissance ballrooms evoked as much pure joy from Harlemites as when "stompin' at the Savoy." The Savoy jam sessions broadcast over radio were to American

Amateur jitterbuggers dominate the floor at the Savoy Ballroom in 1947. Often two bands played—one at either end of the ballroom—encouraging "battles of the bands."

popular music what Dearborn, Michigan, was to transportation, and Fletcher Henderson's Rainbow Orchestra symbolized the debut of jazz as a product for national consumption. Until the end of the '20s, the national jazz sound was the swinging syncopation of Henderson's orchestra, with Duke Ellington's Cotton Club Orchestra placing a close second.

The Apollo opened under the new management team of Sidney Cohen and Morris Sussman in the old Hurtig and Seamon's New Burlesque Theater in January 1934. The people who filled the Apollo on Amateur Nights were not quite as tony as the patrons of earlier entertainment palaces such as the Alhambra, Savoy, and Renaissance. Although the Cohen-Sussman management team advertised its new house as the "finest theater in Harlem" and a "resort for the better people," the "better people" were to be a minority in a time of unprecedented economic distress. Management was compelled to reduce the price of tickets. The Apollo quickly became a place where the unemployed, hardworking poor, aspiring young people, and socially uprooted found emotional uplift or escape—a forum where ordinary Harlemites passed judgment on the talents of people like themselves and where there was even a slim chance that the dream of appearing before the footlights on Amateur Night might be realized. Those who survived the verdict of the audience had certified talent. The Apollo's Amateur Nights, showcasing the vocal and performance genius of Ella Fitzgerald, Billie Holiday, Sarah Vaughan, and scores to come, shaped the popular vocal and performance tastes of generations of Americans of every color.

The Long Road Traveled to Harlem's Apollo

James V. Hatch

The Apollo Theater opened as a home for black entertainment in early 1934. Originally the theater's shows were loose-knit revues, but soon the bill of fare settled into an even looser collection of acts featuring singers, bands, dancers, comics, jugglers, magicians, and other novelty performers. This format had its roots in several different black theatrical styles dating from the mid-nineteenth century, and the Apollo's stars were themselves descendants of a long distinguished line of performers. The Apollo was also influenced by the nightclubs and earlier theaters, especially the southern vaudeville circuits such as TOBA (an acronym the actors dubbed "Tough on Black Asses").

Comedians Bert Williams and George Walker perform a skit. After Walker's death, Williams became one of the most beloved African American solo performers of the vaudeville era.

The cakewalk originated during the era of slavery: dancers imitated their white masters, and the winning couple received a cake.

Pioneers of the Black Theater: 1900–1920

Among the first stars of the black theater were comics Bert Williams and George Walker, Walker's wife, Ada (who used the stage name of Aida), and composer Bob Cole. At the turn of the twentieth century, to emphasize their racially distinctive talents, Williams and Walker advertised themselves as "Two Real Coons." They wrote a series of story-based musicals satirizing, among other things, nouveau riche blacks, as well as those who said they were descendants from African royalty. The *Boston Guardian* described Bert Williams and George and Ada Walker as "the most popular trio of colored actors in the world," and the curmudgeon W. C. Fields declared that "Bert Williams was the funniest man I ever saw and the saddest man I ever knew." Williams was such a big star that he was hired in 1910 by impresario Florenz Ziegfeld to star in the *Ziegfeld Follies*, the first black performer to be featured in this popular revue.

George Walker's wife, Ada, was crowned "Queen of the Cakewalk." Today she is recognized as the first professional black woman choreographer. She boldly created a sanitized version of Salome's dance for herself and inserted it into William and Walker's successful show *Bandanna Land* (1907). At a command performance for the queen of England, she sang "I Wants to Be an

Actor Lady." Ada had begun her career in soubrette roles and never lost her perky provocation. It is said that she taught the soubrette style to Florence Mills, the great African American star of the 1920s.

Bob Cole, recognized as a multitalented performer-composer-director-producer-playwright, began his professional career with Sam T. Jack's *Creole Show* (1890), which featured lavishly costumed Creole women. This casting of light-skinned beauties set a precedent that continued for forty years, down to and including the '20s musical *Shuffle Along* and the Cotton Club. The *Creole Show* toured for seven years, and its lovely women were its biggest draw. In performance Bob Cole himself never wore blackface, but he created Willy Wayside, a ragged and humorous tramp, whom he played in whiteface.

Lyricist and composer Noble Sissle (front) with the chorines of *Shuffle Along*. Right: Original sheet music for "I'm Just Wild about Harry," one of the show's hit songs.

Shuffle Along

The work of Williams and Walker and Bob Cole laid the groundwork for the first Broadway hit show written, scored, and performed by African Americans: *Shuffle Along*. The show's genesis came from the well-established lyricist Noble Sissle, pianist-composer Eubie Blake, and two blackface comedians, Flournoy Miller and Aubrey Lyles. After World War I, Sissle and Blake had formed their own Society Orchestra in Philadelphia, where they met Miller and Lyles, who had developed an original farce, *The Mayor of Dixie*, about a struggle for the mayor's office in fictional Jimtown. Under its new title, *Shuffle Along* arrived in New York from Philadelphia with a debt of $18,000. The four performers negotiated a deal with the producer-owner of a run-down venue, the Sixty-third Street Theatre at Broadway, far uptown from the Great White Way. Backstage they found trunks of used costumes for which they promptly set about writing songs: "Bandanna Days," inspired by cotton pickers' clothes, and "Oriental Blues," a rendition that was neither oriental nor blue but stunning in its costumes. The entire show turned out to be a mixture of old and new genres: folk, blues, ragtime, jazz, and a sentimental ballad "Love Will Find a Way," a duet that

Sheet music for "In My Old Home" from the hit musical *Bandanna Land* (1908) features inset photographs of Williams and Walker.

Florence Mills's career was launched in 1921's *Shuffle Along*. She died of appendicitis at the height of her fame six years later, at the age of thirty-one.

permitted a pair of black lovers to sing a serious love song on a "Broadway" stage for the first time.

At its New York opening in 1921, a variety of critics found something to praise in *Shuffle Along*. All the talents were splendid—Miller and Lyles, Gertrude Saunders, Roger Matthews, Lottie Gee, and, of course, Sissle and Blake. During the run of the show, the chorus line sparkled with names that would soon be famous: Josephine Baker, the darkest and funniest one in the line, would soon fly to Paris and become a sensation in the Folies Bergère. Another lovely chorus girl, Fredi Washington, later starred in the 1934 film *Imitation of Life* as Peola, the miscegenated daughter who could pass for white. Caterina Jarboro, a lyric soprano who would play the lead in *Aida* at Milan's Puccini Theater in 1930 and at Carnegie Hall in 1944, was too dark to appear in *Shuffle Along*'s very light chorus line, so she sang backstage. Paul Robeson's bass voice secured the male quartet; he later starred in *Show Boat* (1927), and twenty-five years later,

he would create a Broadway record for performances of *Othello*, one that still stands today.

The show's greatest discovery was Florence Mills, whom producer Lew Leslie snatched up for his revue *Blackbirds of 1926*. In that show, Mills broke hearts with a song written especially for her: "I'm a Little Blackbird Looking for a Bluebird." Leslie took her abroad, where she broke more hearts in London and Paris. Then *Blackbirds* sailed home to New York City, where Mills died of appendicitis, leaving not a single recording of her voice. Even without her, however, Leslie's revue reinvented itself for a decade. The show and its successors helped to lift Broadway's iron curtain for black musical talents in *Green Pastures*, *Run, Little Chillun*, *Porgy and Bess*, and *Show Boat*.

Harlem Night Clubs and Cabarets

In the '20s, more than forty theaters and cabarets blossomed in Harlem. Many disappeared during the Depression, but others linger in memory: the Lafayette Theatre, Connie's Inn, the Ubangi Club, Small's Paradise, the Alhambra Theater and Cabaret, and finally the queen mother of all cabarets, the Cotton Club.

In 1910 boxer Jack Johnson had knocked out the Great White Hope, Jim Jeffries. Johnson retired in 1915 and opened Club Deluxe on the second floor of Lenox and 142nd Street. In 1923 gangsters eased Johnson out of his ownership and rechristened his nightspot the Cotton Club. Only whites were admitted. Close relatives of the chorus line could sit in a booth near the kitchen.

The shows were professional, the service impeccable. Duke Ellington's band—introduced by a radio announcer as "jungle music"—began broadcasting half-hour sets nightly from the club, spreading its fame across America. Cab Calloway, with his "Hi-De-Hi-De-Ho" banter, later replaced Ellington. Ethel Waters introduced "Stormy Weather" there. Perhaps the club's greatest discovery was Lena Horne. Coffee-light in color, fashionably slim, with "good"

Cab Calloway (far right) leads his popular band at the Cotton Club on New Year's Eve 1937. The whites-only audience danced the night away.

hair (it would blow in the wind) and a fine voice, Horne sang in the chorus from the age of sixteen—despite the club's rule that its chorus members "must be eighteen but not older than twenty-one." After some months singing in the line, Lena was given a duet on the arm of Avon Long, "As Long as I Live." Marion Egbert reported in an interview that "Lena Horne was a show girl, not a chorus girl. Show girls paraded with costumes, things that only a tall girl could

wear. Show girls were like models. Lena couldn't dance, but when the owners heard Lena sing, she took over Ethel Waters' place singing 'Stormy Weather' with Duke Ellington."

The heart of the Cotton Club's success was its atmosphere and style. No profanity or loud talking was permitted at the guest tables. All the workers serving or performing were black, all the patrons white and wealthy. One patron, a bookmaker, would come in late and change twenty dollars into fifty-cent pieces; he'd then throw the whole bag of coins at the feet of a singer or dancer he admired. Many Hollywood stars such as George Raft and Joan Crawford came to be seen. The columnist Walter Winchell came to report whom he had seen. European aristocrats dared not sail home without a tale of venturing into the exotic Harlem club. Twelve chorus girls danced and sang in beautiful costumes measured, sewn, and fitted in the basement between shows. One time on a special occasion, fifty chorus girls danced and sang onstage with Bill Robinson. The bands all had a modern jazz sound—Calloway, Jimmie Lunceford, and Ellington, whose music set the tone and personified the style: "Sophisticated Lady" in a sophisticated club.

Lena Horne performs at the Savoy-Plaza Hotel, 1942. Her 1936 appearance at the Apollo helped establish her singing career.

Marquee of Harlem's Lafayette Theatre, 1935. The stump of the Tree of Hope is seen in the foreground. The legendary tree was supposed to give luck to performers who touched it.

The Lafayette Theatre

In 1912 the Lafayette Theatre was built at 132nd Street and Seventh Avenue, then a white neighborhood. Initially the theater was segregated, and it failed until drama critic Lester A. Walton and C. W. Morganstern, a Broadway booking agent, took it over and dropped the segregation policy. Walton brought Anita Bush and her Lincoln Theatre Players to his house, changing their name to the Lafayette Players. During this period, the theater became a mecca for black talent. Under Walton's new policies, actors were able to be trained and judged strictly by other black performers, and they were allowed to explore mime, singing, and dramatic scenes. (Frank Wilson remembered that when he auditioned for an acting role in a white theater, the director would point to the floor and say, "Act!" That was his cue to dance!) In its heyday, over 360 actors passed through the Lafayette, including Charles Gilpin, Edna Thomas, Abbie Mitchell, and Evelyn Preer. Anita Bush, who became known as "the Little Mother of Negro

Drama," eventually left the Lafayette—as did other actors—to audition for Hollywood films.

In 1915 Robert Levy, a new manager at the Lafayette, introduced "tabs," short versions of Broadway plays. This strategy enabled the company to act in dramatic plays, although all the roles were white. The audience roared when the dark and unmistakably deep-voiced Clarence Muse appeared in a blond wig and white face as Dr. Jekyll and Mr. Hyde. To increase attendance, Levy introduced matinee movies and a new play every Monday, enabling the Lafayette Players to work full seasons in straight plays and melodramas. Among the 250 plays the group produced were *The Octoroon* and *The Count of Monte Cristo*. These "tabs" sometimes piggybacked on the original Broadway costumes and sets.

One day *Variety*, the show business weekly, announced in October 1929 that "Wall Street Lays an Egg." The Great Depression had opened downtown, and rave reviews did not translate into full houses uptown. Lead actors took jobs in other theaters, and the official Lafayette Players moved to Los Angeles, where they successfully opened a fifty-two-week run of Somerset Maugham's drama *Rain*. Back in Harlem, attendance at warmed-over Broadway dramas dropped dramatically. In 1933 Frank Schiffman and Leo Brecher, then managers of the Lafayette, hired Ralph Cooper to try out a "new" idea: Wednesday Night Auditions. Amateurs eager to have an audience and perhaps break into showbiz presented their talents live—dance, song, or monologue—before audiences eager to reward them with applause or reject them with boos. Cooper himself emceed the show. A roly-poly stagehand named Norman Miller, later famed as "Porto Rico," shooed the unready and the unloved offstage. Wednesday Night Auditions was prospering; the *Pittsburgh Courier* noted that "If an amateur can score on the Lafayette stage, he's marked for a glittering career." But Wednesday night's successes did not fill the theater seats on Thursdays. Management turned to films, but the times they were a-changin.'

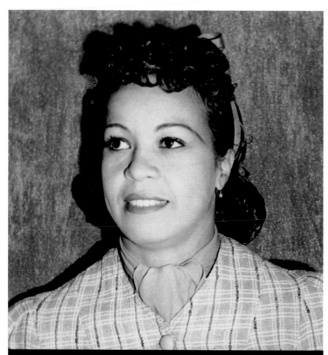

Vivian Harris began her career as a chorus girl on Broadway and at the Cotton Club. In addition to her work onstage at the Apollo she served as the off-stage "Voice of the Apollo" from 1935 until the mid-'50s.

It Happened at the Apollo

Schiffman and Brecher eventually disposed of the Lafayette and acquired the Apollo at 253 West 125th Street between Seventh and Eighth, a new neighborhood where whites were moving out and blacks were moving in. It was a neighborhood with a future, where cabarets still drew audiences for songs, pretty chorus girls, and dance acts. The new Apollo hired Dusty Fletcher and Dewey "Pigmeat" Markham, burnt cork comics, and audiences loved them. The managers also embraced emcee Ralph Cooper and his creation, the Wednesday Amateur Night. However, the Harlem Opera House, the Apollo's competitor, had also initiated a Tuesday Night Amateur Hour. Finally, in 1935 WMCA radio sent the Apollo's Amateur Night over the top with its weekly broadcast of the contest. Many young talents applied. As the legends of Redd Foxx, Jackie "Moms" Mabley, Sarah Vaughan, and Sammy Davis Jr. spread, dozens of unknowns came to try out. The Apollo became *the* place to be seen, be heard, be famous.

Vivian Harris and her sister Edna Mae, who worked for Frank Schiffman onstage and off for many years, loved the Apollo. In an interview with Delilah Jackson, Vivian recalled her roles onstage as a foil for the burnt cork comics. She also served as the offstage announcer, greeting the audience before each performance:

Good afternoon (evening), ladies and gentlemen. We have Count Basie and his Band, Billie Holiday, James Rushing, Butterbeans and Susie. We have a midnight show on Saturday and Amateur Night broadcast on Wednesday. So relax, everybody, and…"Here we go!" The band would strike up the theme song: "I may be wrong but I think you're wonderful. You came along, say, I think it's marvelous, etc." I sang that three or four shows a day, including Wednesday Amateur Night. It created an electricity!

The second balcony became the hawk's nest, where seats were twenty-five cents. Like Shakespeare's groundlings, the audience members expressed their approvals or dislike with direct dialogue to the talent. They were potentially "hanging judges" to a singer's career. Luther Vandross had to appear on five different occasions to win their approval. If you won the talent contest on Wednesday, you were rewarded with a spot on the Apollo stage for the next week. The many winners included Sarah Vaughan, Pearl Bailey, Frankie Lymon, Leslie Uggams, James Brown, King Curtis, Wilson Pickett, Ruth Brown, Dionne Warwick, Gladys Knight, Smokey Robinson, and Ella Fitzgerald. If there had been no Apollo Theater, many of these stars would never have been given their first chance—or indeed been able to become major draws for audiences around the world.

Leslie Uggams wows the Amateur Night crowd on her first Apollo appearance in 1952, when she was eight years old.

The Empress Bessie Smith

Karen Chilton

This famous portrait of Bessie Smith was taken by arts critic, author, and photographer Carl Van Vechten in 1936.

In December 1936 patrons streamed into the Apollo Theater to witness that which was promised: "Harlem's finest colored stage show!" The weeklong engagement featured the Mills Brothers; Leonard Harper's musical comedy hit *League of Rhythm*; the Phantom Steppers; a screening of *Can This Be Dixie?* with Jane Withers and Hattie McDaniel; Erskine Hawkins and the Bama State Band; and the unmitigated blues sung courtesy of the show's headliner, the one and only Bessie Smith.

Prior to the evening's performance, trouble brewed. Once the highest paid black entertainer of her era, Bessie had seen her career suffer owing to the Depression and the advent of radio and talking pictures. Hard-pressed for cash, she requested a pay advance from the Apollo Theater's owner, Frank Schiffman. When he refused, Bessie unleashed her characteristic brashness. Fueled by alcohol and a penchant for a good fight, she stormed out of his office and commenced to give patrons a little something extra for the price of admission. She threw her substantial six-foot-tall frame onto the lobby floor, kicked, screamed, and hollered, "I'm the *star* of the show, I'm Bessie Smith!"

Born in the impoverished Blue Goose Hollow section of Chattanooga and raised by her eldest sister after the death of both parents, Bessie rose through sheer will and the thrust of a tremendous talent from her meager circumstances to become one of the greatest singers of the twentieth century. She hit the vaudeville circuit as a teen, joining her comedian brother Clarence in the Moses Stokes Company. Although she was hired as a dancer, she was schooled in the art of performance by the troupe's lead vocalist, Gertrude "Ma" Rainey (the "Mother of the Blues"), who became mother, mentor, and friend to Bessie. In 1923, after nearly a decade on the road, Bessie signed her first record deal with Columbia. Her debut recording of Alberta Hunter's "Downhearted Blues" (with "Gulf Coast Blues" on the B-side) was an instant hit, selling over 780,000 copies; it was the first spark of a prolific recording career.

From a plaintive swoon to a guttural growl, Bessie brought the brass and the beat. "I don't need no drums," she told record producer John Hammond. Her blues had hypnotic power—raw, unrelenting, poignant. Bessie would slide up to a note, lean into it, then sit on it until the listener was flushed with emotion. Eventually Bessie would transcend the blues idiom as swing became the most popular music of the day. She was accompanied by some of the best jazz

Smith performs with chorus boys in the late '20s. She wears a gold lamé suit with matching top hat, one of her many stunning stage costumes.

musicians on the scene—James P. Johnson, Joe Smith, Coleman Hawkins, Sidney Bechet, and, most notably, Louis Armstrong. Their collaboration on W. C. Handy's "St. Louis Blues" is now considered a blues classic. Bessie later appeared in the 1929 film of the same title. It is the only footage available where she can be seen in live performance.

Following her engagement at the Apollo in 1936, Bessie set out to revive her career. With the help of John Hammond, recording sessions were in the works, as well as an appearance at Carnegie Hall. But it was not to be. In autumn of the following year, Bessie and her common-law husband Richard Morgan were in a car wreck outside Clarksdale, Mississippi. Soon after, a rumor began to spread that Bessie had been refused entry to a whites-only hospital and bled to death on the hospital steps. Actually Bessie had been hospitalized but died days later as a result of her injuries. She was forty-three years old. Her funeral was held October 4, 1937, in her adopted hometown of Philadelphia, with over 7,000 mourners in attendance.

After Bessie's untimely death, John Hammond produced a Carnegie Hall concert that documented the history of black American music. It was called "From Spirituals to Swing." Dedicated to Smith's memory, the concert became a touchstone in the acceptance of this music into mainstream American life.

Familiar with both tragedy and triumph, Bessie sang out her demons as she wrote down her life story in the lyrics. She placed her inimitable stamp on 160 recordings, including "Backwater Blues," "'Tain't Nobody's Bizness If I Do," and "Nobody Knows You When You're Down and Out." Bessie's vocal style, phrasing, and intonation would later inform the sound of many jazz vocalists, including Billie Holiday and Dinah Washington. From the time of her early recordings to today, Bessie Smith's music has remained an important part of the American songbook, a testament to her enduring legacy as the "Empress of the Blues."

Smith in her heyday, ca. 1925. Her recordings outsold all other blues performers of the era.

James Reese Europe's Band's Triumphant Return to Harlem

Robert G. O'Meally

Masses lined the parade route along Fifth and Lenox avenues on February 17, 1919, to greet the 369th Infantry Regiment "Hell Fighters" following their heroic performance in World War I.

Ragtime composer for large ensembles, bandleader and conductor extraordinaire, pathfinding musical entrepreneur, James Reese Europe (1880–1919) made an indelible mark on twentieth-century musical culture. Jazz music could not have developed without his example; nor would Broadway musicals be what they are without his imprimatur. Though his is hardly a household name, Europe's place is nonetheless secure in the distinctive African American—and thus in the definitively American—musical pantheon.

The year 1919 is rightly known as the time of the "Red Summer"—a nadir in U.S. race relations when, between June and December alone, at least seventy-six black Americans were lynched and twenty-five race riots were recorded. But it was also a year of spectacular triumph for James Reese Europe and for black Americans in general. On February 17, 1919, a crowd of perhaps one million gathered along Fifth Avenue from Madison Square Park to Central Park North, and from there uptown along Lenox Avenue to 145th Street. New Yorkers black and white had come out to welcome home the black soldiers who had fought so valiantly in France as the 369th Infantry Regiment of the American Expeditionary Force. The city's elite joined ordinary Manhattanites to cheer the World War I heroes as they marched to booming drumbeats in uncannily straight military lines up the broad avenues.

Europe's biographer, Reid Badger, explains what the 369th fighters had accomplished as soldiers: "[The unit] had survived 191 days under enemy fire, received the Croix de Guerre, and was chosen by the French high command to lead the victorious Allied march to the Rhine. The 369th never lost a prisoner or a foot of ground that it was expected to hold.... One hundred seventy-one of the regiment's officers and men received individual citations for bravery, a record among the American forces." Valor had exacted its price: "800 of the original 2,000…did not return. Many of those who did suffered serious and permanent injuries."

These black soldiers marched to the jaunty music of Lt. James Reese Europe and his world-famed 369th "Hell Fighters" Band. The brilliant tap dancer Bill "Bojangles" Robinson was the band's high-stepping drum major. As the regiment stepped not in the usual direction from midtown down Fifth Avenue but rather up Fifth into Harlem, most of the marches played were traditional ones. But many observers reported that even the conventional brass band music had something of a modern dance beat orientation, if not an uptown strut; and that as the Hell Fighters turned up Lenox toward Sugar Hill, they were rocking contemporary tunes and Sousa marches alike. According to the *New York Age*, by the time the band broke into the locally popular song "Here Comes My Daddy Now," the response of the Harlem crowd "bordered on a riot." At points along the parade route, "so many wives, mothers, and sweethearts had dashed out into the street with flowers and kisses for the men that the regiment's commander was forced to halt the march and wait for the police to escort the civilians back to the curb so that the parade could continue."

It was a momentous day in Harlem. Not only were those who wondered if American blacks could soldier on the international field furnished with a resounding answer. But also the band that had introduced jazz to France had returned to tell their story in sound. Europe later recalled the response to the band at Paris's Théâtre des Champs-Élysées: "Before

we had played two numbers the audience went wild….French high officers who had heard us insisted that we should stay in Paris, and there we stayed for eight weeks. Everywhere we have a concert it was a riot, but the supreme moment came in the Tuileries Garden. We played to 50,000 people at least, and, had we wished it, we might be playing yet."

Born in Mobile, Alabama, to highly musical parents, Europe moved with his family to Washington, D.C., when he was nine years old. As a third grader, he began to study the violin under the tutelage of Joseph Douglass, grandson of Frederick Douglass. He also studied piano with Enrico Hurlei, the assistant director of John Philip Sousa's celebrated U.S. Marine Band. In 1902 or 1903 Europe took off to seek work in New York, the capital of musical America. His efforts put him in touch with Tenderloin and Tin Pan Alley musicians, as well as those who played for private parties and Broadway shows. Reese took his turn in all these arenas, but no experience was more significant than his involvement with Ernest Hogan's Memphis Students, a singing, dancing New York orchestra that featured vaudeville star Hogan,

James Reese Europe (center rear) poses in uniform with two members of the Hell Fighters Band and their instruments, ca. 1919.

Europe (center rear) leads New York's Clef Club Orchestra, 1914. This band was a breeding ground for the next generation of black musicians and composers, notably Eubie Blake and Noble Sissle.

Europe (left) leads the Hell Fighters Band on the streets of Paris, ca. 1917. The band helped introduce syncopated dance music to the French.

Will Dixon, the original dancing conductor, and Will Marion Cook, the group's original composer.

Cook was a black violin prodigy who had studied with Antonín Dvořák and who shared the Czech composer's desire to create a musical style that could translate local vernacular forms into American symphonies. Cook used an unusual array of instruments to present music with a strong rhythmical drive that rang true to "the Southern African American musical tradition from folk music and spirituals through minstrels." Europe's tenure with the Memphis Students showed the possibility of creating music that was artistically uncompromising and disciplined, as well as vibrant with the cadences of centuries of African American living.

In 1910 Europe helped found the Clef Club, a combination black musicians' union and booking agency. The organization's greatest evening came in May 1912, when Europe conducted a 125-piece orchestra that featured violins, cellos, and horns side by side with mandolins, banjos, and ten upright pianos. James Weldon Johnson recalled that "when the Clef Club opened its concert with a syncopated march, playing it with a biting attach and an infectious rhythm, and on the finale bursting into singing…the applause became a tumult."

Europe did not attempt to lace American tunes and effects into the fabric of European symphonic forms, as Dvořák did in his "New World" Symphony. Europe went another, more radical way, proclaiming that African American vernacular sounds could be used to create a concert music more idiosyncratically native than any reordering of European concert music. To put it another way: Europe showed that American forms *themselves* constituted concert music.

Because of this bold departure, Europe is the father of the contemporary jazz band and of jazz as America's classical music—a true native form that, drawing freely on European as well as African and Indian traditions, finds its richest sources in brass bands, funeral marches, minstrel bands, hard-dancing parties, and church songs. "We have developed a kind of symphony music that, no matter what else you think, is different and distinctive," Europe explained, "and that lends itself to the playing of the peculiar compositions of our race." Here was the national symphony that Walt Whitman had predicted, some twenty years earlier, would derive from "the speech of the slaves." Here was the sound that would pave the way for Louis Armstrong, who took Europe's model and turned its algebra of percussive and melodic innovation into a higher calculus of improvisation and swing. Here too was the context into which Duke Ellington, who started out as a ragtime pianist, arrived. Ellington put Europe's audacious conception of a jumping dance orchestra together with Armstrong's gospel of swing and created a multicolored music that was definitive of American life and of the twentieth century.

James Reese Europe was just as important to popular American theater music as he was to jazz. After his association with the Memphis Students ended, he served as composer and musical director for many musical comedies, including productions by Bob Cole and J. Rosamond Johnson and by Bert Williams and George Walker. There is a direct line, too, from the music of James Reese Europe to the composer-musicians Eubie Blake and the 369th's multitalented Noble Sissle, creators of the first major hit Broadway musical staged and acted by African Americans: *Shuffle Along.* The irresistible music of that show and of shows like it—the inextricable linkage of Afro-song and Afro-dance—were part of the legacy of James Reese Europe.

Furthermore, what would popular dance in America have been without the work of James Reese Europe? According to dance historian Jacqui Malone, he was a central figure in the social dance craze that swept the United States between 1912 and 1916. Credited with inventing the foxtrot (credit he shifted to W. C. Handy), Europe showcased the white dancers Irene and Vernon Castle, who became internationally famous for their presentations of black social dance steps to the broad American public. Virtually overnight, Americans began to trade European waltzes and schottisches for such African American dances as the shimmy, the Texas Tommy, and the turkey trot.

It remains to be added that the Hell Fighters Band was an African American unit—with an important international twist.

Along with the U.S. black musicians James Reese Europe recruited to join this army band were several Puerto Ricans—notably certain fine clarinet players. One of these Puerto Rican recruits was the composer Rafael Hernández, one of the most important figures in the history of Puerto Rican music. According to musicologist Ruth Glaser, Hernández "created songs with complexly weaving vocal patterns, minor to major shifts, and highly poetic sentiments."

From Carnegie Hall to the Savoy Ballroom to the Apollo Theater, American music owes much to James Reese Europe. Whether bouncing in their seats at Carnegie, stomping at the Savoy, or rocking in the aisles at the Apollo, audiences have been drawn by the Afro-dance beat orientation of this composer— and those in his tradition. Whatever the venue, something of the homebound Harlem march—the proud "Here Comes My Daddy Now" strut—altered forever the contour and cadence of American musical culture. A black man named Europe had brought black music back home to America.

Sheet music for Europe's "On Patrol in No Man's Land," 1919.
This song was a hit from the band's tour of America following their World War I duty.

Popular Dance of the 1920s and Early '30s
From Animal Dance Crazes to the Lindy Hop

Thomas F. DeFrantz

While leading scholars and artists stretched the boundaries of black expression in the Harlem Renaissance of the 1920s and '30s, African American social dances flourished. Embraced by the people themselves, eccentric and animal dances—when polished up—became the basis for popular singers and dancers in Harlem's clubs and the landmark theaters of the day, including the Apollo. These dances drew on earlier dances created by southern African Americans. Newly

In 1938 amateur performers Myrtle Quinland and Lucas Smith dance the big apple, one of many popular swing era dances.

arrived in New York City, they brought country names and styles to the bustling cosmopolitan popular dance traditions of the urban North. Increasing northern migration and industrialization made individual expression more possible for African Americans, and these social dances reflected the hard-won expansion of personal freedoms. Like most African American expressive forms, these dances began in the small confines of apartments and dance clubs but were quickly adapted for stage performance and soon gained international attention.

Eccentric dances derived from the highly valued individuality at the heart of black creative expression. In these forms, dancers created idiosyncratic movements that made the body appear strange in its motion. These dances built on the extraordinary variety and flexibility common in African American movement styles. Exaggerated rolls of the shoulders or neck; unexpected contortions of the spine or bending of the knees; and strangely mechanical locomotions or freezes formed the core of this style. These were solo dance forms practiced in theatrical settings and in social dances that allowed individuals to "shine" singly. Typically viewed as comic dances performed at a high level of virtuosity, eccentric dances moved from African American contexts through vaudeville to Broadway and Hollywood, as individual entertainers realized the value of creating dance expression that no one else could perform in exactly the same way.

The '20s also produced an unprecedented number of animal dances, which were fanciful vestiges of recently abandoned rural living. These dances drew on the legacy of the nineteenth-century buzzard lope, popular among African Americans in the South, especially in the Georgia Sea Islands. A solo form danced by individuals in a group for fun, the buzzard lope featured hopping steps and gestures that mimicked the awkward movements of a bird eating its prey. It certainly influenced the rise of the early twentieth-

century turkey trot, a partnered dance widely practiced as the movement component of ragtime music. Danced in close proximity, with partners face to face, the turkey trot featured a basic hopping step on each musical beat. Its dancers rocked back and forth while traveling in a large circle around the dance space, essentially following a modified ballroom dancing format. Flapping the arms like a turkey added the distinctive movement that gave the dance its name. Dancers also stylized their movements by adding trotting

Josephine Baker starred in *La Folie du Jour* at the Folies Bergères in 1926–27.
Lower: Whitey's Lindy Hoppers were one of the best-known professional swing dance groups of the '30s.

steps, foot-flicking gestures, and abrupt freezes between phrases. As in other eccentric dances that featured individualized movements, the turkey trot encouraged invention. In a breakaway section, the couple separated, and each dancer explored his or her own rhythmic ideas before returning to partner formation.

Like many African American social dances, the turkey trot was derided by some for its so-called lewd and uncivilized, bent-kneed hopping and pecking gestures. But these distinctive gestures made the dance fun for everyone who did it. Mimicking the imaginary behavior of animals became a way for dancers to enjoy a release from the pressures of crowded urban life and to playfully engage a creative response to the new sounds of jazz music. Animal dances became a string of fads, each aptly named for some distinctive gesture. The camel walk, the chicken scratch, the grizzly bear, the bunny hug, the kangaroo hop, and the various "wing" dances—chicken wing and pigeon wing—each illustrated in playful exaggeration an aspect of animal behavior. Many of these dances had analogues in southern plantation settings that transferred to the Harlem of the '20s.

Some social dances of this era traveled from rent parties and nightclubs to the theatrical stage and back again. These dances, including the black bottom and the Charleston, featured extravagant body part isolations, especially in sinewy or sudden motions of the pelvis and spine, and rolling gestures of the torso, shoulders, elbows, and knees in unexpected continual waves or accented, rhythmic jerking. The snake hips dance, popularized by the impressive performances of Earl "Snake Hips" Tucker, a soloist with Duke Ellington's orchestra, emphasized successional movements that included the hips and pelvis, coupled with twisting motions of the feet.

The black bottom—named for districts in various American cities—allowed dancers a simple solo structure that encouraged improvisation. The dance involved slapping your hips and hopping forward and back, touching the ground, and letting your backbone slide from side to side. As a social dance, the black bottom originally had little cachet, but when stage performers started demonstrating personable, virtuoso versions of the dance, it gained currency for general audiences of African American social dancers. Stage shows that played at the Apollo Theater

in the '30s featured the dance with specially written music that called out its steps, so that audiences could learn it and repeat it at home. These popular versions of the dance, arranged by musicians including Jelly Roll Morton and sung by entertainers including Gertrude "Ma" Rainey, encouraged its adoption by white Americans and international audiences.

The most widely circulated popular dance of this era was the Charleston. Danced with a partner and named for the city in South Carolina, it gained popularity among African Americans in the 1910s and arrived on Broadway in the early '20s. (The 1923 song "Charleston" by James P. Johnson and Cecil Mack was added to the musical revue *Runnin' Wild*, featuring star entertainers Flournoy Miller and Aubrey Lyles.) The twisting footwork and unexpected swinging arms and kicking accents of the dance ushered in the era of flappers, so called for the exaggerated movements of their limbs. The Charleston held great sway over the popular imagination of the day, and celebrities including Josephine Baker performed the dance in international venues.

Indeed, these popular dances brought distinctive African American gestures to international populations. The rise of the Charleston and other eccentric dances on theatrical stages demonstrated a cycle in which social dances first emerged in regional locations; traveled to New York, where they were further refined; were transmitted to the New York stage, where they became the toast of the town; and then were performed abroad to great acclaim. The Savoy Ballroom provided dancers with a space to develop many new social dances that then became featured acts on the Apollo stage, including the Harlem stomp, peckin', the Lindy hop, and the big apple.

The Lindy hop clearly related to earlier black social dances, including the turn-of-the-century Texas Tommy, but it differed in its close relation to the propulsive rhythms of swing music and its intricate rhythmic footwork patterns. "Shorty" George Snowden, a celebrated dancer, has been credited with naming the dance after the aviator Charles "Lindy" Lindbergh, who made the first successful nonstop solo flight across the Atlantic. Various groups, including the Shorty Snowden Dancers and Herbert "Whitey" White's Lindy Hoppers, performed it on international tour and in the movies. Frankie Manning, who later became a professional choreographer, has been credited with innovating the spectacular "air" steps in the mid-'30s for professional dance exhibitions.

The Lindy hop included breakaway steps that encouraged individual expression. Lindy hop movements contributed to the big apple, an African American group social dance, briefly popular in the late '30s. Related to the even earlier ring shout and the cakewalk in form, the dance began when couples marched in a counterclockwise circular formation. A caller directed steps to the dancers and, at times, allowed couples to enter the center of the circle to demonstrate spontaneous virtuosic movements.

The big apple, which derived its name from the Big Apple Nightclub in Columbia, South Carolina, spread across the country when it became the centerpiece of traveling stage shows featuring teenage dancers. By 1937 the dance had reached the Savoy Ballroom in New York, where its format solidified further to include comic, eccentric steps from earlier dances. These included a modified version of the Charleston; the Suzy-Q, in which dancers traveled sideways while twisting the feet with one foot on the toe and the other on the heel; spank the baby, in which dancers fanned their bottoms with one hand as if scolding a naughty child; the peck, in which dancers facing each other thrust their necks forward, imitating the pecking motion of chickens and roosters; the Shorty George, in which dancers slunk from side to side with their arms pointing downward at the sides of their bodies; and truckin', an exaggerated walking locomotion that traveled around a circle with one admonitory finger raised upward.

Like the cakewalk, the various animal dances, the Charleston, and the Lindy hop before it, the big apple achieved huge international popularity and produced an industry of distinctive fashions, special-event dance parties at nightclubs, and courses of dance study offered by teachers who taught its steps to cultural outsiders. In this way, the popular dances of African Americans produced routes of understanding and exchange that influenced the marketplace, the social status, and the physical capacities of an international public.

Irene and Vernon Castle helped introduce African American social dances to whites through performances and their dance school.

Earl "Snake Hips" Tucker, who created the dance bearing his nickname, was often featured with Duke Ellington's orchestra.

2

New Deal, New Swing: The Apollo Theater in the 1930s and 1940s

1935

April 19
Billie Holiday makes Apollo debut.

May 13
Frank Schiffman and Leo Brecher take over the Apollo. Announced as a "merger" with the Harlem Opera House, which becomes a movie theater. Brecher gives Schiffman a half interest in the Apollo. Usually thirty-one shows per week: four per day, plus extra shows on Wednesday, Saturday, and Sunday; sixty to ninety minutes per show.

Bessie Smith headlines at the Apollo on three weekly bills.

1936

Lena Horne makes Apollo debut singing with Noble Sissle's Orchestra.

1937

March 19
Count Basie Orchestra makes Apollo debut.

1938

Sister Rosetta Tharpe first plays the Apollo with the **Cab Calloway** Orchestra.

1940

Late June
Coleman Hawkins leads Friday after-hours/end-of-show jam session at the Apollo featuring Count Basie, Tommy Dorsey, Harry James, Bunny Berrigan, John Kirby, and Gene Krupa. Presages and parallels development of bebop in uptown clubs.

December
Lionel Hampton's sixteen-piece band appears, featuring Dexter Gordon and Illinois Jacquet.

ca. 1942–45

Apollo sets aside thirty-five tickets daily for **soldiers** at the Harlem Defense Recreation Center. Tuesdays at the USO are "Apollo Night."

1942

October
Sarah Vaughan wins Amateur Night, discovered by Billy Eckstine.

1943

April 23
Sarah Vaughan debuts with Earl Hines's band at the Apollo.

1944

Billy Eckstine's band debuts at the Apollo.

1945

Dinah Washington makes first Apollo appearance.

Billy Eckstine receives award as Outstanding Male Vocalist on Apollo stage. He goes solo in 1947.

September 21
Nat King Cole begins a weeklong engagement which is so popular that his stay is extended into the following week.

Late 1940s– early '50s

Frank Schiffman's elder son, Jack, runs the Apollo.

1947

Sammy Davis Jr. first appears at the Apollo as part of the Will Mastin Trio.

Rev. Adam Clayton Powell Jr. organizes boycott of 125th Street stores to protest various forms of discrimination by white-owned businesses.

1948

Louis Jordan's band is so popular that they are held over for a second week.

It's Showtime!

The Birth of the Apollo Theater

Tuliza Fleming

Playing the Apollo was different than playing anywhere else because of the setting and where it was...the theater being in New York, and the prestige of the theater, and the history of the theater. I mean, it was not only black acts that went up there [to] play; white acts played up there [as well].... It was the place to play if you were going to play up in Harlem.

—John Levy
Interview with Steve Rowland
April 24, 2009

Legendary tap dancer Bill "Bojangles" Robinson was a major star onstage and in films throughout the '30s.

The legendary Apollo Theater emerged in the wake of the Harlem Renaissance, in the midst of the Great Depression, and during a time when Harlem, New York, was considered the "Negro capital of America." When the Apollo first opened its doors to an integrated audience in 1934, the theater was uniquely poised to take full advantage of Harlem's abundance of African American entertainers and burgeoning black community. According to Apollo emcee Ralph Cooper, "Harlem...was the one place in the whole country where black men and women could express themselves and do their thing. Black talent and black culture could flourish in Harlem like nowhere else in the land....Harlem music, dance, and even language helped turn American culture black."

During its first sixteen years of existence, the Apollo presented almost every notable African American jazz band, singer, dancer, and comedian of the era. Although white and other nonblack performers were always welcome on its stage, the Apollo Theater was best known as the nation's leading showplace for black entertainment. In addition to presenting the best and brightest in African American entertainment, the Apollo's tradition of hosting its weekly Amateur Night contest was, as Bobby Schiffman (son of Apollo owner Frank Schiffman) noted in 1965, "without question the most productive program of its kind...as far as spawning talent for show business in general is concerned, going all the way back to Ella Fitzgerald, Billy Eckstine, Sarah Vaughan, Billie Holiday, all the way up to 30 or 40 percent of those major black attractions that are working today." Whether they were discovered during Amateur Night or bolstered by the advantage of appearing on the Apollo

stage at the beginning of their careers, the cachet of a successful Apollo performance
was considered a tremendous boost to any show business hopeful.

Perhaps the most important element contributing to the mystical star-making
power of the Apollo Theater was its audience. Apollo's audience was renowned
for its ability to catapult entertainers to stardom, alert them to the inadequacies of
their art, or doom them to the realm of obscurity. Performing before an Apollo
audience has been universally identified by professional and amateur entertainers
alike as either extremely unnerving (if they dislike you) or spectacularly gratifying
(if they approve), but never a dull or lifeless encounter. Although the tradition of black
audiences accepting or rejecting a performer in theaters was common during the
heyday of the TOBA vaudeville circuit (the Theatre Owners Booking Association),
satirically dubbed "Tough on Black Asses" by many of its contracted entertainers,
the outspoken behavior of the Apollo's audience was by far the most notorious.
For example, Sammy Davis Jr., who first appeared at the Apollo in 1947 as a dancer
in the Will Mastin Trio along with his uncle and his father, found his experience with
the audience to be particularly memorable. "It was really kind of special," Davis
recalled. "There was a marvelous rapport. The audience talked back to the performer.

125th Street Apollo marquee in
the late '30s. Featured that week
were swing bandleader Count Basie,
tap star Honi Coles, and comedian
Jackie "Moms" Mabley.

Audience members enjoy Amateur Night at the Apollo, 1947. The audience was as much a part of the show as the performers, who enjoyed the cheers (and often endured the jeers) of the highly critical spectators.

The performer talked back to the audience. It wasn't heckling so much as we know it now. But the guy in the audience would say, 'You ain't shit.' And the performer would say, 'Yes, I am' right back at him." Comic Flip Wilson stated that "Many instances, while performing,…it sounded as if the whole world was going to explode with laughter and any second the balconies would fall. It's a sound I've never heard anywhere else, and it made such an impression that I compare the sound of every audience to that sound….It's a sound I think I'll never forget."

The Apollo's location, timing of its opening, interracial policy, Amateur Night contests, and its discriminating and vocal audience all contributed to the creation of an unparalleled entertainment venue that would eventually eclipse all other black theaters in both reputation and longevity. Singer Ernestine Allen said, "You could make it at the Howard [in Washington] or the Royal [in Baltimore], but you *never, never, never* really made it until you made it at the Apollo." Like Allen, countless other African American entertainers viewed the Apollo as the ultimate launching pad for their budding careers, hopes, and dreams.

The entertainment venue known as the Apollo Theater was built in 1914 by burlesque theater operators Jules Hurtig and Harry Seamon, and was initially called Hurtig and Seamon's New Burlesque Theatre. This whites-only music hall was purchased in 1928 by rival burlesque entertainment mogul Billy Minsky, who renamed it the 125th Street Apollo Theatre, while retaining the burlesque format and whites-only policy. In 1934 Sidney Cohen and his manager Morris Sussman transformed the Apollo into a showplace for African American music, dance, and comedy. Keeping the name 125th Street Apollo Theatre, it opened to an interracial audience for the first time on Friday, January 26. That night the Apollo presented a "colored revue," *Jazz a la Carte.* Emceed by Ralph Cooper, it showcased the music of Benny Carter and His Orchestra and an all-black chorus line called the Gorgeous Hot Steppers.

The idea to convert their 1,500-seat burlesque theater to a venue that showcased African American entertainment for a black audience served two purposes. It complied with Mayor Fiorello La Guardia's campaign against burlesque in New York City, and it took advantage of the growing African American population in Harlem that had tripled in size between 1910 and 1930. This critical decision fostered a new cultural phenomenon: a legendary theatrical institution whose featured artists, musical genres, and entertainment styles reflected and affected the political, social, and cultural developments both in Harlem and in the broader American sphere.

The hard times of the Depression led people from all walks of life to seek escape through inexpensive popular entertainment. The Harlem community felt the effects of the Great Depression more acutely than other New York City neighborhoods, which all but erased the hard-won financial gains made by African Americans during the boom times of the 1920s. The Apollo emerged from this environment as a refuge that, even if only temporarily, eased life's burdens by providing its patrons with sidesplitting laughter, good music, acrobatic dancing, and theatrical entertainment, all for the price of fifteen cents (fifty cents for Wednesday and Saturday nights).

Season tickets for the Apollo Theater when it was still a whites-only burlesque house, prior to 1934. The theater then featured a combination of scantily clad beauties and broad comedy.

Cohen and Sussman modeled the Apollo's theatrical format after the vaudevillian tradition, a tradition called "presentation." The second owners of the Apollo, Frank Schiffman and Leo Brecher, continued this tradition at the theater for decades after it lost favor throughout the rest of the country. The Apollo would open around 10 a.m., offering four to five shows each day. These shows would usually start with a short film, a newsreel, or a feature film, followed by a revue. These revues would consist of six or seven separate live performances surrounding a headliner act, which during the '30s was generally a big swing or jazz band. Secondary forms of entertainment featured in these Apollo revues included singers and musicians, dancers, female impersonators, animal acts, one-act plays or scenes from plays, athletes, chorus line dancers, acrobatic acts, and comedians who would often joke with the hosts, Ralph Cooper and Willie Bryant, throughout the show. For a single ticket, a patron could stay for one show or for the duration of the day.

COMEDY

Almost all of the Apollo's early comics were seasoned

professionals who emerged from the black vaudeville tradition, and many of them continued to perform in traditional blackface. These comics based their routines on

Comedians Mantan Moreland and Pigmeat Markham played perfect foils. They were popular in the comedy skits that made up an important part of the Apollo's stage shows from the '30s through the early '50s.

recognizable characters within situational skits that made use of multiple props and setups. Apollo comedian George Wiltshire remarked, "Back in the late '30s up until the early '50s, we were doing big comedy situations that called for six and seven people in the cast with special scenery built for us. There were usually two comedians, a straight man, a straight woman, a character man, and a character woman....Vivian Harris...was then, and still is in my estimation, the best straight woman we ever had." In addition to Wiltshire and Harris, the Apollo also featured such notable comedians as Stepin Fetchit, John Mason, Dewey "Pigmeat" Markham, Crackshot Hunter and Edna Mae, Butterbeans and Susie, Mantan Moreland, and Eddie "Rochester" Anderson.

According to Cooper, "The Apollo soon became famous for our comedy bits. Half the stars in vaudeville used to come up here looking for new material. Milton Berle came so often, he started bringing his secretary along to take notes on what we were doing." Cooper adds that although Apollo regulars such as Berle, Joey Adams, and Jackie Gleason came both to enjoy as well as steal material, they would have to refashion the Apollo material to suit the tastes of white audiences. "A lot of our humor" Cooper added, "was double entendre, stuff that was a little too racy for middle-American radio."

The Apollo Theater continued its signature vaudevillian comedy routines through World War II. Following the war, in an effort to save money, Apollo management began to scale back significantly its large-scale comedy skits, reducing its cast members from seven members to three. This extensive reduction in cast, props, and scenery ushered in a new era of African American humor, the beginning of stand-up comedy. At this time a younger generation of comics entered the field who were more in tune with the Apollo audience's increased sense of social and political awareness. This new generation of comics, called "talkers," rejected many of the more outlandish traditions of black vaudeville, such as blackface and funny costumes, in favor of appearing in a more dignified manner manifested by their preference for wearing fashionable suits and tuxedos.

One of the earliest black stand-up comics from this new generation was Timmie Rogers. An Apollo regular known as both a comedian and musician, Rogers was one of the first black comedians to deliver a monologue directly to a white audience, which was considered less aggressive, instead of to another black comedian onstage. Rogers partially attributes the demise of blackface on the Apollo stage to his persuasive arguments against the practice. He stated:

> When I came along in 1944, I says to John Mason, Crackshot Hunter, and Pigmeat Markham, "It's time to get the black off your face; you don't need it."
> They gave me hell....I only had one valid point that stuck in the guys' minds. That was, "Suppose you were on radio? Would you wear black on your face?"...
> About two years later they all took the black off their faces, and they were just as funny without blackface, because the makeup, the clothes don't make you. What you say makes you.

Rogers is probably best remembered for his clean stage acts, political commentary, and his signature phrase, "Oh, yeah!" which he coined at the Apollo Theater.

Most important, humorists like Rogers as well as later Apollo regulars such as Redd Foxx and Slappy White radically altered the Apollo's comic tradition by speaking directly to the audience, delivering jokes that were more critical of American society, racial inequities, and white society in general. Overwhelmingly male, these newcomers laid the foundation for contemporary black stand-up comedy.

Dancer/comedian Timmie Rogers, who took a strong stand in the '40s against blackface makeup, was influential in convincing his fellow comedians to eliminate it from the Apollo stage.

Like comedy, swing was an extremely popular form

of music that served as an affordable means of entertainment for Americans across
the country seeking respite from the economic turbulence of the Great Depression.
Swing music emerged from the dance halls, nightclubs, and theaters of Harlem
in the '20s and '30s. During this period, swing evolved into a number of variations
and styles. Even though each swing band had its own distinctive flavor, they often
shared certain commonalities. These included large band ensembles, improvisational
solos by individual band members, strong emphasis on the rhythmic quality of
the arrangements (beats that would "swing"), the pervasiveness of the riff (a short
melodic phrase played repeatedly), and the practice of musical dialogue (often called
counterpoint, where soloists or units such as the brass
and reed sections played riffs against one another
in the tradition of call and response).

For the first few decades of its existence, the
Apollo built its stage shows around big swing bands.
Apollo headliners included bandleaders such as Duke
Ellington, Count Basie, Don Redman, Chick Webb,
Lucky Millinder, and Fletcher Henderson. Glamorous
lead singers including Ella Fitzgerald, Lena Horne,
Bessie Smith, and Billie Holiday often performed
with these bands, increasing their audience appeal.

Although big bands remained an
integral part of the Apollo presentation, during the
'40s swing began to fade from the spotlight in
American popular culture, forcing the theater to
adapt. The United States' entry into World War II,
the recording ban of 1942–44, and the rise
of bebop were all factors in the demise of the
big swing bands. Many bands lost as many
as two-thirds of their musicians to the war, and
the recording ban imposed by the American
Federation of Musicians, which prevented its
members from making records (until the recording companies devised a suitable
arrangement for paying fees for records played on the radio and jukeboxes), led to
a shift in emphasis from the band as the main attraction to the singer. During the
ban vocalists were still allowed to record, leading to a rise in their popularity and
enabling solo singers to steal the spotlight.

The rise of bebop also siphoned away musicians from the relatively regimented and impersonal arrangements of swing music to the more complex melodies, harmonies, and improvisational style of bebop. Many of the big bands continued to play with a reduced number of gigs, lower pay, and almost no recording contracts, but only Ellington's and Basie's bands were able to grow and thrive during this period, as both leaders created arrangements that featured and catered to the individual styles of their musicians.

Another exception to the general demise of swing was the rise of the all-girl bands during the '40s. All-girl bands had played professionally throughout the '20s and '30s, but they didn't become national attractions until the American involvement in World War II. Across the country African American girl bands began to fill the gap left by their male counterparts while they fought overseas. A few of these bands branched out from the local spotlight to perform nationally, receiving widespread acclaim. The Prairie View Co-Eds, the International Sweethearts of Rhythm (the first integrated all-women's band), and Eddie Durham's All-Star Girl Orchestra were the most distinguished of these groups. All three groups played multiple performances at the Apollo during the '40s. Even though these bands were composed of relatively young women (many of them still in college), their accomplishments as musicians afforded them the same treatment as other feature bands at the Apollo: they performed at least four shows a day, playing their own repertoire as well as numbers for the various other secondary acts in the presentation.

The Prairie View Co-Eds, an all-female jazz ensemble from Prairie View A&M College in Texas, were marketed as a novelty, but the band's solid musicianship ensured their popularity throughout several Apollo engagements.

While the vast majority of swing groups were disbanding, other newer musical innovations, such as rhythm and blues and bebop, were bursting onto America's cultural scene. Jazz saxophonist, vocalist, songwriter, and bandleader Louis Jordan is considered to be the major innovator of a genre known as jump blues, whose rhythmic foundation was derived from classic jazz, blues, and swing with a dance-oriented, up-tempo beat. Widely acknowledged as a primary innovator of rhythm and blues and one of the most popular musicians of his era, Jordan laid the foundation for what would become rock and roll.

By 1946 Jordan was a perennial crowd favorite at the Apollo, headlining multiple shows throughout the year, playing to packed and appreciative audiences, and receiving top pay for his performances from Schiffman, who often praised his

Louis Jordan (far right) and several of his Tympany Five musicians on the Apollo stage. In the late '40s Jordan pioneered "jump blues," an up-tempo, highly danceable music credited as one of the major precursors of R & B.

talent and showmanship in his notes. Even though he loved the Apollo audience, Jordan did have more than a few complaints about the theater's shabby and dirty conditions, which he believed made him repeatedly hoarse. He was more generous in his appraisal of the owner, stating that Schiffman was "one of the best managers of theatres I have ever worked for; he could get out of you what you think you can't do...

made a lot of Negro stars. A great manager! But as for the theatre—it stinks."

While Jordan was regaling audiences with his jump swing sound, a more complex and improvisational style of jazz, which would later be called bebop, slowly began to enter the Harlem music scene. Because bebop was developed by Charlie Parker, Dizzy Gillespie, Thelonious Monk, and others during the recording ban, it was not widely available to the general public. However, those fortunate enough to see these artists play at the Apollo as well as at other jazz clubs and after-hours venues witnessed the complete transformation of big band swing into a new style of jazz, emphasizing extended improvisational solos and complex harmonies, while a rhythmic beat defined the bass and drummer (who accentuated melodic phrases through accents on a snare drum). Smaller ensembles became more common.

According to musician and Apollo legend Lionel Hampton, the first time bebop was played on the trumpet was when Dizzy performed the song "Hot Mallets" at the Apollo. Saxophonist Charlie Parker also conducted a few bold musical experiments during his engagements at the Apollo. In 1950 Frank Schiffman reflected on Parker's atypical musical presentation, noting that "[Parker] appeared with an unusual combination of 3 violins, a viola, an oboe, and the rhythm section. Presentation well liked." A year later, however, after a similar appearance, Schiffman wrote, "Parker is an excellent musician. Has some drawing power. Doubt continued value of the 'strings.'" In spite of the criticism he received from Schiffman as well as from jazz critics of that era, the string experiment performed at the Apollo eventually produced the album *Charlie Parker with Strings*, a recording meant to bridge the gap between jazz and classical music.

DANCE

During the '30s and '40s there were approximately

fifty nationally performing dance soloists, teams, and troupes working on entertainment circuits in black theaters throughout the northern and southern regions. The Apollo was considered the premier American stage for dancers and dance innovation, a distinction that diminished with the demise of the presentation format and big band music during the late '40s and through the '50s. Apollo legend Honi Coles recalled that, in the heyday of dance at the theater, dancing acts "were usually used as the opening act to assure a fast and flashy start before the revue. However, if the middle or even the closing spot in the show needed bolstering, the dancing act could fill the need." In addition to bookending revues, many of the country's most admired dancers, such as the music and dance team of Ford "Buck" Washington and John "Bubbles" Sublett, Bill "Bojangles" Robinson, and Eddie Rector, were billed by the Apollo as headlining acts.

Regardless of their accomplishments, all Apollo dancers were accompanied by the featured jazz or swing band of the week and, as a result, the musicians and dancers developed a type of symbiotic relationship onstage. "Playing the Apollo was

The Nicholas Brothers, 1943. Brothers Fayard and Harold were famous for their acrobatic tap routines, including dramatic leaps and splits.

Cholly Atkins and Honi Coles were famous for their "class act," combining intricate tap moves with a smooth, debonair attitude. The duo were popular performers on the Apollo stage through the early '50s.

different from playing a dance hall, because in a dance hall the dancers had to dance to your music," recalls musician and bandleader Andy Kirk. "At the Apollo, with a star like Bojangles, we had to play music for him to dance to....We always had regard for the artist, whatever he was doing, and our music was background. We wanted to play it right—the way he wanted it."

According to dance scholar Jacqui Malone, the Apollo featured a wide variety of dancing acts and dance styles during the '30s and '40s, including ballroom, comedy, acrobatics, adagio, flash, eccentric, and tap. They also had a line of chorus girls and a line of chorus boys (who were called the Linen Club Boys, according to famed dancer and choreographer Cholly Atkins). All these dancers were accompanied by the week's featured band, although some of the bandleaders were more sympathetic to dance than others. Atkins recalled, "All the dancers loved to work with Basie because his music was very earthy and had so much feeling. And see, Basie got a big kick out of the whole thing because he loved dancers, especially tap dancers."

The dramatic innovations practiced by Apollo dancers influenced countless other dance groups around New York and the nation. According to Coles, "Tap dancers were always highly competitive, and any dancing act opening at the Apollo would always be confronted by the first two rows being filled with rival dancers. Consequently you were always on your toes." In addition to the proclivity for dancers in the Apollo's audience to appropriate new and inventive styles, the talented performers in the Apollo chorus lines also were known to steal a move or two from the dancers that traveled with the big swing bands. Coles recalled, "A dancing act could come into the Apollo with all original material, and when they left at the end of the week, the chorus lines would have stolen many of the outstanding things that they did."

Perhaps the most important and sophisticated jazz-influenced dance innovation to emerge during the swing era was rhythm tap, invented by Apollo regular John "Bubbles" Sublett. Bubbles infused tap dancing with the complex rhythmic structure and improvisational freedom that not only defined the era's jazz music but also is thought to have served as precursor to the distinctive rhythmic quality of bebop. His inventive style of tap dancing influenced countless generations of dancers, including Michael Jackson. Even though the rhythmic and melodic structures of jump swing and rhythm and blues continued to facilitate dancing among listeners as well as performers on the Apollo stage, the demise of the big swing bands and the tighter arrangements and complex polyrhythmic configuration of bebop (which was generally perceived as incompatible with the art of dance) marked the closing stages of the greatest age of tap.

THE END OF AN ERA

When the Apollo Theater opened in 1934, it was one

of the first entertainment venues in New York City to have a fully integrated audience (in the balconies as well as on the main floor) and to employ African Americans both onstage and behind the curtain. For the next sixteen years it became a bastion of African American talent, a star-making vehicle, and one of the only theaters in the country to feature the dying art of black vaudeville. By the late '40s, as Frank Schiffman grew older, first his son Jack and then Bobby began to assume greater responsibility for the Apollo's management. Upon the recommendation of WWRL disc jockey Dr. Jive (Tommy Smalls), Bobby began to replace the vaudevillian-based presentation format with what became slowly known as the R & B revue—where six or seven groups with hit songs were featured in a row. Bobby's decision to replace the theater's tradition of featuring headlining acts coupled with ancillary acts (comedy and dance) with this new format presaged the end of a unique and important era in American entertainment.

Crowds outside the Apollo in the late '40s. Featured acts that week included the all-female band International Sweethearts of Rhythm and pioneering jazz tenor saxophone player Illinois Jacquet.

Impresario Frank Schiffman

John Edward Hasse

Apollo owner/manager Frank Schiffman at his desk. Schiffman was an astute businessman and community legend who guided the theater from 1935 until his death in 1974.

Born of immigrant parents into a large, poor family, Frank Schiffman managed to earn a degree from the College of the City of New York, then tried various jobs before opening a motion picture film delivery service in the early 1920s. Through his work, Schiffman met Leo Brecher, who owned a number of movie theaters and clubs in Harlem. In 1925 Schiffman and Brecher became partners in the management of Harlem's famous Lafayette Theatre, refurbished it, and turned it into a house for black vaudeville. In 1934 they took over the Harlem Opera House, seven blocks south, and ran it briefly as another vaudeville house for the African American market.

The Opera House's biggest competition was Sidney Cohen's Apollo Theater, located on the same block of 125th Street. Cohen had opened the Apollo on January 26, 1934, and it had been an immediate success. However, his reign was short-lived, as in mid-1935 he died suddenly of a heart attack. Seizing an opportunity, Schiffman and Brecher took over ownership of the Apollo Theater on June 9, 1935—just two months after Harlem's first race riot. They thereupon ended vaudeville at the Harlem Opera House and converted it into a movie theater. Brecher was essentially a silent partner in the Apollo, and Schiffman, assisted from the late '40s by one of his sons, Jack or Bobby, ran the theater until he semiretired around 1960 and Bobby took the helm. Frank Schiffman died in 1974 at the age of eighty; the theater closed under the Schiffman family's management in 1976.

When Schiffman began running the Apollo, he continued the policy that the theater had established when it opened in 1934—welcoming people of color at a time when many businesses on 125th Street, including the landmark Hotel Theresa, did not. The tallest building in Harlem, the hotel didn't admit blacks until 1937, although it would later become known as the "Waldorf of Harlem" and Malcolm X had his headquarters there.

With the United States moving only slowly out of its Great Depression and Harlem worse off economically than white areas, it must have been difficult to successfully operate a theater playing vaudeville, which was slowly dying (many vaudeville houses were being converted into movie houses). The *Pittsburgh Courier*, in a June 1937 article, appreciated what the Apollo had brought to Harlem: "It isn't strange to see a good show at the Apollo, for… aside from building a better theatre for this section day by day, the Apollo management has gone ahead with the building of better and finer musical stage presentations."

In the late '40s and early '50s Jack Schiffman helped his father run the Apollo, and then brother Bobby took over this role. Bobby started booking around 1959, bringing in more youth-oriented acts such as Motown entertainers. Bobby was not only younger and more in tune with the Harlem audience, but friendlier, too. The entertainers preferred working with him. He played golf with Smokey Robinson and hung out with Marvin Gaye.

Frank Schiffman was not fundamentally a showman or producer, but first and foremost a businessman. His son Jack wrote that "in a business where good booking can spell the difference between success and disaster, my father has few peers for combativeness—and at times, inventiveness." Calling his father's spirit "pugnacious," Jack wrote, "He was the supreme anachronism for a show-biz type: he was educated, articulate, and straight-laced. He could ooze charm; but he could also cut you down with a glance or skewer you with a phrase." In his 1971 book *Uptown*, Jack admitted, "There is nothing benign about this impatient, intense man, and most performers regard him with a soul-bending mixture of awe, dislike, fear, love, and reverence."

The ability of the acts to fill seats was paramount to Schiffman, a conclusion that is underscored by the over twelve hundred five-by-eight-inch cards—now housed at the Smithsonian's National Museum of American History—that he maintained, beginning in 1946, on all Apollo acts. One looks in vain for his details of an act's style, repertory, and soloists. What one finds, besides the fee he paid each act, are pithy comments about drawing power, polish, affordability, freshness or staleness, how each act registered with the audience, and sometimes a note about a musician's cooperativeness or troublesomeness. Nor are there personal diaries or self-revealing letters to verify the assumption that the shrewd Schiffman must have been keenly aware of his

tenuous position as a white Jewish businessman operating in a struggling black neighborhood.

Schiffman's file cards do offer a fascinating glimpse into the variety of performers who appeared at the house. His use of terms like "cooperative"—to indicate that an act didn't complain about the theater's low booking fees or often run-down facilities or otherwise challenge him—reveals that as a manager he was interested in drawing audiences as large as possible for acts who caused little trouble and whose fees were affordable. Many acts had a varied history at the theater, sometimes drawing well and sometimes doing poorly, occasionally within the same time period. Schiffman applauded tenor saxophonist Gene Ammons's December 27, 1950, appearance ("Pretty good band"), but by the following June 22, he wrote, "Very troublesome. Repeated same routine as previously. No drawing card." Many of the cards reveal Schiffman's preference for big-band style jazz over the newer R & B styles. These younger performers were also less likely to kowtow to management. Of singer-guitarist Chuck Berry's March 13, 1958, appearance, he wrote, "Very bad experience. No drawing power at all." Schiffman also had little tolerance for the raw sensuality of contemporary rock. Of singer-guitarist Bo Diddley's December 31, 1965, appearance, he wrote: "Drums, guitar, 3 girls—doesn't really fit this show but after taking out filth—closed very well." And of rock singer Buddy Holly's famous August 16, 1957, appearance—where the audience was shocked to discover that the Crickets were white, but nonetheless gave them a warm welcome—Schiffman simply wrote: "Four White boys. Very bad." Some of the acts, he noted, drew poorly enough to not offset their fees, and he took a "substantial loss." The facts that running the Apollo was a tenuous business requiring sustained risk taking and that some of his shows lost a lot of money did not occur to his critics—at least they didn't mention such matters in print.

Schiffman was a tough negotiator and could be a difficult man to work for: Lena Horne had several run-ins with him and by the late '40s reportedly decided to never perform at the Apollo again. One of those whom Schiffman clashed with, before taking over the Apollo, was Ralph Cooper, for many years the master of ceremonies of Amateur Night contests, who recalled bitterly in his 1990 memoirs: "all Schiffman cared about was money....Schiffman was a smart businessman. But he was also a ruthless competitor who would do anything, including take advantage of his black employees and exploit the great black artists who worked for him, in order to increase his profits and beat down the opposition." Cooper charged that "Schiffman offended a lot of black performers and crew people because of his imperious manner. He talked fast and he liked to talk down to people....From the janitors in the basement to the stars on his stage, Frank Schiffman disdained them all."

Before Schiffman assumed control of the Apollo, the theater hosted community events—a policy he continued and expanded. In 1937 the stage welcomed four of the "Scottsboro Boys" who had been released on bail. Beginning in 1938, the Apollo held an annual Midnight Benefit Show for charitable causes—these shows grew to include a glittering array of performers, black and white. Eventually the Apollo would donate its theater for a dozen or so benefits per year for such organizations as the NAACP, Negro Actors Guild, British War Relief Society, Colored Actors Welfare Fund, and Harlem Children's Fresh Air Fund. The festivities, usually starting at midnight, would sometimes run as late as 5:30 am. Schiffman could also be warm to some musicians who had maintained long associations with the theater. After the death of bandleader Jimmie Lunceford in 1947, Schiffman wrote a heartfelt letter of condolence, five paragraphs long, to Lunceford's widow— a letter as polished and poised as a president's.

In 1948 Schiffman wrote a letter to Ed Sullivan, then a leading newspaper columnist, thanking him for describing the reaction of the Apollo audience as a "community effort": "We have tried to make ourselves a part of the community. We help raise funds for many of the desperate needs which exist here. We help promote employment amongst Negro's [sic]. I have found real joy myself in being chairman of the Harlem Children's Camp Fund, a Director of the Urban League...and other organizations."

Schiffman helped found the Freedom National Bank (the first black-owned bank in Harlem), held two lifetime memberships in the NAACP, and earned a citation from the Abyssinian Baptist Church, where Rev. Adam Clayton Powell Jr. preached.

That Schiffman was considered an important figure is attested to by the correspondence he received. One of the most striking items preserved in the entire Schiffman Collection at the Smithsonian is a letter dated December 17, 1963, from Martin Luther King Jr. on Southern Christian Leadership Conference letterhead (see Herb Boyd's essay "The Apollo and Civil Rights" in this book). In 1968 Mel Watkins, an African American writer for the *New York Times*, asserted:

In the eyes of the Harlem community, the Apollo management has an overwhelmingly favorable image. Of foremost importance, the theater's admission cost has been kept at a reasonable level—a $2.75 top. Besides starring black performers and staffing the theater with blacks from the beginning, the Schiffmans have been noticeably active in uptown affairs and civil rights causes. They are actively involved with local youth groups and church boards and have often extended a needed boost to fledgling black businesses....According to Manhattan Borough President Percy E. Sutton, "The Schiffmans have traditionally involved themselves in Harlem community affairs. If all businessmen had done as much, community tension would be considerably lessened." It is noteworthy that during the past three Harlem riots, while many white-owned businesses were stormed, the Apollo remained untouched.

If Schiffman drew criticism from some quarters for his difficult personality and demanding, imperious management style, for the low salaries he paid to the nonstars, and for the increasingly shabby backstage conditions, he can be fairly credited with—besides the contributions noted above—helping to racially integrate a main thoroughfare in Harlem; providing African Americans with affordable, meaningful, big-time live entertainment; being the only theater owner in New York, for many years, to employ black stagehands; and for his willingness to take suggestions from his staff and to experiment.

Speaking about Frank and Bobby Schiffman, singer Gladys Knight said, "They were some of the first people to give us the opportunity. They were *fair* people." Comedian King Coleman remarked in 1963: "Without the Apollo a lot of brothers and sisters wouldn't be making it. Frank and Bobby Schiffman are *soul* people."

PEARL BAILEY
7/3/47   1000.00
   12/31/48   Basie Unit
  10/27/49   1933.33
8/30/50 $200.00. - Excellent comedy, talk, patter and dance. Temper-
mental in demands but a fine performer. Not yet a big
drawing card.

4/18/52 $2000.00 Excellent performance. Disappointing attraction.

q2/20/53   Co-featured with DUKE ELLINGTON. She received guarantee of
$5000.00, made about $1700.00 more as a result made with DUKE
ELLINGTON

6/19/53

      Superb performance. Business disappointing. Partly
due to heat wave

3/24/54 $8,397.09   Very good. Worked throughout show. Very satisfactory
business.

1/27/56   Had her own revue. Did an excellent job.

PEARL BAILEY

11/2/56   Had her own revue. One of the greatest shows we have ever
had.   Net receipts $27,588.53 . She got $14,803.12
Held over with entire show for second week. Added Condos
and Brandow to the show.

5/8/59   Held over for two weeks. Total receipts $29,002.08, Excellent
Revue.

10-16-59 Show earned $14,489.52. for the first week.

4/19/63   The usual Brilliant performance. Most of the familiar
songs and bits and some fine new material. Stays on for
an hour and is entertaining all the way.

10/22/65 $15,000.00 for entire revue which included Martin Bros.
and Bunny Briggs plus band.   The absolute mistress of
comedy - song. Has audience in her hands from start to
finish. Excellent!!!

Heyday of the Big Bands

John Edward Hasse

When the Apollo Theater opened in 1934, big bands dominated American musical entertainment. As interest in public dancing had surged in the 1920s, dance bands had been expanding in scope. The larger aggregations sonically filled dance halls and ballrooms—which were growing in size and number—and provided composers and arrangers with more resources to create and sustain musical interest. By the mid-'30s, there were three thousand "name" bands performing and often touring the United States. Bands now competed keenly for popularity, much like that of great athletic teams. It was the Swing Era.

While big bands played mostly for dancing, the best ones also executed stage shows, during which musicianship and showmanship became more important than keeping a good beat for dancers. Some of the black bands toured houses on the Theatre Owners Booking Association (TOBA) circuit, but they also played predominantly white theaters, too, such as the Earle in Philadelphia and the Oriental in Chicago.

When the Apollo Theater opened on January 26, 1934, big bands immediately became the main drawing card for the theater—as signaled by the appearance of Benny Carter's band on opening night—and would remain so well into the '40s. When Leo Brecher and Frank Schiffman took over management of the Apollo in May 1935, they continued and solidified the policy of featuring black bands. They had experience at booking big bands; as managers of Harlem's Lafayette Theatre, before the Apollo opened as a variety theater, they had engaged bands such as those of Duke Ellington, Benny Carter, and Cab Calloway. Brecher and Schiffman's first booking at the Apollo was the big band of Don Redman. Soon the Apollo would become, like Harlem's Savoy Ballroom, one of the most important and celebrated venues for jazz musicians and both a proving ground and a launching pad for many African American entertainers.

All the best-remembered African American bands played at the Apollo, and some that never became widely popular were solid Harlem favorites. Not only were the big bands the main drawing card, as the financial ledgers in the Schiffman Apollo Theater Collection at the Smithsonian's National Museum of American History attest, they were the Apollo's largest expense. Among the better paid were Cab Calloway ($6,500 plus a percentage) and Duke Ellington ($4,700); others received between $950 and $2,000. In the '30s, admitted Frank Schiffman's son Jack, there wasn't any "rhyme or reason to band salaries." They probably had to do as much with band managers' skill at negotiating with Schiffman as with their drawing power.

The Apollo's shows ran from Friday through Thursday. On opening night the stakes were high, and the air crackled with electricity as crowds came in expectantly to check out the new

Benny Carter on the Apollo stage, 1942. Carter's band played the Apollo's inaugural opening night in 1934, when the theater first became an integrated showcase for African American entertainment.

band, singers, dancers, and other acts. In August 1939, the *New York Amsterdam News* reported that "Friday, the front row and boxes at the Apollo were plentifully peopled by hot music critics for many of the big national magazines and publications as well as theatrical editors, nightclub managers and others." They had come that night to assess the band of ex–Benny Goodman pianist Teddy Wilson.

Some musicians arrived in a highly competitive spirit, ready to jump in if they could. In a Smithsonian Jazz Oral History Program interview, the virtuoso drummer Roy Haynes recalled: "They would always wait in the front row—a group of drummers—so if the drummer couldn't play the show [well enough], they would get the gig for the week. If a new drummer with a band or a young guy come in that couldn't play the show, [he] wouldn't work that week."

Besides a Wednesday night amateur show, broadcast from 11 to 12 p.m., the Apollo produced, at least around 1940, a Monday night jitterbug show, as well as a special Saturday night midnight show, which bandleader Charlie Barnet called "another big attraction at the Apollo. It was patronized by many white folks from downtown. The theater would close after the regularly scheduled shows, and the midnight performance was strictly a matter of reserved seats. We had an hour and a half off before it, and we used to get into a very mellow condition, so those midnight shows really jumped, especially since the audience was usually just as mellow as we were."

Swing music provided a context for forward strides in race relations, as did the Apollo in its own fashion. While most of the bands that played the Apollo were black, several white bands became popular, notably Barnet's—the first white band at the Apollo, in 1934. Five years later, when he returned during the popularity of his hit "Cherokee," he recalled that the audience was so hip they sang his solo along with him. Barnet was the most popular white bandleader in Apollo history. In the words of Jack Schiffman, "Charlie, as more than one jazzman pointed out, led 'the blackest white band of all.'" He hired a number of African American musicians, including bassist Oscar Pettiford and singer

Bandleader/singer Cab Calloway, along with a caricature on an Apollo handbill. He was famous in the '30s for his version of "Minnie the Moocher."

Lena Horne, and won a reputation for being musically color-blind. Barnet played the Apollo regularly until the early '50s.

The band business was dominated by men, but several female-run bands performed at the Apollo. One was led by Blanche Calloway, Cab's sister, who, according to some observers, had at times a better band than her much better-known brother. Others were trumpeter Valaida Snow's all-female orchestra of the '30s, and Eddie Durham's All-Star Girl Orchestra, which was active during World War II. The best-remembered of such groups, the International Sweethearts of Rhythm, played the Apollo through 1953, but never really took off; according to Jack Schiffman, "Only the prevailing prejudices prevented the Sweethearts from becoming a major attraction." In addition to racial discrimination against African Americans, there was also bias within the business against jazzwomen. (The leading jazz magazine of its day, *Down Beat*, called women musicians "skirts" and women singers "chirpies," and even Harlem's *Amsterdam News* called the great Billie Holiday a "chirper"—mild signs of the rampant sexism of the day among both black and white males.)

During the heyday of the big bands, the Apollo's shows typically stuck to a formula: an opening number or two by the featured band would warm up the audience, followed by a "sight act" such as an acrobat or tap dancer, a singer, perhaps a novelty act, a comedy act, and then the headliner performing its most popular work. The shows required the talents of a producer, and the Apollo employed such veteran African American showmen as Leonard Harper and Clarence Robinson. In addition, recalled Charlie Barnet, "The Apollo always had a third-run picture that was shown between stage shows. Nobody paid any attention to it, but it usually cleared the house for the next show."

In a normal week, the Apollo presented thirty-one shows. But during the memorable week of November 28, 1941, featuring Billie Holiday and bandleader-vibraphonist Lionel Hampton, he played forty-five shows, each ending with his sensational finale, "Flying Home." "Some funny things happened at the old Apollo," recalled Hampton. "There was a time when a guy in the second balcony was high on too much reefer. When we were playing 'Flying Home,' he got inspired. He climbed up on the rail and

The International Sweethearts of Rhythm, with bandleader Anna Mae Winburn, 1946.

starting shouting, 'I'm flying, I'm flying.' And then he jumped. It was a miracle that no one was hurt." Another time, on the 1944 opening-night show of Count Basie, a twenty-seven-year-old man jumped out of the second balcony—and was promptly taken by the police for observation and a jail sentence.

"Back then," recalled Hampton in his memoirs, "playing the Apollo was the big-time for black musicians. I was luckier than most, because I'd played the white big-time places with Benny Goodman, but there was something about the Apollo. If you were a black entertainer of any kind—musician, singer, comedian— being a headliner at the Apollo was your proudest achievement."

What made it so? A combination of shrewd booking, management, and promotion by Frank Schiffman; the Apollo's pivotal location in the heart of Harlem; the comparative lack of other theaters where African American entertainers could perform—and polish—their acts for a week at a time; extensive coverage by the African American and entertainment press; and the legendary Apollo audiences: hip, critical, demonstrative, forming an organic interaction with the performers akin to the

Blanche Calloway, 1930s. Overshadowed by her brother, she was a talented singer, bandleader, and composer who ranked among the earliest women to lead a coed band.

call-and-response between a preacher and congregation in a down-home church.

The Apollo audience knew what it wanted. On one hand, the younger members generally favored something new and novel, while, on the other hand, there were those who wanted to hear something familiar, as Duke Ellington was reminded in 1938: "In preparing my big song of the season for the Apollo, I decided to do a new arrangement with rather a strong countermelody. Opening day, I soon learned that the audience, as always, wanted to hear the version they had heard on the air. So we took out the new chart after the first show and went back to the old arrangement, and that's the way it stayed."

"The Apollo audience was a trip," recalled writer Dan Morgenstern. "No other audience was so attuned to what transpired onstage, be it music, dance, or comedy." The audience in the second balcony, where tickets were least expensive, was legendary, as recounted by the *New York Amsterdam News* in 1944:

> *The second balcony…where [sit] the most hardboiled critics of swing—critics without portfolio but who know their music by instinct—is literally the civil service examiners for the poets and peasants of hot music. Cab Calloway, Duke Ellington, Earl Hines, Lionel Hampton, and other emperors of jazz…have sought and won the romping, stomping approval of the Apollo roofers before they swept into swing glory; while the little fry who weren't so hot won disapproval and were shot down the shaft to oblivion.*

> *Every music aggregation that ever played Harlem's Apollo knows what it means to satisfy the balcony boys who will boost you up or bounce you out by their riotous reaction.*

Band battles were a celebrated feature at Harlem's Savoy Ballroom, where two stages at either end of the ballroom provided for alternating bands, and music battles were also sometimes staged at the Apollo. For example, in July 1935 the Cuban American flutist and bandleader "[Alberto] Socarras appeared in a 'battle of music,'" according to the *New York Amsterdam News*. "Luis Russell and his orchestra were Socarras' adversary. Reports are that Socarras won a decisive victory."

In 1940 a heated jam session prompted the *New York Amsterdam News* to headline a review "Two 'Hawks,' Barnet, Carter Jam with Basie Band: Cops Stop Ticket Sale at Apollo When Jitterbugs Swarm All Over the Place":

> *Nearly 1,000 swing fans and jitterbugs were turned away from Count Basie's Million dollar jam session at the Apollo theatre Friday morning when an overflow house witnessed and heard what many observers called "the greatest jam session in swing history." Coleman Hawkins, Charlie Barnet, Benny Carter, and Erskine Hawkins were on hand to jam out Count's famous "One O'Clock Jump" at the opening show. It ran for 15 minutes.*

When Lionel Hampton first played the Apollo, he revved up his showmanship to its maximum: "I jumped up and down on

```
COUNT BASIE BAND
 & Revue      March 20, 1947
50%   10,541.87
      Sept. 25, 1947   9639.89
March 18, 1948    9,177.69
 Dec. 31, 1948   9,122.61
6/7/49    7754.65    With James Rushing, Earle Warren, Johnny Moore's
                     3 Blazers, Stump & Stumpy the Two Hot Shots
4-5-51 $8642.95   With Bill Bailey, Rose Hardaway, Joe Turner, Chittison
                  Trio with Irene Williams, & Pigmeat & Norma Miller's
                  chorus.  Large band.  Played show well.  Basie excellent
                  Band only fair.  Business helped materially by excellent
                  show including Bill Bailey.

11/9/51    2441.84    Played well.  Nice personality.  Unfortunately, no
                      drawing power by himself.
           2699.57    A good band.  No draw.
5/9/52     3163.90    EXCELLENT band.  Still unsatisfactory business.
4/17/53               Excellent band with greater popularity than he
                      enjoyed for several years.
```

Earl Hines (foreground) with Count Basie (seated right) at Basie's apartment, 1945.
Both were master pianists, with Basie's minimalist style contrasting to Hines's more intricate playing.

my drums, and I made an arrangement with Bob Hall, the Apollo electrician, to let loose with his smudge pot so it would look like the stage was blowing up. The first time he did that, everybody ran out of the theater. But word got around that it was just a special effect, so the next time everybody stayed in the seats."

One of the theater's most memorable jazz shows came in the spring of 1948, when the band of Buddy Rich—a popular drummer and showman—debuted at the Apollo. "Buddy was a big attraction in the black theaters," remembered vibraphonist Terry Gibbs. "Buddy could only use his right hand because his left arm was in a cast [at that time]. When he played his drum solos, he used his right foot as his right hand and his right hand as his left hand. What he was doing with his foot and his hand were

Vibraphonist Lionel Hampton was a member of Benny Goodman's first integrated band. He later became a famed bandleader and showman on his own.

unbelievable....It was the most amazing thing I have ever seen or heard a drummer do and some of the greatest drum solos I ever heard Buddy play." After seeing this display, Jo Jones, Count Basie's drummer and a friend of Rich's, quipped: "If his left arm heals, somebody ought to break it again."

The Harlem community held Rich in high esteem, as was shown by an amazing story related by Rich. One night while he was performing at the Apollo, his new Cadillac was delivered to the theater and was totally dismantled by thieves. As soon as word got around that it was *Rich's* car, however, the car was quickly put back

together *and waxed.* Said Rich, "The car was put back in perfect shape—better, really, than when it was first delivered that day."

The Apollo's policy of building shows around name bands was not without controversy. Dan Burley, an influential writer for Harlem's *Amsterdam News*, mounted an editorial campaign in 1940 to get the Apollo to change course, arguing that focusing on "'presentation' shows in which the 'name' orchestra is the box-office lure is fundamentally unsound and not stable in entertainment values." Burley argued for bringing actors and other entertainers onto the stage "where they belong instead of in holes-in-the-walls and on the street corners." In response, Frank Schiffman experimented in 1941 with playing musical comedies with a band in the orchestra pit (not onstage), but he continued to feature big bands.

Each band that played the Apollo successfully purveyed something distinctive. For Ellington, it was his music's unique sound, his brilliant and highly varied soloists, and his originality and class. "Duke Ellington," observed Jack Schiffman, "was never a gate-buster, but he always attracted an interesting crowd… during his engagements. You could look at the patrons—a little more conservatively dressed, a little more sophisticated, a bigger sprinkling of whites—and know that Duke was headlining." Reporting on a 1938 Apollo engagement by Ellington, the African American *Pittsburgh Courier* wrote, with no little pride, "Resorting to but a few of the many marvelous tunes he and his crew have written, Ellington's engagement can be considered more or less a musical concert, during which the most pleasing type of Negro music is presented; negroid in all its features."

The golden era of the big bands came to an end right after World War II—in late 1946, eight "name" bands temporarily or permanently disbanded—but some big bands soldiered on and continued to play the Apollo. In the postwar years, the Apollo periodically employed the classic bands of Barnet, Rich, Hampton, and Basie, as well as newer groups led by Dizzy Gillespie, Maynard Ferguson, and, in the '60s, Quincy Jones. Ellington performed there until 1963. But the glow was fading from the trumpets. Frank Schiffman made these telling notations on the cards he kept, after World War II, on each act: Charlie Barnet, 5/14/54: "No drawing power"; Cab Calloway, 5/18/56: "Business about the worst ever with a loss exceeding $6,000";

Duke Ellington, 9/23/55: "Usual unprofitable business." The demographics of Harlem were changing by the '50s, and fewer whites came there. Concurrently, popular taste—especially among young African Americans—had shifted to singers such as Billy Eckstine, Dinah Washington, and Johnny Mathis, and to rhythm-and-blues vocal groups such as the Orioles.

But the big bands had helped the Apollo establish itself not only as a springboard but as *the* must-play venue for black entertainers, growing and grooming audiences to become perhaps the hippest, most critically attuned in the land. And if the Apollo was important to the careers and success of some of the bands, the big bands were crucial to theater's early success, establishing a standard and reputation that would endure for decades.

Duke Ellington conducts his saxophone section, 1963. Ellington's was perhaps

Great Jazz and Pop Singers

John Edward Hasse

If big bands were the mainstay of the Apollo Theater during the 1930s, singers also played vital roles in drawing and entertaining audiences. Most of the big bands included singers who stayed with the bands and did not venture out on their own: Duke Ellington's orchestra featured Ivy Anderson, for example, and Andy Kirk had June Richmond.

Perhaps no other singer is more associated with the Apollo Theater than Ella Fitzgerald. Other than Ethel Waters, Fitzgerald boasted the longest performing career of any female singer at the Apollo, where, records indicate, she appeared more than thirty times between 1935 and 1959.

After her win at the Apollo's Amateur Night on November 21, 1934, Fitzgerald made quite a name for herself, but Fletcher Henderson refused to hire her. He was unimpressed with her appearance, as was Chick Webb. Webb relented, however, and Fitzgerald joined his band in April 1935, singing with him until his death in June 1939. During that time, Fitzgerald and Webb's band performed at the Apollo at least once or twice a year. A review in the *New York Amsterdam News* of one of her earliest Apollo appearances, in November 1935, applauded her singing: "Miss Fitzgerald, an outstanding local favorite, came back

with 'Judy' which, to my mind, is about the spiciest bit of vocal doings I've come across of recent date." ("Judy" was the Hoagy Carmichael song with which she had won the Amateur Night contest.) By 1937 the *New York Amsterdam News* was proclaiming that Fitzgerald had "displaced Connie Boswell [a white singer then at the peak of popularity] in the minds and affections of the theatre goers." In 1938 Fitzgerald rewarded Webb's faith in her by penning and recording a huge hit, "A-Tisket, A-Tasket," which, by 1950, reportedly had sold one million records.

After Webb's death, Fitzgerald took over his band and sang with it at the Apollo at least four more times. In the summer of 1942 she began a solo career and thereafter was paired with various bands on the Apollo's stage. Her value to the Apollo box office was on the rise, as indicated by Frank Schiffman's notations on the five-by-eight-inch cards he maintained on the acts that performed for him. Her weekly pay rose from $1,500 in 1946 to, seven years later, $2,500—an increase of 167 percent.

"Until Queen Ella walked onto this stage, this was just another good Apollo show," wrote *Metronome* of an October 1947 show: "After she had finished, the packed house was in an uproar.…The buxom gal is unquestionably the greatest singer

ELLA FITZGERALD	5/31/46	1200.00	1500.00
	9/13/46		1750.00
			1750.00
	3/27/47		1750.00
	10/30/47		1750.00
	8/19/48		1750.00
	7/7/49		2000.00
	9/15/49		2000.00
	3/24/50		With Illinois Jacquet

1-10-51 $2250.00 Registered very very well.
6-7-51 Illinois Jacquet show. Registered very well. Business very bad.
2/1/52 $2000.00 Gave a wonderful performance. A pretty good draw and very cooperative.
7/11/52 $2250.00 Added at the last minute and worked with trio. The best in the business.

Very disappointing business -

Ella Fitzgerald appears with drummer Chick Webb's band at the Apollo in 1937.
Webb appeared frequently at the Apollo until his untimely death in 1939.

Billie Holiday, 1951. Holiday's distinctive approach, superb styling, and warm, mellow tone marked her as a major vocal innovator.

of them all today....The pièce de résistance was of course Ella's now famous vocal jam on 'Lady Be Good' and good for at least six sensational choruses. She has some set riffs that would make many top musicians' eyes bug out."

Ever the careful businessman, Schiffman kept notes on Fitzgerald's early '50s appearances, which—while musically triumphant—were not always economically successful. In January and June 1951, he noted that the singer "registered very very well," but for the June show "business [was] very bad." Things apparently improved financially for a February 1952 appearance, when Schiffman noted: "Gave a wonderful performance. A pretty good draw and very cooperative." But by November that year, apparently the singer's drawing power was down: "Very disappointing business—actually a substantial loss. Salary [$2,500] included her Trio. The girl is great. We should play her but we should try to get her...for...a reasonable salary."

At about the time of Fitzgerald's discovery, the Apollo's master of ceremonies, Ralph Cooper, took note of another unpolished, struggling young singer, Billie Holiday. After hearing Holiday sing at a Harlem dive called the Hot-Cha, Cooper told Apollo management, "You never heard singing so slow, so lazy, with such a drawl—it ain't the blues—I don't know what it is, but you got to hear her!" Holiday was booked to perform in November 1934. When it was time for her to go on, she was so frightened that comedian Pigmeat Markham had to push her onstage. "I had a cheap white satin dress on and my knees were shaking so bad the people didn't know whether I was going to dance or sing," she recalled in her memoirs, *Lady Sings the Blues*. Somehow Holiday managed to sing "If the Moon Turns Green" and "The Man I Love." "The house broke up," she remembered, though other accounts vary about how well her first few appearances at the Apollo were received. But by March 1937,

she "raised the roof at the Apollo Theater," raved the *New York Amsterdam News*. She became an Apollo perennial, performing there at least twenty-three times over the course of her career. In 1944 one newspaper reported that "Billie's annual appearances at the Apollo are always gala occasions. Six and seven songs per show are the rule."

At the Apollo Holiday shared her nonpareil gifts for moving an audience. Frank Schiffman's son Jack remembers when she sang the antilynching song "Strange Fruit": "When she wrenched the final words from her lips...a moment of oppressively heavy silence followed and then a kind of rustling sound I had never heard before. It was the sound of almost two thousand people sighing. One of those sighs was my own. I felt as if I had just had a noose removed from my neck." The Apollo took on special significance to Holiday when, in the late '40s, drug problems caused her to lose her New York City cabaret card, denying her the right to perform in nightclubs there. The Apollo Theater remained one of the few New York City venues (along with an occasional concert at Carnegie Hall) where she could perform.

The Apollo's business records paint a picture of a general decline, after World War II, in Holiday's value to the box office. Her fees ranged from a high of $3,000 for the week of October 14, 1948, to a low of $1,500 for the week of July 26, 1951. In May 1950 Schiffman wrote, "Unless a miraculous change takes place Billie's value to us is lost. She has lost her public favor. She seems unable to remain away from stimulants." In July 1951, however, he noted, "Gave a good show. Very cooperative in finale. Sang fairly well. No misbehavior. Salary received [$1,500] is top value for her." But by August 1953 he was lamenting, "Terrible! She was sick, but she was also under the effect of stimulants. Only a miracle can restore this girl and make her worthwhile playing...again." Nonetheless, Schiffman gave her one more chance in September

Vocalist and bandleader Billy Eckstine, 1940. He led one of Harlem's most popular bands and nurtured many young talents, including trumpeter Dizzy Gillespie.

1955: "Very indifferent lackadaisical performance....Proved absolutely valueless to the box office." This heartbreaking notation was the final one on her card.

By 1940 the Apollo's Amateur Night contests had become legendary. In October 1942 a skinny, seventeen-year-old church singer from nearby Newark, New Jersey, decided to enter the contest. Singing "Body and Soul," young Sarah Vaughan won first place. Singer Billy Eckstine was in the house that night and, upon his urging, bandleader Earl Hines hired Vaughan as second pianist and singer. Reported the *New York Amsterdam News* in January 1943: "Miss Vaughan…came, saw and conquered the Apollo's critical audience better than anyone since the early days of Ella Fitzgerald…the audience 'brought her on' in a manner seldom seen at the Apollo." Within a couple of years, Vaughan had graduated to a solo career. She performed at the Apollo until 1960, earning as much as $8,500 for one week. Schiffman's last notation

on her card reads: "Sang beautifully, but her box office value is not great enough to stand alone."

Most of the other jazz singers of the era—from Helen Humes and Nat "King" Cole to Lambert, Hendricks, and Ross—and the pop singers—from Johnny Mathis to Dinah Washington—played the Apollo. A few deserve special mention.

Ethel Waters—who had made her first recordings in 1921, developed her own influential blend of blues, jazz, and vaudeville styles, and in 1927 started singing in Broadway musicals—had performed for Schiffman at the Lafayette Theatre in 1932. Between 1935 and 1938 she performed eight times at the Apollo—in 1938 as part of the Cotton Club revue, a show emanating from the famous nightspot (which, after the Harlem riots of 1935, had moved to midtown Manhattan). The Apollo paid her as much as $3,550 in 1936. Her last appearance was in 1952, with a fee of $2,500 and the notation from Schiffman, "Superb performance. Disappointing business." But her engagements had spanned twenty years—in show business, quite a long run.

In 1934 a young singer named Pearl Bailey won Amateur Night at the Apollo. By the '40s she had developed a stage act as a singer, dancer, and something of a dry comedienne. She gradually became a darling of Apollo audiences. Her show the week of August 30, 1950, prompted Schiffman to write (see cards p. 87): "Excellent comedy, talk, patter and dance. Temperamental in demands but a fine performer. Not yet a big drawing card." The week of November 2, 1956, her show earned this praise from Schiffman: "Had her own revue. One of the greatest shows we have ever had. Net receipts $27,588.53. She got $14,803.12. Held over with entire show for second week." She was still performing at the Apollo in October 1965: "The absolute mistress of comedy—song. Has audience in her hands from start to finish. Excellent!!!" Exclamation points were unusual for Schiffman; three were extremely rare.

Sarah Vaughan on the Apollo stage, 1964. She was one of the few vocalists who could keep up with the rapid-fire improvisations of Charlie Parker and Dizzy Gillespie.

Pearl Bailey on the Apollo stage, 1963. After winning an Amateur Night contest in 1934, she appeared many times as a headliner through the '60s.

The star of suave, handsome Billy Eckstine was rising in 1945 when, on the stage of the Apollo, he was presented with a plaque as Outstanding Male Vocalist for the success of his hit records "Prisoner of Love" and "Cottage for Sale." By the late '40s the youngsters at the Apollo were calling him "Mr. B" or just "B," and he became perhaps the first matinee idol for both black and white teenagers. Jack Schiffman recalls that "the kids screamed and bounced in their seats as though they were on so many trampolines. B would lower his eyelids, smile, and utter a throaty 'Steady now,' which was all that was needed to send the kids into paroxysms." Throngs would anticipate his annual appearance after the Apollo's August closure; Eckstine would reopen the theater with the words, "Thank you so much. It's so good to be at the Apollo again—so good to be home." A true Apollo charmer, he performed there into the '70s.

Betty Carter debuted at the theater in December 1948 with the band of Lionel Hampton, who called her "Betty Bebop." Jack Schiffman recalls that "Hampton introduced a small girl, hair bobbed short, eyes seemingly larger than her face, [who] burst out on stage, took a deep breath, and sang bebop riffs, a whole machine-gun load of them, that turned the house upside down. I never saw an audience turned on so quickly to a new sound." After her debut as an Apollo soloist in October 1952, she made twelve more appearances in thirteen years, and Schiffman tripled her fee from $250 to $750. As she developed her craft and became more adventurous, Schiffman's notations changed from "Excellent bee-bop singer" (October 1952) and "Good voice, nice personality, registered well" (February 1953) to his final notation, "Too modern and far out for this set. Has strayed too far for understanding" (New Year's Eve 1965).

By the mid-'50s, singers such as these were being crowded by the new sounds of such R & B vocal groups as the Orioles, Coasters, and Drifters, with James Brown, Wilson Pickett, Aretha Franklin, and the Motown acts just over the horizon. But during the several previous decades, the Apollo had launched the careers of Fitzgerald, Bailey, and Vaughan and had tested the mettle of many others, thereby proving crucial to their success. The Apollo gave African American audiences affordable and often rare opportunities to hear these singing stars in person. No wonder that, in the blur of their careers, their Apollo engagements stood out like beacons.

A People's Theater

Guthrie P. Ramsey Jr.

"Porto Rico" (Norman Miller, arm raised) plays the "executioner," about to pull a would-be singing star offstage at an Amateur Night performance. Emcee Ralph Cooper (left) watches.

Since its beginning the Apollo was a quintessentially American institution, drawing on diverse historical forces that were packaged as "new." The combination of race, money, "foreigners," music, humor, and other forms of expressive culture have always fascinated Americans. The Apollo represents but one example of these obsessions coming together in the perfect cocktail. As the theater developed, it became a barometer for the changing sensibilities and social standings of African Americans. Situated in the center of one of the nation's largest and most diverse black communities, the Apollo existed as the spiritual heartbeat of New York's live entertainment.

Through the years, fans worldwide—particularly those in the black American community—have recognized the singularity of the Apollo, treating it as a kind of "headquarters"

for popular culture, as two recent events demonstrated. After James Brown, "the Godfather of Soul," passed on Christmas morning 2006, one of his memorial services was held at the theater three days later. All along the streets of Harlem, Brown's music saturated the airwaves, causing celebratory dancing among the thousands who attended. More recently, after pop icon Michael Jackson died suddenly at age fifty, a spontaneous memorial formed over many days outside the theater, with fans leaving voluminous flowers, notes, and a makeshift remembrance wall. In both cases, the Apollo was clearly the people's choice of venue for expressing their grief and appreciation for these fallen musical giants.

In order to understand the Apollo's ability to continue drawing the people—the famous, the infamous, and the "round the way" folk—into its spell, one must consider the cultural forces that created it. Throughout the late nineteenth century, this nation's music culture gradually shed its European pedigree and became more American in its style, tenor, and goals. As the focus of music making became less centered on home parlors and more on public spectacles, venues were built to accommodate these changing tastes. A big part of this appeal for new entertainments could be attributed to the allure of the music of black citizens, who had since the days of blackface minstrelsy provided an important element in the aesthetic makeup of the "popular." But, of course, as a nation with a constant flow of immigrant cultures, Americans have always been enamored of all the different ethnic groups that have constituted our human mosaic. So by the time that Sidney Cohen and Morris Sussman decided to open a theater with an African American focus, they did so within a long tradition of entrepreneurs who cashed in on America's obsession with cultural difference.

The business world already had an infrastructure in place, and Frank Schiffman, who took over the Apollo with Leo Brecher in 1935, knew how to work it. By the 1930s the loose network of varied popular entertainments had gradually coalesced into an integrated system of songwriters, performers, agents, managers, attorneys, publishers, theater owners, and recording labels—a modern industry that sought to dispel the preciously held notion that art and commerce were irreconcilable forces. Indeed, before its latest status as a nonprofit foundation, the success of the Apollo's formula had resolved this complicated, yet wholly American assumption about the presentation and dissemination of artistry. Schiffman knew audiences, and he knew business and what he liked in "the show." He assured the Apollo's success by harnessing the variety show format that had been so

The Stanley Theatre in Pittsburgh was part of the circuit of performance halls serving African American communities in major cities across the country.

familiar and beloved by American audiences since minstrelsy and later perpetuated in vaudeville. But it wasn't solely Schiffman's chosen format that made him a success.

Harlem's demographic shifts also contributed to the Apollo's allure. By the '20s Harlem was well on the way to becoming a primarily black neighborhood, and the conditions there created a need for entertainment. Schiffman recognized that he could probably capitalize on the specific yet varied tastes of this constituency. It was perhaps only within the social context of Jim Crow separatism—indeed, within an environment in which black people were brutally policed by law and custom—that such an experiment could succeed. Black artists were making brilliant

Howard "Sandman" Sims performs his famous soft shoe in his later years. He scattered sand on the stage to create a percussive swooshing sound, something resembling a ride cymbal in jazz.

artistic worlds within an environment that tried to contain them to status quo, second-class social positions. As they turned the world on its ear, their works became viable commodities, turning profits for all involved. Indeed, the dam burst at the Apollo, and the flood is still flowing.

It is also important to note that in other cities with large black communities such as Chicago, Philadelphia, and

Washington, D.C., similar developments existed: white entrepreneurs positioned themselves to supply what black communities required as they grew. These theaters became important to an emerging black star system; they provided black artists and their audiences with the space to enjoy prestige and income, which conferred a visibility separate from their white counterparts with whom they were not considered social equals. As such, the Apollo and her sister venues throughout the black archipelago provided an incubator for the showcasing and development of black talent—indeed, they became pinnacles of achievement beyond the less prestigious venues on the "chitlin circuit." Behind the curtain of segregated performance spaces, black artists honed their respective crafts, created their own artistic standards, tutored one another, competed, thrilled audiences, earned living wages, and ultimately created art that became the musical lingua franca of the world.

Historians have noted how African American–run institutions such as black churches operated as hubs of cultural, social, political, spiritual, and economic empowerment in segregated communities. Yet the Apollo, owned and operated by Schiffman, a man of Austrian Jewish heritage, worked in much the same way. As a shining symbol and paradigm for the visibility of black expressive culture and an emerging social integration, this progressive institution has been both a reflection of and an active agent in our nation's artistic, social, and political evolution. As a site of racial cooperation that was, for the most part, mutually beneficial, this venue became more than simply a place to test one's artistic mettle. Performing at the Apollo made one a part of a grander history, the story of how people came together—the triangulation of business people,

The interior of the Apollo Theater, showing its double balconies. The patrons at the uppermost levels are most famous for quickly reacting to an Amateur Night performance, either showering performers with praise or booing them off stage.

performers, and audience members—to produce stars, create legends, and participate in the ever-changing American society as few other venues did.

The will of the people was always a strong factor in the Apollo's history, and this observation can be seen most clearly during the post–golden era years as well as in the phenomenon of Amateur Night, a standing performance format popular since the '30s. In 1934 Ralph Cooper, an accomplished emcee, actor, and dancer, originated the weekly talent contest that introduced some of the best-known entertainers in American history. Over the years it has become a bona fide tradition in American popular music. In his memoir, Cooper describes his philosophy: "With nothing but talent and a lot of heart, you can make it. You can be somebody. That is the American dream, and it is the Harlem dream—and we can make it the Apollo dream." One cannot miss

the strong connection between Cooper's idea and the *American Idol* reality show that has captured the public's imagination for the better part of a decade.

In 1934, when he was still at the Lafayette Theatre, Cooper had appointed one of the stagehands to become the first of a long line of "executioners" who would do the audience's bidding and shoo shaky upstarts offstage, making it less horrifying to be rejected. Amateur Night became a big hit for business, with local radio picking it up as a live broadcast. Audiences participated in judging who had what it took to make it in show business. And aspiring performers got their big opportunity to show their wares. One enthusiastic columnist praised Cooper: "It is the Cooper personality that is being felt over the airwaves and radio listeners are catching the spirit. This broadcast must mean much to the Apollo and it means a great deal to Harlem too. It is putting

Apollo audiences today continue the tradition of being actively engaged in approving — or strongly disapproving — stage acts, particularly during Amateur Night.

Harlem on the map and spreading the knowledge and realization of Harlem, or, I should, say colored, talent." Cooper believed that radio made both Harlem and the Apollo's audience famous.

When black businessman Percy Sutton purchased the Apollo in 1981, he promptly reinstituted Ralph Cooper's original Amateur Night. The format became the basis for *It's Showtime at the Apollo* (1987–2007), a syndicated television show that secured the Apollo's presence in the mass media in the same way that the earlier radio show had. Many believe that Sutton's work saved the Apollo from permanent ruin, securing its future in Harlem for years to come. By this time an entirely new generation of musicians, musical styles, and fans had come of age. Collectively, they were known as hip-hop culture.

With hip-hop, New York became home once more to cutting-edge musical innovation. And miraculously, the Apollo's

legacy proved large enough to include more traditional R & B acts as well as hip-hop groups such as Run-DMC, LL Cool J, and the Beastie Boys, who performed from the mid-'80s on to enthusiastic crowds. This wide umbrella of styles and performers continued after the establishment of the Apollo Theater Foundation in 1991, which to this day manages the theater's finances, bookings, and educational programming. Under the foundation's auspices, the legacy of audience reign still rules as Amateur Night maintains its position as a modern-day marvel of endurance and appeal.

As a people's theater, the Apollo has served many constituencies with its durable format of big talent, discerning audiences, and flexible formats that worked well on radio, stage, and television. And as it moves into the future, one thing is a surety: the people will continue to make their desires and choices known on 125th Street and around the world.

Rap artists who have appeared at the Apollo beginning in the mid-'80s include (clockwise from top left) LL Cool J, Run-DMC, and the Beastie Boys.

Ella Fitzgerald at the Apollo

Willard Jenkins

Ella Fitzgerald at the microphone in 1947, while Dizzy Gillespie listens.
She was a favored singer for boppers because of her remarkable scat-singing talents.

On November 21, 1934, a somewhat intimidated young woman of decidedly modest means and demeanor from Yonkers, New York, crept timidly onto the Apollo Theater stage. Her name was Ella Fitzgerald, and the world of jazz and popular song would never be the same from that point forward. That night she joined the illustrious pantheon of Apollo Amateur Night winners.

Amateur Night actually started at Harlem's Lafayette Theatre in 1933. Its originator was the indefatigable Ralph

Cooper, who became the legendary Apollo master of ceremonies. When Frank Schiffman and his partner took over the Apollo, Ralph Cooper was quickly contracted. Given the Apollo's renowned tough, opinionated, and interactive audience, such an Amateur Night policy was apropos. Amateur Night at the Apollo went viral in 1935, when WMCA began broadcasting on Wednesday nights from 11 p.m. to midnight. The broadcasts generally included seven or eight contestants, plus a couple of numbers from that week's featured attraction.

Also essential to the whole Amateur Night schematic was an otherwise undistinguished stagehand named Norman Miller, who at the appointed time morphed into "Porto Rico," the specter every lackluster contestant dreaded. This by equal turns feared and hilarious character was the audience-appointed hanging judge of Amateur Night. If the audience believed you came up short, woe be unto you as Porto Rico, brandishing a blazing cap pistol, would give you a quite unceremonious heave-ho, to the delight of the audience/jury. At the end of the contest, the winners were awarded by audience acclaim as Porto Rico held a cloth over each contestant, requesting either audience scorn or their applauded acclaim, the volume of which determined the victor.

On that fateful fall night in 1934, Ella Fitzgerald signed up as a dancer to compete on Amateur Night on a dare from two girlfriends. A professional dance team called the Edwards Sisters, one of that week's featured acts, preceded the seventeen-year-old Ella's turn onstage. As the trumpeter Buck Clayton, who worked the Apollo with the Count Basie band at the time, recalled in his book *Buck Clayton's Jazz World*: "The Edwards Sisters were two little geniuses who had been taught to dance by their father and were pretty well known to be the best kid dancers around. When Ella saw that she was to follow the Edwards Sisters she did the best thing she could have possibly done; she decided to sing, not dance."

When it was Ella's turn to follow the Edwards Sisters, she developed a huge case of stage fright, to which the stage manager insisted "Do *something*." In a 1989 Smithsonian archival interview, Fitzgerald revealed her response. "I looked and saw all those people [in the audience] and I thought, 'Oh my gosh, what am I gonna do out here.' I was real thin, skinny legs…and everybody started laughing, saying 'what is SHE gonna do,'" Ella recalled. "I couldn't think of nothing else to do so I tried to sing 'The Object of My Affection.' But I was imitating Miss Connee Boswell, and I always loved her and respected her for that [inspiration]," she said of one of her biggest influences from the popular Boswell Sisters singing group. Somebody in the audience, in typically demonstrative Apollo fashion—like call and response between preacher and congregation in a black church—hollered "Hey, that little girl can sing." So Ella won first prize, and later proceeded to do the same at the nearby Harlem Opera House amateur contest.

Different variations on Fitzgerald lore have been written, but either bandleader Chick Webb's guitarist, Benny Carter—who legend has it was in the Apollo audience that night—or bandleader Bardu Ali recommended young Ella to Webb, though Chick wasn't exactly keen on hiring a girl singer. But he relented, trying Ella out on a gig in New Haven, Connecticut, and she got the job. Webb, diminutive and frail owing to a tuberculosis-related spinal infirmity, was nonetheless the king of the Savoy Ballroom and a

Fitzgerald decided to sing on Amateur Night in 1934, leaving the dancing to Baby Edwards (right) and her sister.

drummer mighty in stature. He became mentor and later guardian to young Ella, and when Webb died in 1939, Fitzgerald took over leadership of the band.

From that point she grew to become a pillar of American song, with her perpetual youthfulness, freedom, and joy. Ella always looked like she was having such fun; her girlishness, warmth, and perfect pitch were her hallmarks, along with an impeccable sense of timing. Her uncanny inventiveness enabled her to hang with even the most wizardly modern jazz instrumentalists. Her ability to make a trifle like "A-Tisket, A-Tasket" one of her trademarks, let alone the mastery she brought to more consequential vehicles like "Mr. Paganini" and "Lush Life," spoke clearly to her mastery. As Duke Ellington described Ella's singing, "Her majesty…all heart…beyond category…total jazz."

Pioneering Comedians

Mel Watkins

Comedian Stepin Fetchit, born Lincoln Perry, was a hit on African American stages and in films from the late '20s through the '40s.

When its doors first opened, the Apollo Theater was billed as "the only stage show in Harlem." It usually presented what Jack Schiffman, son of owner Frank Schiffman, called "Broadway type extravaganzas" with big bands, a chorus line, and the top musical and dance acts of the era. Its lavish productions included original musical scores and scripts.

Initially, comic performers were rarely billed as headline acts. Jackie "Moms" Mabley, one of the most popular entertainers to ever play the Apollo, began appearing in and writing comedy skits in the 1930s, for instance, but she was not billed or paid as a headline act until 1962, when she was sixty-eight years old. "Wouldn't you know it," she told Frank Schiffman, "by the time I finally arrive at the big money I'm too old and sick to enjoy it."

There were, of course, a few glaring exceptions. Comic actor and hoofer Lincoln Perry, better known as Stepin Fetchit, received top billing as "the Greatest Colored Screen and Stage Star" several times during the '30s. Eddie "Rochester" Anderson, who had risen to fame as Jack Benny's radio sidekick in the late '30s, and the comedy dance team of Buck and Bubbles (1936) were also among a select few comedians who were given headline billing during the Apollo's early years.

Despite not being billed as headliners, comics were a central part of those variety shows from the outset. "The comedian was the most important part of the show," Redd Foxx said of the era's black stage presentations. Apollo management apparently agreed, since comedy permeated nearly all the shows. Between acts, emcees, many of whom were seasoned comedians, regularly engaged in lighthearted banter with band members and other performers. Their off-the-cuff quips punctuated and heightened the theater's gala atmosphere. Performers such as Moms Mabley frequently interacted with the headliners, offering impromptu lines that inevitably broke up the audience: "Count [Basie]," she'd drawl suggestively, "I sure would like to know what that drummer is doin' after the show."

The featured comedy acts usually adhered to familiar black variety show formats, presenting skits, blackout bits, and situational humor in which two or more comics worked and reworked established routines. One classic routine was "Open the Door, Richard," made famous by Dusty Fletcher. Fletcher would stagger onstage carrying a ladder and announce, "Yeah, it's me, and I'm drunk again," before beginning to plead with his unseen roommate to open the door to their apartment. Failing to get Richard's attention, Fletcher would begin an acrobatic simulation of climbing up to the apartment window—wavering precariously on the freestanding ladder and occasionally tumbling to the ground as he begged or demanded that his roommate open the door. Finally, with the frustrated Fletcher lying entangled in the ladder and still yelling at the unresponsive Richard, a policeman would enter and haul him off to jail. The bit was an enduring favorite among Apollo audiences.

This routine, like much of the showplace's early comedy, had been shaped in the raucous atmosphere of minstrel stages, traveling carnivals, and tent shows, and honed on the Theatre Owners Booking Association (TOBA) tour, which booked most black acts during the early 1900s. Similar but original routines were written specifically for the Apollo stage by such stalwarts as Moms Mabley and Flournoy Miller, two of the era's most influential comedians. Usually these sketches relied on the pratfalls, sexual innuendo, and broad comic approach popular in black circuit venues. Reflecting their minstrel show origins, comics nearly always appeared in clownish attire and blackface makeup.

From the '30s to the '50s, such situational, sketch humor was a mainstay on the Apollo stage. And while comic stars and perennial favorites such as Mabley, Fletcher, Tim "Kingfish" Moore, Butterbeans and Susie, Mantan Moreland, and Pigmeat Markham eventually rose to stardom, perhaps the most remarkable aspect of Apollo Theater comedy was its ensemble makeup. The cast was composed of a raft of such talented, lesser-known comics

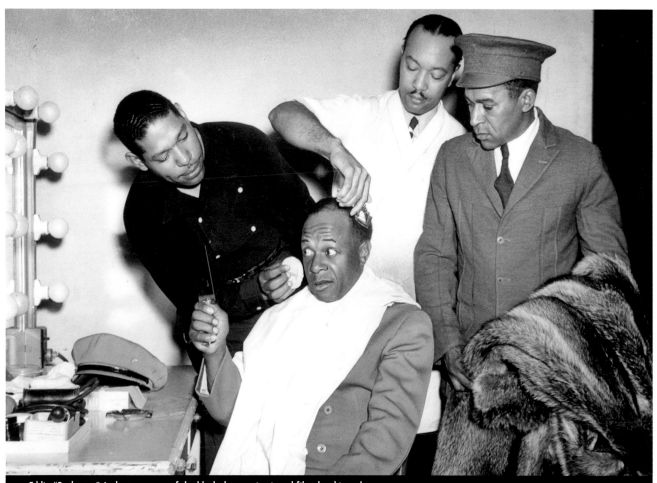

Eddie "Rochester" Anderson, a star of the black theater circuit and film, has his makeup

Comedian Pigmeat Markham (center) performs his famous "Here Come de Judge" routine with Edna Mae Harris (right), 1940s. The sketch would remain a staple through the '60s, when it was revived on television's *Laugh-In*.

and straight people as John "Ashcan" LaRue, Johnny Lee Long, Jimmy Baskette, Eddie Green, Sandy Burns, Edna Mae Harris, Crackshot Hackley, Spo-Dee-O-Dee, Monte Hawley, John "Rastus" Murray, John "Spider Bruce" Mason, and Vivian Harris. All these performers contributed to the scores of sketches and burlesque type blackout skits that became a hallmark of the Apollo stage.

Perhaps best known among them is Pigmeat Markham's "Here Come de Judge" bit. Like many of these classic routines, its origins were disputed. Some insist it surfaced during the early days of the TOBA, but Markham contended that "de Judge" evolved out of a routine that originated at Harlem's Alhambra Theatre in 1928, in which he appeared as a magistrate. "Negroes loved it," Markham wrote, "probably because the judge, the pompous oppressor of the Negro…was being taken down a peg by a Negro

comedian. I added little bits and pieces down through the years—and new jokes all the time but the format is always the same."

On the other hand, emcee and original Amateur Night host Ralph Cooper claimed that "Pigmeat became famous for that routine, written by yours truly," and offered a more elaborate version of its opening:

Hear ye, hear ye, the Court of Swing
Is now about ready to do its thing.
Don't want no tears, don't want no jive,
Above all things, don't want no lies.
Our judge is hip, his boots are tall
He'll judge you jack, big or small.
So fall in line, his stuff is sweet,
Peace, brothers, here's Judge Pigmeat.

Pigmeat then entered into a mock courtroom where he joined a group of comedians cast as lawyers or defendants. Usually he began by loudly announcing that everyone would be doing some time. ("I'm goin' start by givin' myself thirty days—next case!") And if one of the lawyers objected, de Judge might proclaim: "*Object*! You object! You all the time comin' in here and objectin' me outa decisions. Why man, I got all these years in my book and somebody's gotta do 'em! Ain't gonna be me! Where's you client… he's *guilty*!"

After being introduced in the '30s, "Here Come de Judge" became one of the Apollo audience's favorite comedy bits, and Pigmeat Markham remained one of the theater's most popular comedians until the '60s, when network television appearances revived his career.

Another popular routine was the "Go Ahead and Sing" skit developed by John "Rastus" Murray and Henry Drake, in which one comic goads his buddy into defying a policeman's order to stop performing on a street corner, with predictably disastrous results. (The bit was widely copied and was used in 1944 by Abbott and Costello in *In Society*.)

Flournoy Miller, a noted comedy writer as well as performer, was among the major contributors to the stable of routines presented on the Apollo stage. In 1908 he had joined Aubrey Lyles to form Miller and Lyles, a preeminent comedy team that was in demand as both performers and writers. The duo's credits included the groundbreaking Broadway show *Shuffle Along* (1921), which they wrote, produced, and starred in. When Lyle died in 1932, Miller continued performing and appeared frequently at the Apollo. Among the team's comic scenarios was the popular "Mulsifying and Revision" bit—a mathematical poser in which they prove that 13 multiplied by 7 equals 28. That routine was also widely imitated, appearing in the acts of Abbott and Costello and Amos 'n' Andy portrayers Freeman Gosden and Charles Correll.

Miller and Lyles also created the classic "Indefinite Talk" routine. The setup was deceptively simple. Two men begin a casual conversation, but before either one can finish a sentence the other interrupts, taking the conversation into unexpected directions.

Comic 1: *Who he goin' marry?*

Comic 2: *He goin' marry the daughter of Mr.—*

Comic 1: *Yeah, she's a nice girl. Lemme tell you, I heard once—*

Comic 2: *Nah, that was her sister. I'm keepin' company with her.*

Comic 1: *You are?*

Comic 2: *Oh yeah, I been with her now every since—*

Comic 1: *I didn't know you knew her that long.*

Comic 2: *Sure!*

Comic 1: *And I thought all the time she was—*

Comic 2: *She was! But she cut him out.*

Comic 1: *Well, you know, I was talkin' to her father the other day, and the first thing—*

Comic 2: *That was your fault. What you shoulda done was—*

Comic 1: *I did!*

This routine, depending on the comics' imagination and quick wit, had endless possibilities and was a favorite from the '30s until the '60s. Introduced initially by Miller and his partner in their vaudeville act during the '20s, it became a staple in Miller's act and was reprised in Hollywood films and on the Apollo stage by numerous comics.

Miller and Lyles (right and left) starred in *Shuffle Along* in 1921. Although they wore blackface, their routines didn't rely on stereotypes.

Singing, dancing, and comedy husband-and-wife act Butterbeans (right) and Susie (left) were widely admired at the Apollo for their bawdy, humorous songs and satirical skits on married life.

Butterbeans and Susie were another of the legendary acts that graduated from the TOBA circuit to become regulars at the Apollo. Jodie Edwards ("Butterbeans") and Susie Hawthorne met in the early '20s and, shortly afterward, married and formed a song and dance team. They soon shifted the emphasis of the act to comedy, and Edwards began appearing onstage in tight, high-water pants, a bowler hat, and oversized, floppy shoes, which were in marked contrast to Susie's elegant attire. The act usually began with a duet, and, after performing a cakewalk or some other dance routine, they segued into a stream of comic patter.

Susie's rendition of the somewhat ribald tune, "I Want a Little Sugar in My Bowl," was among their most requested routines. Susie would belt out the lyrics, "I want a hot dog without bread you see. 'Cause I carry my bread with me… I want it hot; don't want it cold. I want it so it fit my roll." And while dancing suggestively, Edwards would answer with quips such as, "My dog's never cold! Here's a dog that's long and lean"—to which Susie would reply, "I sure will be disgusted, if I don't get my mustard."

One of the funniest and most popular of their original songs was titled "A Married Man's a Fool If He Thinks His Wife Don't Love Nobody But Him." That tune, like much of their work,

was punctuated with the snappy asides, lighthearted signifying, and boisterous threats that were hallmarks of their act. The verbal sniping and cutting quips were always followed by a conciliatory tune from Susie, however, and the humorous stage spats were inevitably exposed as a sham. Their act always closed with Edwards performing his hilarious comic dance, the "Heebie Jeebies" or "Itch," while Susie looked on affectionately and the audience roared.

Many other comic stars who appeared at the Apollo were also deft dancers. Pigmeat Markham, for instance, incorporated several catchy dance steps into his routine, including the shim sham, the Suzy-Q, and a shoulder-bobbing, hand-waving strut that he named truckin'; the latter became a national craze in the '30s. And, to her audiences' delight, Moms Mabley rarely left the stage without doing the down-home shuffle that had become her signature dance step.

By most accounts, Mabley, who began her career as a singer and dancer in the '20s, has the distinction of being the most beloved comic ever to play the Apollo. She turned to comedy in 1921 at the suggestion of Butterbeans and Susie, and they helped jump start her career as a comedienne on the TOBA circuit. In early Apollo appearances, she participated in ensemble cast skits. Soon, however, she began donning oversized clodhoppers, tattered gingham dresses, and oddball hats, and affecting the persona of a sage, elderly, but slightly racy earth mother. Although she still occasionally worked with other comics, it was clear that she was at her best alone—delivering monologues with just a microphone and what one journalist described as "an outfit Phyllis Diller might wear if she was black."

Mabley was brilliant at establishing a mood of comforting familiarity with her audience; onstage she could become the grandmother that most everyone knew at one time or another. But she could shift abruptly from soothing reassurances like, "Hi, children. How y'all doin' tonight?…Yeah, *I know*! I know how y'all feel. Moms is tired, too," to racy retorts such as "An old man can't do nothin' for me, 'cept take a message to a young one."

She was also one of the pioneers of social satire at the Apollo. One of her most popular stories concerned two bank robbers, one black and one white, who are arrested and sentenced to death for robbing a bank and killing several tellers. The white man is terrified and immediately begins whining, "I don't want to be hung!" "Ah man, we done killed up them people and you talking 'bout you don't want to be hung....They goin' kill you, so why don't you face it like a man?" his partner asks. "That's easy for you to say," the white robber replies. "You're used to it."

Jackie "Moms" Mabley in the late '40s. Her popular routines included folksy homilies, ribald double entendres, and deft social and political satire.

Mabley's ability to move easily from folksy homilies to ribald double entendres and on to social and political satire was remarkable. Perhaps more than any of the early Apollo comics, she foreshadowed the shift to direct social commentary that would define black humor by the early '60s.

Increasingly, the broad, often bawdy, knockabout style that characterized most of the era's traditional black stage humor came under attack during the '50s. But many of the Apollo's veteran comics fought back, defending their approach. "My laughs grow out of situations, while the stand-up gets his out of what he says," Pigmeat Markham argued. "But what does he get? Giggles. The situational comic gets a *belly laugh* every time. Listen to Mort Sahl, say, and then listen to Red Skelton. Then you'll see what I mean. Man, I could never work for giggles."

He also described the origins of his comic style and asked a penetrating question during an interview in the *New York Post*:

> I was born and raised black. I learned my comedy
> from black comedians. The earliest skits I did
> onstage or under a tent were invented by black men.
> The audiences I learned to please, all of those years in
> small towns and big cities, they were mostly black,
> too....Who kept our people together in the real bad days
> so that they could survive during those Depression
> days...when the rats were huger and hungrier, when
> a sense of humor was all we had to feed on?

Despite such entreaties by Markham and others, the old-style burlesque approach that had dominated Apollo Theater humor fell out of fashion and gradually disappeared. Minstrel-style blackface makeup, the most visible symbol of that approach, was also abandoned. Pigmeat Markham stopped corking up in the late '40s, and Crackshot Hackley, reportedly the last popular black comic to perform in blackface, quit in the mid-'50s.

A new breed of young, assertive black stand-up comics emerged to take center stage. By the early '60s, they dominated comedy at the Apollo and at most other venues, reflecting the mood of an African American community that demanded equality in the streets and less demeaning images onstage.

Tap and the Apollo Theater

Zita Allen

Bill "Bojangles" Robinson in a famous photo by Edward Steichen, taken for *Vanity Fair* magazine in 1935. By then Robinson was a film star known for his performances with the young Shirley Temple.

The Apollo has held a special place in the hearts of hoofers since Bill "Bojangles" Robinson bolted out of his seat, leapt onstage, and declared his love for the theater shortly after it opened. True, the Apollo stage was not the Hoofers Club—the old pool hall next door to the Lafayette Theatre several blocks away —where dancers challenged each other, fueling tap's innovative evolution. Yet the roster of performers who appeared at the Apollo represents milestones in the history of tap and its stylistic spectrum.

What did they love about the Apollo? "The Apollo stage has always been just right. The right sound. It's not too slippery. Just perfect. Different stages had different sounds," Gip Gibson once confided.

Then there was the audience, that secret ingredient that made performances at the Apollo different. John W. Bubbles once compared audience reactions while playing, uptown and on Broadway, in *The Ziegfeld Follies*: "I was doing the same steps in both places, but with a different feeling. Downtown it was a battle between the acts; uptown, between the dancer and the audience. In Harlem, the audience practically dared you to dance, and you had to swing. Downtown they just watched and you couldn't fail. I danced loose and rhythmic uptown, simple and distinct downtown." Bubba Gaines went even further: "Playing the Apollo was such hard work. You really had to give out there. But, they understood you there more than anyplace else…. They knew what you were doing. If you had something, you were gone. They'd make you." The Apollo made a lot of dancers.

Audiences weren't the only ones who knew what they wanted. Apollo owner Frank Schiffman was pretty demanding himself. Bubba recalled how his act, the Three Dukes, tried to retire the crowd-pleaser of laying down intricate tap rhythms while jumping rope. "We got away with it for a while. But, working back at the Apollo Theater, Schiffman came backstage saying, 'Hey, Dukes, can I speak to you for a minute?' I said, 'Oh, my God, here it comes.' Schiffman said, 'You're not doing your act. I want

Pianist/dancer Ford "Buck" Washington and dancer John "Bubbles" Sublett. The duo was known for their comic routines, graced with moments of rhythmic tap dancing.

you to do your act the next show.'" For him, no ropes, no act. He called the bands down to the rehearsal hall, and the Dukes had to make the necessary adjustments before their next show that same night. When asked why, Bubba simply said, "He owned the theater, didn't he?"

What's more, in its heyday, the theater was a mandatory stop on the African American performer's touring circuit. "The Apollo in Harlem, the Howard Theatre in Washington, the Royal in Baltimore, and the Lincoln in Philadelphia. That was called 'Around the World.' You did it in four weeks, and you had a whole season," said dance great Honi Coles.

Playing the Apollo in the '30s and '40s might have been a sign a performer had arrived, but, with what some called "the grind"

of four, five, and six shows per day, it was no walk in the park. Still, the dancers strove for perfection even if they did it in what might seem to have been a rather unorthodox way. Buster Brown confided, "We'd go into rehearsal and do our routine easy like, no sweat." Sometimes they'd just talk through their routines. "We all know the same routines, like the BS chorus, shim sham, ole soft shoe. So, you just call it off," Honi Coles added. If they were really pressed for time, they'd use yet another kind of shorthand: "We're going to do number one or number three." But more often than not, they would just get down, because, as Buster said, when you prepared to perform at the Apollo, you had to "come ready to sweat!"

Dancers were a staple of Apollo shows. In fact, Jack Schiffman said there was never an Apollo show without them: "There they were beating out the rhythms of the day, performing the gymnastics, meeting the jazz beat with simultaneous and contrapuntal beats....It was as though sparks from their flashing feet lit up the firmament as they pranced out on the Apollo's stage." In tap's heyday, great hoofers shared the stage with some of the hottest bands, pumping up the volume of a music and dance dialogue. As one tap dancer said, "It's the rhythm that counts, and when we danced all we wanted to do was pick up that beat, play around with it, and ride it out!"

The roots of this indigenous American art form can be traced back to a time when African captives were loaded onto slave ships and the brutality of the Middle Passage and beyond. Over four hundred years tap evolved in America's cultural pressure cooker, where West African music and dance mingled with British step dances, Irish jigs, clog dances, and other influences, creating a remarkable fusion of movement and rhythm. Tap's popularity peaked between the '20s and '40s as jazz swept the nation, and its dance counterparts stole center stage in performance venues that ranged from cramped nightspots to spacious stages such as the Apollo.

Bojangles tops the list of tap icons who graced the Apollo's stage. When he started out as a kid dancing for pennies on street corners, many buck dancers wore burnt-cork blackface;

Clayton "Peg Leg" Bates, 1932. His wooden leg (the result of
a childhood cotton mill accident) was an integral part of his act;
its sharp crack played off the percussive sound of his tap shoe.

Bojangles did not. Flat-footed shuffling steps were hoofers' stylistic
signature; Bojangles changed that by shifting his weight to the balls
of the feet, allowing him to make what Langston Hughes called
"the finest sound in jazz music." And, instead of steel-plated taps
on the heels and toes of his shoes, Bojangles had a loose wooden
half-sole attached from the toe to the ball of the foot. The result
was what Hughes called his "little running trills of rippling softness
or terrific syncopated rolls of mounting sound, rollicking little
nuances of tap-tap-toe, or staccato runs like a series of gun-shots."

At a time when black performers were stymied by
stereotypes, Honi Coles said, Bojangles "taught upright class."
He would have known. When tap ruled the day at the Apollo, Honi
was one-half of the consummate class act, Coles and [Cholly]
Atkins. One admirer said, "There is hardly a step he doesn't own,

and all are done with an ease that is almost careless." Tall, thin,
and elegant, Coles was one of Frank Schiffman's favorite dancers.
Not only did he hire Coles and Atkins before they had danced
together professionally, Schiffman made Coles the theater's
production manager after tap was no longer a box-office draw.
Even after many of the usual venues closed and gigs were scarce,
Coles didn't stop dancing. Along with Buster Brown, Charles
Cook, Clayton "Peg Leg" Bates, LeRoy Myers, and Bubba Gaines,
he formed a group called the Copacetics to honor Bojangles's
memory and keep tap alive.

Not too many dancers headlined at the Apollo but,
according to Jack Schiffman, one dance team was the exception
to the rule: Buck and Bubbles. "Bubbles," declared dancer,
choreographer, and teacher Henry LeTang, "was the daddy of the
modern rhythm tap," creating the style of tap that echoes jazz's
complex polyrhythms and its blend of structure and improvisation.
Gregory Hines agreed: "He is the first tap dancer who dropped
his heels in a syncopated way in the middle of a combination rather
than at the end, like a period to a sentence. He enlarged the
vocabulary so that you could tap to any tempo." Bubbles also cut
the tempo in half by switching from a two-to-a-bar to a four-to-a-
bar rhythm, allowing twice as much time to lay down dazzling new
combinations.

Paul Draper described Bubble's nonchalant performing
ease: "You'd think he's just going to stroll around the stage, when
presto, he'll toss off a burst of sight and sound that you just can't
believe." Bubbles's taps would explode in counterpoint to Buck's
piano playing, which was so slow it seemed the next note would
never come. All the while, Bubbles pulled an amazing assortment
of riffs out of a bottomless bag of tricks, such as dropping his
heels or clicking his toes or heels together for added accents,
and tapping while doing complex turns. He could take one of
tap's basic building blocks, the time step, and do endless
variations. To Coles, who once said there are two types of tap
dancers—ad lib and routine—Bubbles was "one of the greatest
ad lib dancers around."

But Bojangles and Bubbles were just two of a host of
hoofers who wowed Apollo audiences. Pete Nugent's group—
Pete, Peaches, and Duke—was one of the top class acts. Their soft

The Apollo chorus girls onstage with a performer, 1940s. The dancers were among the theater's most popular attractions, known for their beauty, grace, and ability to master the latest routines.

shoe was something special. "All of us did a soft shoe, but each is different," Buster Brown once said. "Pete was a master with his whole group. Three guys dancing like one. They looked like they were tied together with string. Precision." Nugent believed that "good dancers lay those rhythms right in your lap." Eddie Rector's was a class act with a twist: with the exception of Howard "Sandman" Sims, who followed his lead, few hoofers sprinkled sand on the stage before launching into a classic soft shoe.

Not all the great hoofers agreed with Cholly Atkins's opinion that "with taps, you have to sound good as well as look good." Some hoofers were more concerned with the sound and the rhythm. Bunny Briggs's sharp staccato seemed to come from nowhere, since his feet barely left the floor. Jimmy Slyde spent almost as much time slipping and sliding across the stage as he spent slapping it with the soles of his tap shoes. Baby Laurence was another whose taps "were delivered with machine-gun rapidity without strain...and with flawless ease." These dancers made an

easy transition from the big band sound to bebop, from dancing with Duke Ellington, Jimmie Lunceford, or Count Basie to dancing with Charlie Parker, Art Tatum, or Dizzy Gillespie. Their delivery owed a lot to old-timers such as Bubbles and has given something to today's hoofers such as Savion Glover.

Tap at the Apollo was not a men-only affair. Former chorus girls Mae Barnes and Lavinia Mack were among a handful of women whose acts stood out. Of course, during the Apollo's heyday, most female performers, like singer Lena Horne, who had been a Cotton Club chorus girl before graduating to soubrette roles, needed to know a little time step and shim sham shimmy. But a few dancers, such as Barnes, Mack, Candi and Pepper, and the Whitman Sisters knew a lot more, earning the ultimate compliment male tap dancers paid female hoofers: "That girl can dance her ass off!"

Mildred "Candi" Thorpe and her partner, Jewel "Pepper" Welch, earned that praise when they made their 1941 Apollo debut

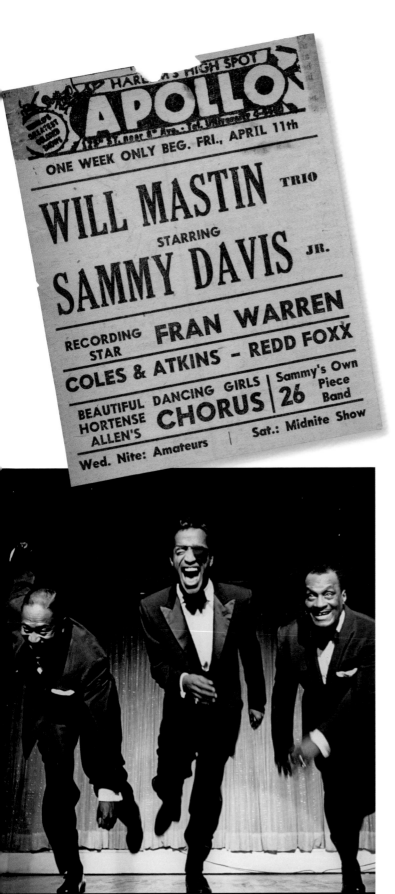

The Will Mastin Trio with Sammy Davis Sr., Sammy Davis Jr., and Will Mastin in 1955. Young Sammy was always the standout for his versatile singing, dancing, and comic abilities.

as an opening act for Fats Waller and his band. "We tore 'em up," remembered Thorpe, adding that they were called back for so many encores that they ran out of routines. That debut launched a career that included working with Louis Armstrong, Erskine Hawkins, and others. Alice Whitman, whom fellow hoofer Bill Bailey called "the prettiest thing in show business," was part of the impressive Whitman Sisters act. Called the "Queen of Taps," she performed with her blond, fair-skinned sisters, Essie, Alberta, and Mabel, doing "tricky little tap steps" and closing with the shim sham.

Whether the hoofers were men or women, tap at the Apollo Theater often left a lasting impression. For Maurice and Gregory Hines, a trip to the Apollo with their dance teacher, the legendary Henry LeTang, to see the Nicholas Brothers was a revelation. Gregory was only seven and Maurice was nine when they saw the brothers "attack a step, pause between steps, and start on an upbeat," before unleashing a flurry of acrobatics. Maurice said that made him realize tap "wasn't going to be just about the feet." Gregory, on the other hand, realized that folks who said the Hines Kids would be the next Nicholas Brothers were wrong: "When they came on, a roar went up, like a bullfighter made a pass....I remember the ease with which they did the act… they just were so relaxed, and seemed to do everything so effortlessly. I realized then that nobody was gonna be the next Nicholas Brothers."

After tap's heyday, occasional (and always successful) reunions, such as one at the Apollo in 1962 and others in the 1980s at the Brooklyn Academy of Music, brought many of the hoofers together, to the delight of audiences and critics alike. But even Honi Coles, who worked with the Copacetics and a young white hoofer named Brenda Bufalino to keep the art alive, confided to an interviewer that his generation of hoofers was a dying breed. Then along came a young dancer with fast feet, a passion for tap, a compelling presence, and the good fortune to have worked with some of the best hoofers who ever lived: Savion Glover. In 2003, when Gregory Hines passed, Maurice hosted a star-studded tribute at the Apollo. At that event Glover brought the house down with a moving tribute to his mentor. His performance showed that there is no better place to prove that tap is alive and well than the stage of the Apollo Theater.

The young Nicholas Brothers, twenty-one-year-old Fayard (left) and
fourteen-year-old Harold (right), at the beginning of their career, 1935.

The Apollo Chorus Girls

Zita Allen

Apollo chorus girls in a lavish number, 1935. Chorus girls not only danced between acts but also posed in grand costumes and took bit parts in the comic skits.

From the moment the Apollo Theater opened, sixteen sepia-toned dancers, hailed as the most beautiful chorus girls on the "Broadway of Harlem"—125th Street— were the glue that held together a roster of ever-changing vaudeville acts and a major draw for the best and brightest of the city's "colored theaters." Some even dubbed them the Apollo Rockettes. Dressed in glitzy costumes, dancing to the era's hottest bands against a backdrop of colorful scenery, the chorus girls dazzled audiences and critics alike as they strutted their stuff in revues created by choreographer Clarence Robinson and bearing catchy titles such as *Jazz a la Carte*, *A Night in Spain*, or *Babes in Toyland*.

Three chorines—Catherine Campbell, Marion Egbert, and Maudine Simmons—featured in the *Amsterdam News*, shortly after the Apollo opened, captured the typical look. Snapped backstage between shows, they wore sequined dresses with fur trim that circled a hem short enough to accentuate their long legs

and show off tap shoes adorned with bows across the instep. Fashionable bobs framed their smiling faces, described as "proof of the claim so lavishly made by the dramatic editor that the Apollo Theatre houses the best looking chorus of all."

It goes without saying that, like most black chorus girls performing in 1930s nightclubs, theaters, and chorus lines, they had to be "high yaller" (fair-skinned). According to Mary Bruce, a Harlem-based dancer and dance teacher at the time, producers always asked for light-skinned girls. "If I showed them a group of dancers and one was very dark," she recalled, "that dancer was almost always eliminated, even if she was one of the best workers you can have on the stage."

The routines looked elegant, but they were far from effortless. In an interview years after her days as a chorus girl were over, Marion Coles (née Egbert), who at seventeen had danced at the Apollo when it first opened, said rehearsals were so demanding the dancers practically lived in the theater. There were even

Earl Bolling, the first usher in Harlem to rise to a managerial position as manager of the Apollo Theater, poses with the chorus girls, early 1940s.

cots backstage so they could catch a quick nap to recover from a rigorous regimen that often began at 10 a.m. and ended more than twelve hours later every night of the week. Those were the days of four or more shows a night. "You'd be down here until three o'clock in the morning. And we opened every Friday morning with a brand new show," Coles said.

"Chorus girls made this house," declared one of the original chorus girls featured in a documentary entitled *Been Rich All My Life*. The film follows Coles and former chorines Bertye Lou Wood, Cleo Hayes, Elaine Ellis, and Fay Ray in their more recent incarnation as "The Silver Belles," still kicking up their heels well into their seventies, eighties, and even nineties. The claim that chorus girls were the backbone of the Apollo was no idle boast. They held their own in productions featuring such impressive showstoppers as the big bands of Chick Webb, Duke Ellington, Cab Calloway, Count Basie, and Jimmie Lunceford and countless legendary singers and comedians.

For many chorus girls, working at the Apollo was a dream come true. They got to pick up steps from tap legends. They performed the famous stair dance with Bill "Bojangles" Robinson. Some even appeared with him in '30s movie musicals. Lunceford wrote a tune especially for them called "For Dancers Only." Jazz great Louis Armstrong created a catchy little rhyme for one dancer: "He said, 'Dear Faye, Roses are red. Violets are blue. Faye's are pink 'cause I saw them hangin' on the line.'" Others found love. Marion Egbert married hoofer Honi Coles, who had made a name for himself as part of the legendary class act Coles and Atkins before becoming the Apollo's production manager. But they all took particular pride in one thing: "We held those shows together, because the audiences came to see us."

Life on the chorus line was not all glitz and glamour. One 1934 newspaper article entitled "The Price a Show Girl Must Pay" described a young dancer's journey from a small southern town to the big city. With stars in her eyes and $250 to her name,

Apollo service staff, 1937. The Apollo ranked high among Harlem businesses in employing blacks, particularly in roles of responsibility.

she arrived seeking fame and fortune but found "the bitter taste of disillusionment behind the gaiety of the marquee; the misery that lurks under the rouge and powder and paint of the smiling girls in the line." Hers was not an unusual story. After all, when the Apollo opened, the country was still under the cloud of the Great Depression. Black folks flocked to the North to escape the South's Jim Crow repression, only to find that jobs were scarce, opportunities were tainted by racism, and life was no crystal stair.

One Harlem newspaper kept track of which businesses hired blacks and how much responsibility they had. The Apollo ranked near the top. Owner Frank Schiffman employed blacks from backstage to the front of the house. In the '30s, that mattered. In 1939 Schiffman's theater was called "a bulwark between performers and a crackup of local show life." One week after the 1940 closing of the legendary Cotton Club, the Apollo was described as "the only theater in America devoted to the presentation of

revues with colored hands and colored stage casts." Years later, Bobby Schiffman, who took over the helm after his father retired, commented, "Every craftsman, every outside repair man, every service organization that the Apollo uses, has its roots in this community. We are a spur of economic activity in this community so we don't let our dollars move outside if we can help it."

Still, during the economic squeeze of the '30s and '40s, that didn't keep the Apollo chorus girls and twenty-two of the theater's thirty-two employees from going out on strike. The strike was organized by the American Guild of Variety Artists, which had only recently gone against the grain of other AFL-CIO theatrical union affiliates and declared that "all performers, white and black, had the same right to protection from exploitation." Honi Coles was on the strikers' bargaining committee. When they met with Schiffman to discuss raises and changes in the chorus girls' working conditions, he demanded proof that a majority of them

were represented by the union. One committee member called it a
typical delay tactic designed to give Schiffman time to root out
and fire the instigators.

It didn't work. The dancers meant business. "The
strike was called at 6:30 p.m. Saturday. The girls went up to their
dressing rooms, changed their clothes, and walked out. At the
midnight show, only 143 patrons were in the theater, which holds
2,000," recalled one committee member. Labor and community
groups rushed to support them. A Harlem local of the stagehands'
union, the International Alliance of Theatrical Stage Employes,
let the strikers set up temporary headquarters in its offices.
Harlem's female movers and shakers, including Paul Robeson's
mother-in-law, also came to their aid. So did most Apollo patrons.
"Nearly every white patron who saw what was taking place refused
to cross the line and went home," reported one newspaper.

After a week or so, Schiffman caved. The strikers won.
The chorus girls' minimum salary was hiked to $30 a week,
and rehearsal time was shortened. Dancer Frenchy Bascomb,
who some called "the spark plug of the picket line," was one of
many who rejoiced. "We're glad, darned glad, we won the strike.
The $30 in place of $25 is mighty, mighty nice in these days," she
said. With the strike settled, the dancers went back to work.

Schiffman put on a brave face: "If the girls want the
union, then I'm for it. If it aids us in putting on a better show, then
I'm for it 100%. Now that this thing is settled, our main program
is to give our patrons the finest entertainment obtainable."

But times were changing. Vaudeville was dying. By the
late '40s the Apollo in Harlem and the Howard in Washington, D.C.,
were the only two theaters with live revues that catered to black
artists and talent. Performance venues for African American
chorus girls were drying up. Other venues around the country could
absorb only a limited number of the sepia-toned beauties. Soon
the Apollo Theater chorus girls would become a thing of the past.

Amsterdam News, March 2, 1940. Lower: Apollo chorus girls practiced
long hours and were paid low salaries. They went on strike and won
better terms, but the days of chorus lines at the Apollo were numbered.

The Apollo Theater and the Chitlin Circuit

Mark Anthony Neal

For much of the twentieth century, the Apollo Theater stood as one of the most visible emblems of the formal and informal networks of theaters, clubs, restaurants, dance halls, and after-hours clubs that constituted the so-called chitlin circuit. Though the term "chitlin circuit" has been considered pejorative in some circles, the circuit itself was indispensable to the development and circulation of African American culture in the late nineteenth and twentieth centuries, particularly in the arenas of theater, dance, comedy, film, and music. The Apollo emerged one of the most cherished of chitlin circuit institutions, often viewed alongside Chicago's Regal Theater and Washington, D.C.'s Howard Theater as the ultimate venue for black performers who, well into the twentieth century, were denied access to spaces that primarily catered to white audiences.

Chitlins or, more formally, chitterlings are delicacies in which pigs' intestines are cooked in an assortment of ways. In the United States, chitlins are largely synonymous with the South and with African American cuisine in particular—soul food—as the byproduct of a historical legacy: enslaved Africans on plantations in the American South were often given leftover scraps of meat such as pigs' intestines. It was, in part, the ingenuity within these slave societies that helped transform many of the plantation's throwaways into something of substance that enabled slaves to

Washington, D.C.'s Howard Theatre, one of the premier venues on the TOBA circuit, rivaled the Apollo in the roster of talent it presented.

express themselves in unique and meaningful ways, be it cooking or expressive arts.

Thus, in its earliest formations in the period after emancipation, the chitlin circuit was the literal place where one could consume African American cuisine, including chitterlings. It was often understood within mainstream culture that the chitlin circuit was something inferior, part of an underbelly of American society. Such interpretations were inevitable, as Doris Witt argues in her book *Black Hunger: Food and the Politics of U.S. Identity*, given the reality of the functions of a pig's intestines. The chitlin circuit was always going to be associated with filth, waste, and stench. But the early chitlin circuit, particularly with regard to de facto and later legally enforced segregation in the late nineteenth century, also became the location where blacks could let down their guard and discard the masks they wore in the face of antiblack racism and violence. It was within these physical confines that blacks began to hone performance sensibilities that celebrated the pursuit of leisure, attempted to speak back to the political realities of the day via trickster narratives (often with comic undertones), countered the popularity of blackfaced minstrelsy and its distortions of black life and culture, and crafted a more nuanced sense of their public selves as represented in the expressive arts. Writing about black minstrels in the postemancipation period, Mel Watkins states, "Although the narrowly defined, primarily demeaning images of blacks that [black minstrels] commonly fostered were no different in most respects from those projected by white minstrels, as professional entertainers, they brought a measure of dignity to themselves and therefore, indirectly, to other blacks."

The chitlin circuit began to take on more formal attributes in the early twentieth century with the emergence of the Theatre Owners Booking Association (TOBA)—the collective of white theater owners who catered to black audiences, largely in the South. The quality of life on the TOBA circuit led many black performers to refer to the acronym TOBA as "tough on black asses." Nevertheless, it served as a training ground for a generation of black performers, allowing them to hone their artistic skills in ways that were competitive as well as collaborative. Part of the value of the chitlin circuit was the rapport developed between performers and audiences. The close proximity between audiences and performers meant that the former could impact and even dictate the trajectory of black expressive culture on the basis of their response to artists. As Watkins suggests, "Audiences were outspoken and inhospitable to acts that either were lackluster or strayed too far from preferred black performance style." Joe Sample, pianist and cofounder of the Jazz Crusaders, recalls such an experience opening for a rhythm-and-blues tour, somewhere in Texas. According to Sample:

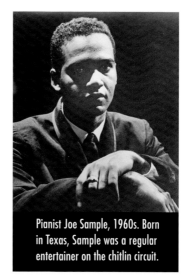

Pianist Joe Sample, 1960s. Born in Texas, Sample was a regular entertainer on the chitlin circuit.

> It was 1954, 1955. I'm either 15 or 16 years old. The place is somewhere in a barn with a bandstand along the east Texas/Louisiana border. We are in sugar cane country…. I am the piano player in a band, the house band….These blues artists could have been Gatemouth Brown, T-Bone Walker, Big Walter, Little Walter, Johnny Copeland, Percy Mayfield or any number of those particular men that were prominent at that particular time. The custom was the band played a warm-up set and of course the singer finally comes up on to the bandstand and the show commences.

> We of course wanted to play our Jazz. We were doing anything to play Jazz and we would force Jazz on the top of these rhythm and blues grooves. Suddenly men would start walking from the back of the room and approach the bandstand. This man said to me, "Look I want you niggas to understand something right now. We paid 25 cent at the front door and we came in here to have a good time. Now it sounds to me [that] you guys are playing a bunch of bullshit and we're not getting our money's worth. So we're gonna tell you now. We will take your instruments from you, whip your ass and destroy your vehicles and more than likely you will have to walk and beg your way back to Houston, Texas. Now we will do this to you unless you make us feel real good, real suddenly…"

Sample's recollections are a reminder that many of the customers at chitlin circuit functions were spending their hard-earned money to have a good time—it was one of the few moments

A roadside juke joint (left), customers enjoying drinks inside (middle), and an informal dance (right). Small joints formed the backbone of the chitlin circuit up until the '60s.

of leisure afforded them in their lives—and their desires dictated, in this case, what kind of music would be played.

The TOBA was unable to survive the economic crisis of the late 1920s and '30s, but the need for black performers to find an outlet for their practice—even as a few were integrated into the vaudeville stage and the burgeoning motion picture industry—and the need for black communities to be entertained remained. In the midst of the mass migration of African Americans from the South to northern cities such as Chicago and New York,

beginning during the '20s on through to the late '50s, theaters such as the Regal in Chicago and the Apollo in New York began to take on more prominence. Despite the lore associated with the most popular chitlin circuit institutions, the bulk of those venues were greasy, overheated, badly ventilated, badly protected, and overcrowded spaces that kept most black artists to a second-tier status within the entertainment industry. Before the Apollo Theater's opening in 1934, theaters such as the Lincoln Theatre and the Lafayette, which catered to whites but allowed black

T-Bone Walker, 1960s. One of the most innovative guitarists of his day, his recordings influenced blues and rock musicians from B. B. King through Jimi Hendrix and beyond.

patrons, were the most prominent in New York City's most populated black enclave, Harlem. Shortly after its opening, the Apollo began its Amateur Night programming, which was broadcast live on the local radio station WMCA. Hosted by dancer Ralph Cooper, the show, with its active audience participation, was emblematic of the value of the chitlin circuit.

With audiences that ran the gamut of class, social standing, and regional background, Amateur Night at the Apollo and similar programming at other chitlin circuit outlets were examples of the hyperdemocratic tendencies that existed within black political and social thought. A breadth of opinion and sensibilities helped shaped what was deemed acceptable to black communities. As such the chitlin circuit had the power to police black expressive culture, with the understanding that part of its authority was its ability to prime performers for the labor of representing the best face of the race, if some of these artists made the transition to mainstream stages.

Ralph Cooper recalls one of example of such gatekeeping when a white performer sang Jerome Kern and Oscar Hammerstein's "Ol' Man River"—a song that would become an emblem of political resistance for the legendary performer and activist Paul Robeson. While audiences were open to the performance of the song by a white performer, many black performers substituted Hammerstein's use of the word "nigger." As Cooper recalls, "this fellow was a purist, and he wanted to sing the song as written....No explosion could have been as loud as the silence that followed." This same rigor was of course regularly experienced by black performers, particularly those who lacked originality or mimicked more popular artists. Some performers who later achieved fame failed in their initial outings at the Apollo, but their later success was a testament to the chitlin circuit's capacity to season young performers—a rite of passage that ultimately improved the quality of their performances.

Clarence "Gatemouth" Brown performs in a black club, 1955. He became popular in the '70s and '80s on the blues revival circuit.

But the chitlin circuit wasn't simply about black performance; it also spoke to the desire for economic self-sufficiency and control of community institutions, issues that were not mutually exclusive from the political push against segregation and the attainment of voting rights. The chitlin circuit was a metaphor for the capacity among African Americans to generate something of their own from the larger culture's scraps and to put their unique cultural stamp on those institutions. Even as black culture became more prominent within mainstream culture in the post–civil rights era, remnants of the chitlin circuit continued to nurture emerging cultural practices in black communities, whether with rap music in the '70s or the gospel musicals of David Talbert and Tyler Perry in the '90s.

African[s] and World War I[I]

Robert L. Allen

The Tuskegee Airmen were the first black members of the U.S. Army Air Corps, including Benjamin O. Davis Jr. (third from left). Nearly 1,000 pilots graduated at Tuskegee Army Air Field during World War II, 450 of whom served overseas.

World War II proved to be a significant turning point for African Americans and for the Apollo Theater. The onset of the war lifted white America out of the Great Depression, but it left African Americans searching for a lifeline. Commentators often refer to World War II as "the Good War," the war fought against an obviously evil enemy overseas, the war for a good cause—to defend freedom and democracy against tyranny. For white America this view of the war may be valid, but for African Americans World War II was a war on two fronts—against fascism overseas but also against racism in American society. The enemy was at home as much as overseas, and what good came out of the war was due as much to the battle against racism on both fronts as it was to the battle against fascism in foreign lands. In the course of the war, black America became a truly national community with a strong sense of its identity and a fierce determination to never again be cowed by the age-old enemies of racial segregation and discrimination.

During World War II over a million African Americans served in the U.S. armed forces. Thousands of Harlem men and boys volunteered for service in the military, and thousands became workers in the defense industries. The Apollo supported the war effort by setting aside thirty-five tickets each day for soldiers. Each week Apollo performers—including Billie Holiday, Ella Fitzgerald, Cab Calloway, and Lena Horne—

gave shows for the soldiers at Harlem's USO Center. Tuesdays became known as "Apollo Night."

For most of the war, the great majority of black soldiers and sailors were relegated to segregated labor battalions or mess duty, serving as cooks, dishwashers, and busboys. This discriminatory treatment angered many African Americans in the military. As one black sailor said, "I joined the Navy to help defeat the enemy. I came to fight, but all they gave me to fight with was pots and pans."

Some black soldiers did get into combat, and they served with courage and honor. Two all-black Army combat divisions, the 92nd and the 93rd Infantry, were activated after the war began. After training at Fort Huachuca in Arizona, the troops in these two divisions were called upon to fight enemy troops in Italy and to serve with U.S. forces in the South Pacific. More than two thousand soldiers volunteered to serve in all-black combat units that fought bravely and helped push the war into the German heartland. One of the most famous groups of black combatants was the 761st Tank Battalion. Known as the Black Panthers, the 761st helped to spearhead the Allied drive across Europe, and they liberated hundreds of people from Nazi concentration camps. In the air, the Tuskegee Airmen defended American bombers from marauding German planes. Black women also participated in the Allied campaigns. Over four thousand African American women were members of the Women's Army Corps.

The heroism of African American soldiers and sailors was epitomized by Dorie Miller, a mess attendant on the USS *West Virginia* at the time of the Japanese attack on Pearl Harbor. Though not trained as a gunner, Miller seized an antiaircraft gun and single-handedly shot down several attacking Japanese fighter planes. He was killed two years later when his ship was hit by a torpedo in the South Pacific.

Following the bombing of Pearl Harbor, Harlem's *Amsterdam News* ran a front-page editorial declaring: "America is at war. This is no time for superficial distinctions based upon

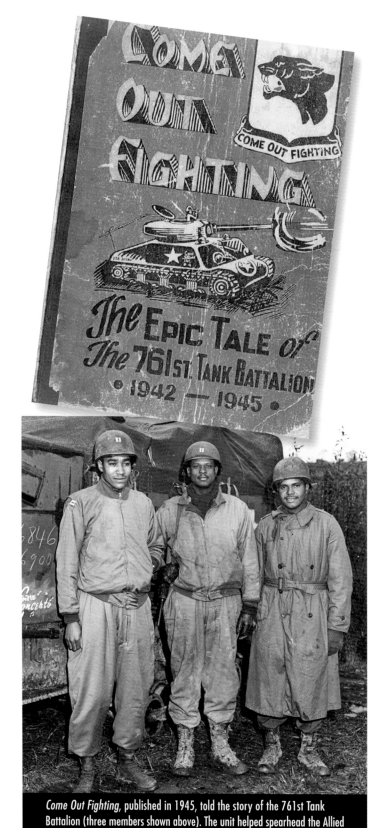

Come Out Fighting, published in 1945, told the story of the 761st Tank Battalion (three members shown above). The unit helped spearhead the Allied drive across Europe, liberating hundreds from Nazi concentration camps.

skin-color. This is no time for subversive race prejudice. We will show those Japs and Nazis that as one nation indivisible, we fight the battle for democracy. We fight to win!" The paper reported that black volunteers were swamping the Navy recruiting office downtown, and a group of black doctors was organizing to go wherever needed to attend the wounded.

Despite their courage and willingness to fight, the vast majority of black soldiers and sailors found themselves discriminated against and limited to doing menial labor or backbreaking work. Black soldiers and sailors protested the mistreatment, but their protests were criminalized and treated as insubordination, refusal to obey orders, and even mutiny. One such incident occurred in 1944 among a group of young African American sailors at an isolated base in northern California called Port Chicago. The Port Chicago naval ammunition depot was the largest and most important ammunition transshipment facility on the West Coast. Only the black sailors, most of them teenagers, were assigned the hard and dangerous job of handling ammunition. All the officers were white; no black man could become an officer. None of the sailors had been trained in handling ammunition, and the officers forced the black sailors to race against each other in loading ammunition. When a terrible explosion wrecked the base on July 17, 1944, killing 320 men,

most of them African American sailors, more than 250 of the surviving men refused to go back to work under the same officers and the same conditions. It was a strike, but fifty men were singled out and convicted of mutiny. Thurgood Marshall, who was then special counsel for the NAACP Legal Defense Fund, filed an appeal brief for the sailors and led a campaign to publicize the injustice. Although the young sailors suffered imprisonment, their protest and the ensuing public outcry compelled the Navy to change its racial policies. By 1946 it had begun to desegregate its shore facilities and Navy ships as well. The Port Chicago incident contributed to a push for general desegregation of the military, which President Harry Truman ordered in 1948 throughout the armed forces.

Such instances of protest and resistance to racism in the military were directly related to the state of black America, which was in a watchful, skeptical mood as the nation entered the war. The Garvey movement had reawakened a sense of racial pride among many African Americans, and the labor and radical movements of the 1930s—in which many blacks participated— had demonstrated the importance of collective action. Italy's invasion of Ethiopia in 1935 and the rise of Hitler's racist regime had attracted black attention to the developing international conflict. Even sports had taken on political overtones with

A headline from the *Pittsburgh Courier* announces the Double V campaign, in which African American leaders promoted service in World War II as a means of securing better treatment at home.

the Joe Louis–Max Schmeling fight and Jesse Owens's Olympic victory in Germany in 1936.

But economic depression and rampant racial discrimination at home continued to preoccupy black leaders, the black press, and the black community in general, shaping the black response to the war. Unlike World War I, in which a leader such as W. E. B. Du Bois could urge black people to "forget our special grievance and close ranks shoulder to shoulder with our white fellow citizens…fighting for democracy," World War II was from the beginning regarded by most black leaders as a struggle on two fronts. A. Philip Randolph took the lead in January 1941 when he called for a march on Washington to protest discrimination in the war industries and segregation in the armed forces. Randolph, the head of the Brotherhood of Sleeping Car Porters union (whose

headquarters in Harlem were only a few doors from the Apollo Theater), confronted President Franklin Roosevelt and demanded that he order the desegregation of the military and the defense industry. Worried that Randolph could deliver on his plan for tens of thousands to march on Washington, Roosevelt issued Executive Order 8802 prohibiting discrimination in the defense plants and the federal government and setting up a Fair Employment Practices Commission.

This was the first success in what the *Pittsburgh Courier*, a widely circulated African American newspaper, would call the "Double V" campaign—calling for victory over the fascists abroad and victory over racism at home. Although Executive Order 8802 was criticized for having no enforcement provisions, it nonetheless opened up tens of thousands of jobs to black men

African American soldiers walk the streets of Harlem, 1943. The community took great pride in the service of young men like these in the armed forces.

Harlem Riot, 1943. Several days of unrest occurred when a white policeman shot a black serviceman in the arm after the soldier had objected to the treatment of a black woman being arrested for disturbing the peace.

and women in defense plants around the country. Entire new black communities sprang up on the West Coast as thousands of African Americans took part in a new great migration in search of work.

In 1942 the *Courier* published a poll of its readers which found that over 80 percent of those questioned believed that African Americans should not soft-pedal their demands for freedom. Another survey found that a surprising one-half of blacks interviewed in New York felt it was more important to make democracy work at home than to defeat Germany and Japan. The issue was not patriotism. Black youth were signing up for military service in record numbers. Moreover, *Life* magazine reported that at least one-quarter of Harlem's residents were doing some kind of war support work. Some fifteen thousand Harlem residents served as air-raid wardens. Thousands of Harlem women were "learning first aid, knitting sweaters, serving in canteens, studying internal combustion engines." For African Americans the issue was racism. Harlem playwright Loften Mitchell put it succinctly when he said, "Irritated black people argued that when colored Ethiopia was attacked, Uncle Sam hadn't raced to her defense, but when white Europe was in trouble, Uncle Sam was right there."

The skeptical, defiant mood of black America was further apparent in the refusal of African Americans in many cities to meekly accept discrimination in housing and employment, or police brutality, or harassment by white mobs. In the summer of 1943 these issues sparked racial disturbances in Los Angeles, Detroit, and New York—the latter precipitated by an incident in which a white policeman shot a black soldier in Harlem. When a rumor spread that the soldier had died, thousands of protestors raged through the streets setting fire to white-owned businesses. The Apollo was saved when a group of Harlem residents formed a protective cordon around the much-loved theater. Unfortunately, the riot meant financial loss for the Apollo, as white patrons who had previously come uptown to Harlem were now reluctant to do so.

By the end of World War II, African Americans were serving throughout the U.S. military in a wide range of jobs. In civilian life the well-paying defense jobs that opened up as a result of President Roosevelt's executive order had given an economic boost to tens of thousands of African American workers and families. These gains were short-lived, however, as the end of the war brought military demobilization, the closing of defense plants, and a consequent loss of good jobs. Black men and women who could get jobs found themselves once again relegated to working as janitors, domestics, nurse's aides, and menial laborers.

But something fundamental had changed. A new spirit of militancy had emerged as African Americans realized that their protests in the military and in civilian life had brought about significant, albeit temporary, changes in their life circumstances. They realized that if discrimination in defense plants could be prohibited by a stroke of the president's pen, and if segregation in the military could be ended by a stroke of the president's pen, then segregation and discrimination were not immutable yokes of oppression. Collective resistance and social protest could compel change for the better. African American veterans and civilians alike were ready to put their bodies on the line for freedom.

Black America had learned a valuable lesson in the war, and with that lesson the seeds of the civil rights movement were sown.

For the Apollo, the latter part of the '40s presented difficulties as it faced new realities. The loss of black and white patrons had taken a toll. Moreover, many of the big bands that were its bread and butter during the war years succumbed to economic stresses and broke up. In 1946 alone, eight big bands fell silent. Black bands in particular could not afford the rising costs and declining incomes they encountered. The rise of bebop as a new musical style featuring brilliant jazz artists such as Dizzy Gillespie and Charlie Parker also undercut the big bands. But bebop and the growing popularity of vocalists such as Billy Eckstine and Pearl Bailey and singing groups like the Orioles would provide another source of exciting talent for the Apollo to spotlight in the coming era.

3

The Soul of the Apollo: The Apollo Theater in the 1950s and 1960s

1949

August 12
Pioneering vocal group, the Orioles, make their Apollo debut and set the stage for the R & B era.

1950

The Johnny Otis Rhythm and Blues Caravan comes to the Apollo on the strength of its hit "Double Crossing Blues," sung by thirteen-year-old Little Esther Phillips.

Seventeen-year-old Clyde McPhatter wins Amateur Night and is hired by **Billy Ward and His Dominoes**.

1951

Big Joe Turner, singing with Count Basie, is "rediscovered" by Atlantic Records' head, Ahmet Ertegun, at the Apollo.

December 19
Josephine Baker debuts at the Apollo.

1953

Clyde McPhatter is signed by Atlantic's Ahmet Ertegun, who first hears him at the Apollo. McPhatter forms the Drifters.

Reuben Phillips takes over the house band, playing for all R & B and later soul groups into the '60s.

1955

April

Fighter Joe Louis knocks out the Apollo with his comedy routine with Leonard Reed. He is brought back three weeks later.

Pearl Bailey's headlining show with Duke Ellington sets Apollo house attendance record.

Disc jockey **Tommy "Dr. Jive" Smalls** and Bobby Schiffman begin R & B revue show format, featuring as many as a dozen vocal acts on one bill. Disc jockeys supplant show producers as Apollo show presenters and packagers. Signals the end of the vaudeville-variety format at the theater, but turns around the Apollo financially.

Spring 1955

Joe Tex wins at Amateur Night.

November

Elvis Presley attends the Apollo and sees Bo Diddley while on his first trip to New York City to visit his record company. He attends again while rehearsing for his January 28, 1956, television debut on the Dorsey Brothers' *Stage Show*.

December 15

Thurman Ruth's Gospel Caravan debuts at the Apollo. These shows become hugely popular in the '50s. Top acts included the Dixie Hummingbirds, Shirley Caesar, Alex Bradford, the Swan Silvertones, the Staple Singers, Clara Ward, and the **Soul Stirrers**.

1956

Bo Diddley breaks Pearl Bailey's Apollo house attendance record.

Screamin' Jay Hawkins freaks out the Apollo crowd with "I Put a Spell on You."

Buddy Holly and the Crickets appear at the Apollo.

Mid-1950s

James Brown wins Amateur Night.

Frankie Lymon discovered on Amateur Night playing drums for the Esquires.

1957

Johnny Mathis debuts at the Apollo.

April
Timmie Rogers is the first comedian to headline the Apollo with his show "No Time for Squares."

1958

The Shirelles make their Apollo debut on Jocko Henderson's Rocket Ship Revue. They were the first of many "girl groups" popular from the late '50s to the mid-'60s.

Ben E. King's the Five Crowns become the Drifters to fulfill a long-term performance contract at the Apollo when Clyde McPhatter is drafted.

Little Anthony and the Imperials make their professional debut at the Apollo.

1960

Nancy Wilson makes Apollo debut.

Harold Melvin and the Blue Notes first appear at the Apollo.

Early 1960s

Gladys Knight wins Amateur Night.

Early to mid-1960s

A transvestite show, the Jewel Box Revue, becomes a major attraction each February, when other artists were put off by winter weather. The shows were stopped after the Apollo was threatened by a black nationalist group in the late '60s.

1961

Bobby Schiffman, younger son of Frank, takes over management of the theater.

1962

October 24
James Brown records live shows at the Apollo, which become the basis for his famous *The Apollo Theatre Presents the James Brown Show* album, released the following year.

December 7
The Motortown [*sic*] Revue debuts at the Apollo, bringing major Motown label artists to the theater.

1963

February 15
Dionne Warwick makes her first professional appearance at the theater.

May
Jackie Wilson claims Apollo house attendance record.

1964

James Brown smashes Apollo house attendance record.

1966–71

Apollo presents some two dozen community activities and educational programs to reach out to the Harlem community.

1968

June 14
Bill Cosby's one and only Apollo professional appearance.

Stephanie Mills, an eleven-year-old singing sensation, wins Amateur Night for six consecutive weeks.

1969

Jackson 5 win Amateur Night, featuring a ten-year-old Michael Jackson.

Late 1960s

The Apollo presents Miriam Makeba and Babatunde Olatunji.

The Apollo's Golden Years

Herb Boyd

The golden years at the Apollo Theater stretch across a generation of exciting but turbulent American history. To some extent, the entertainers, personalities, and acts that appeared on the Apollo's stage mirrored the nation's most significant cultural and political events.

Whenever an era is defined as the "golden years," so much depends on when and where you enter. For those aficionados of the swinging big bands of Benny Carter, Duke Ellington, and Count Basie in the 1930s, as the Apollo was completing its transition from vaudeville and burlesque, those were the theater's golden years. Who can forget those fantastic evenings when Lionel Hampton and his band rocked so hard that their fans' foot stamping literally cracked the theater's balcony? Others would argue for the bebop phase of the '40s with such musical greats as Charlie "Yardbird" Parker and Dizzy Gillespie fronting groups as the most unforgettable period at the Apollo. Critic A. B. Spellman recalled the excitement of this era in his *Four Lives in the Bebop Business:*

> When Bird [Parker] was at the Apollo, we would go early in the morning,
> and stay and watch the show all day long. We would watch him from the first
> show until after three o'clock, when it was time to go home from school.
> We used to go home and put our books up, and then tell our parents that we
> were going to the Apollo, and they'd let us go and we'd split and go watch
> Bird again until nine, when it was time to go home at night.

The fans of doo-wop and the advocates for Motown can also make a strong case for the '50s and '60s as the glory years at the Apollo.

Each one of these phases at the Apollo is worthy of a "golden years" title, and to relegate them to distinct time periods without considering the vital continuum may be a disservice to them all. In effect, the eras blended almost imperceptibly, particularly through the music, dance, comedy, and social commentary so vividly reflected from the Apollo's stage.

In the '30s, America was caught in the throes of the Great Depression and racial turmoil. For several years the plight of the Scottsboro Boys, nine black youths

Multiple exposure of Charlie Parker in performance, 1955. The legendary saxophonist helped create and popularize bebop music in his postwar performances and recordings.

Trumpeter Dizzy Gillespie and vocalist Sarah Vaughan enjoy refreshments backstage. Both were leaders of the new bebop movement in the late '40s and early '50s.

charged and convicted of raping two white women on a train en route from northern Alabama to Memphis, commanded the headlines. When four of them, out on bail during an appeal, appeared on the Apollo's stage on August 20, 1937, their case reached an even larger audience of concerned citizens. Presenting the Scottsboro Boys to highlight their case and to raise funds for their defense was, to some degree, the beginning of the theater's involvement with civil rights, an activity—thanks largely to its owner, Frank Schiffman—that would reach its apex in the '60s.

Paradoxically, while the Apollo was capable of reflecting the issues of the larger society, it also provided a sanctuary from the hostility that occasionally ravaged the community. Despite the riots of 1935 and 1943, the shows went on at the Apollo. As many witnesses of these tumults have reported, the theater, along with Harlem's churches, may have been the only refuge from the violence and mayhem in the streets. "The Apollo was our conjure, our mojo, our voodoo, our Negro empowerment zone…our black magic, in whose hallowed confines we could overcome all enemies, even white folks," wrote playwright and actor Ossie Davis.

The Rev. Adam Clayton Powell Jr. harnessed the spirit of Davis's passion in mounting demonstrations to alter the inherent discrimination of Harlem's primarily white-owned businesses. "Don't Buy Where You Can't Work" were the words emblazoned on placards outside Woolworth's, Blumstein's and other local businesses that refused to hire blacks. On the contrary, at the Apollo Schiffman was surrounded by capable black employees, and it had less to do with Powell's boycotts than with his own sense of fairness.

During the post–World War II period, the Apollo was a hipster's haven, and no one epitomized that style and panache as well as the irrepressible Dizzy Gillespie. If Gillespie's sunglasses, beret, zoot suit, and goatee didn't convince you of his ultramodern attitude, one blast from his lyrical trumpet did the trick. His big band popularized the new bebop music, and as the intricate rhythms and complex harmonies resonated from the Apollo's stage, bebop possessed all the swagger and insouciance of the black men and women returning from military service, having seen the world and made it safe for democracy.

When the big bands, except for Ellington's and Basie's, were no longer in vogue by the '50s, the Apollo, adapting to the changing times, surrendered the stage to the smaller rhythm-and-blues ensembles. At the forefront of this new trend was Louis Jordan and His Tympany Five, which combined a robust, rollicking beat with vocal exchanges among the band members and whatever comedy act was on the bill. But it was the Orioles, Ravens, Flamingos, Drifters, and other doo-wop singing groups who secured the roost at the Apollo, thereby setting the stage for the full arrival of rhythm and blues and the emergence of Los Angeles–based songwriter/promoter Johnny Otis and his entourage.

Of course there were peaks and valleys during the late '40s and early '50s, but one thing was consistent at the Apollo and that was Amateur Night. No matter how troubled the outside world, inside the Apollo on Wednesday night, with emcee and founder Ralph Cooper controlling things and Norman Miller ("Porto Rico") hustling the untalented off the stage, a dream world existed where a victory could catapult an aspiring entertainer to cloud nine.

In his autobiography, Cooper summed up the importance of Amateur Night. It wasn't that the contest "launched so many future stars toward the heavens, or that Amateur Night helped to make the Apollo Theatre the leading showcase for black entertainment," he wrote. "What was most important was that we gave thousands of young people the opportunity to learn something profound about themselves and some lessons about life itself. Some discovered that they would never solo on Broadway. They learned the hard way that they weren't the next Marian Anderson or Paul Robeson. Fame and fortune don't await every kid who walks on the stage on Wednesday nights. But wisdom might."

Amateur Night was never bereft of singers and dancers, and for a few of the dancers who could really cut the mustard, if they weren't good enough to win the contest, there were opportunities in the chorus line or as part of another burgeoning act. Jack Schiffman, the Apollo owner's son, noted in his book *Uptown: The Story of Harlem's Apollo Theatre* that between the '20s and '30s there were as many as fifty topflight dancing acts working the so-called black circuit. Unfortunately, most of these soloists or units of dancers did not get their routines recorded for posterity. All we can bank on is what someone remembered about Snake Hips Tucker, Sandman Sims, Baby Laurence, or Bill Bailey, Pearl Bailey's brother and the putative creator of the moonwalk, later made famous by Michael Jackson. "Dance acts comprised the essence of most shows," Jack Schiffman recalled. "Sometimes as many as three were used, one to get the show to a fast start, one to add pace to the middle, and a third to close it in blazing splendor."

Chuck Berry in the late '50s. Berry's mix of country melodies, jazz chords, upbeat rhythms, and teen-oriented lyrics made him a prime mover in the creation of rock 'n' roll.

The '50s also witnessed another revolution: rock and roll. As any student of American music knows, rock and roll evolved out of rhythm and blues, and such masters of the format as Big Joe Turner, Johnny Otis, Little Richard, and the inimitable Chuck Berry planted the seeds later nurtured and harvested by Elvis Presley, Jerry Lee Lewis, Buddy Holly, and countless other white rockers. The revue format that was developed at the Apollo was given broader exposition and exploitation by the likes of Alan Freed, Robin Seymour, and Dick Clark.

As the civil rights movement gained traction in the late '50s, the Apollo granted its stage to A. Philip Randolph, Bayard Rustin, Dr. Martin Luther King Jr., CORE (the Congress of Racial Equality), the NAACP, and other organizations seeking

Doo-wop and R & B vocal group the Drifters, 1964. Left to right: Gene Pearson, Johnny Terry, Charlie Thomas, Johnny Moore, and Abdul Samad (Bill Davis).

The Orioles were the first great doo-wop group to appear on the Apollo stage. Alex Sharp, at top, wraps his arms around Sonny Til, George Nelson, Ralph Williams, and Johnny Reed, with Charlie Harris at the keyboard.

Little Anthony and the Imperials, ca. 1959, one of the many popular doo-wop groups of the '50s. Left to right: Nathaniel Rodgers, Tracy Lord, Clarence Collins, and Ernest Wright, with "Little Anthony" Gourdine (top).

Singer Sam Cooke crossed over from gospel music in the late '50s to become a pop star. Among his hits were the ballad "You Send Me" and the socially conscious "A Change Is Gonna Come."

to raise funds to bring about change in segregated America. With the movement gathering momentum in preparation for the historic March on Washington in 1963, the Apollo became indispensable, opening its doors to a host of freedom fighters allied with politically conscious entertainers, including Sidney Poitier, Eartha Kitt, Pearl Bailey, Sammy Davis Jr., and Harry Belafonte.

While there was very little that was funny about the social and political climate in Harlem in the early to mid-'60s, a collection of hilarious comedians were on call at the Apollo to make light of the darkness pervading the community. When Fidel Castro and his brigade took up residence at the Hotel Theresa in 1960, Moms Mabley, the mistress of social satire, joked about it at the Apollo, recounting a fictitious meeting with Cuba's leader, who she said told her he didn't understand her by saying *"no entende."* "Well, I didn't intend to, either," Mabley cracked.

Harlem's own Canada Lee was a distinguished actor and producer who also defied the red-baiting critics. A versatile performer in film and on stage, Lee had maintained close ties with the Communist Party at a time when the United States was enduring the Cold War. In 1949 Lee chose the Apollo Theater as the place for his press conference to address the anticommunist hysteria that threatened his scheduled two-week run of Philip Yordan's *Anna Lucasta* there. At the press conference Lee denied that he was a member of the Communist Party but vowed that he wouldn't stop speaking out against racial or religious discrimination. "I am ready to join any group that would expose racial discrimination in the radio and television fields," Lee asserted.

Also in the '50s, gospel music was doing its part to fill the seats at the Apollo. With so many singers crossing over from gospel to rhythm and blues and to pop—Aretha Franklin and Sam Cooke were the more prominent examples—the Apollo was ready to accommodate them, even if they retained their religious fervor, which Clara Ward and Thurman Ruth were not about to relinquish. Complementing the popularity of gospel during these days were the live broadcasts of disc jockeys such as Tommy Smalls (Dr. Jive), which pioneered rhythm and blues from the airwaves at the Apollo for another generation that was ready for a "brand new sound."

In 1964 a contingent of protesters marched by the Apollo on their way to a local police station to voice their concern following a devastating urban disturbance that summer. The courageous defiance of civil rights activists was replicated by the young African Americans, boldly advancing their cause for total liberation "by any means necessary," as their idol, Malcolm X, often declared. Suddenly black self-determination enveloped Harlem, and elements of it found ways to be expressed on the Apollo's stage. Malcolm did not speak at the Apollo, but his militancy was approximated by several entertainers as they sought to capture his audacity. Redd Foxx, an Apollo mainstay who evinced all the combative aura of Malcolm (who was his good friend), was notorious and uncontrollable onstage. Until Richard Pryor came

Famed theater and film stars Sidney Poitier (left) and Canada Lee (right) in *Cry, the Beloved Country*, 1951. Both actors were active in civil rights issues, with Lee particularly active as a member of the Harlem community.

along, Foxx's irreverence and antiestablishment fervor made him the favorite of Harlem's black radicals, including members of the Black Panther Party.

Throughout Harlem and practically all over America, black was beautiful, and the fervor of nationalism found its way into the music from the ghettos of Detroit and Philadelphia all the way to the Apollo. Berry Gordy wasn't one to blatantly promote politics in the music created at Motown, but it was hard to rein in all of his producers, songwriters, and performers. Norman Whitfield was often a thorn in Gordy's side, with his unbridled imagination and an ear for a chart-busting song. When he proposed "War," an antiwar song composed by Barrett Strong for the Temptations, Gordy rejected it. Instead the song was given to Edwin Starr, whose powerful rendition made it an anthem for those opposed to the war in Vietnam.

Ironically, one of Gordy's top acts came to him via the Apollo. "When I had first seen Gladys Knight and the Pips perform at the Apollo in 1966, I knew right away how sensational they were," Gordy wrote in his autobiography *To Be Loved.* "Gladys was smart. She could talk to an audience and articulate what she wanted to say with just the right words." After the initial appearances of the Motown Revues at the Apollo in the early '60s, the endless talent at Motown was a veritable conduit, providing a steady flow of acts to the Apollo, long after several of them had severed their ties with Gordy and his label.

The year 1968 was unforgettable: Dr. King and Bobby Kennedy were assassinated; the Tet Offensive intensified the war in Vietnam; the Black Panther Party was virtually decimated by the FBI and other law enforcement officials; Marvin Gaye and Stevie Wonder topped the charts with "I Heard It through the Grapevine" and "For Once in My Life," respectively; and black pride reached a high point in art and politics. The inexhaustible James Brown harnessed the era's emotional fever with his "Say It Loud, I'm Black and I'm Proud." In a direct and even boastful way, Brown addressed racism, bigotry, and racial discrimination. When boomed from the Apollo stage, Brown's power was even more inciting, and fans would leap from their seats to the aisles, hoping to land on the "good foot."

The music of Curtis Mayfield also resonated for those working to bring about change in society. In the early '60s Mayfield had asked, "If you had a choice of colors, which one would you choose my brothers?" During the civil rights movement, his songs provided spiritual uplift and momentum to Dr. Martin Luther King Jr. and cohorts as they marched to the beat of "Keep on Pushin'." If the Black Power

Apollo advertisement announces disc jockey Dr. Jive's (Tommy Smalls') Rhythm and Blues Revue, 1959. In the '50s, popular DJs became the emcees of shows like this that featured a number of current, chart-topping acts.

Marvin Gaye wows the audience on the Apollo stage, 1964. A favorite Motown star, Gaye was equally at home crooning love songs or asking "What's Going On?"

R & B/soul star Ray Charles in concert, 1966. His melding of gospel intensity with an R & B beat made him one of the pioneers and most enduring performers of soul music.

movement had an anthem, Mayfield's "We're a Winner" was it, and it was hard not to feel somewhat empowered on hearing a boom box blaring "We're movin' on up, Lawd have mercy, we're movin' on up."

For those still unmoved by Mayfield's magic, there was soulful inspiration from vocalist and pianist Nina Simone. Just as Simone had stirred the hearts and minds of the freedom fighters with Dr. King with her cry of "Mississippi Goddam," so she bolstered the often flagging soldiers of the Black Power movement with her rendition of "To Be Young, Gifted and Black." Mayfield and Simone fueled the struggle for Black Power in the same way they blazed the trail for the soul music that would soon sweep the nation and establish an implacable grip on the Apollo's stage.

Soul was now embedded in America's lexicon, and no one consistently invested his total musicality in it more than Ray Charles. During his long career, Charles was a regular at the Apollo, performing his distinctive mix of gospel, soul, blues, and even country music, delivered with his unique and passionate soul. And like many of the true creative geniuses—Stevie Wonder, Duke Ellington, and James Brown—Charles's music was keyed to the times in which he lived, able to meet whatever emotional zeitgeist prevailed. His instinct for integration was evident when he blended his voice with those of Norah Jones, Willie Nelson, Elton John, and others in his 2004 duets album, *Genius Loves Company*, and his love for a country still reeling from the 9/11 attacks soared whenever he sang "America the Beautiful."

By 1969 a harbinger of doom loomed over the Apollo, and its gradual decline culminated in the mid-'70s, forcing the Schiffman family to close the theater. There was no one factor that caused the demise of the Apollo; it was a fatal combination of racism, neglect, and economics—they could no longer afford the escalating contracts offered by agents of the marquee acts. Like the other historic black theaters—the Regal in Chicago, the Uptown in Philadelphia, the Howard in Washington, D.C., and the Paradise in Detroit—the Apollo was no longer a reliable magnet, guaranteed to draw large audiences. The same entertainers whom the theater had supported when times were hard now commanded fees the Apollo could not afford.

Even toward the end, the Apollo had enjoyed some of its most lucrative years from 1970 to 1974. Once those four years were over, however, Apollo lovers had to resort to memories rather than performances. Record producer Ahmet Ertegun fondly remembered those halcyon days. "The Apollo developed an aura of its own and myths of its own," he told Ted Fox. "It represented getting out of the limitations of being a black entertainer. If you're a black entertainer in Charlotte or Mississippi you have great constraints put upon you. But coming to Harlem and to the Apollo— Harlem was the expression of the black spirit in America, it was a haven. The Apollo Theatre stood for the greatest—the castle that you reach when you finally make it."

Nina Simone, ca. 1968. She combined classical, blues, and jazz-inspired piano techniques with socially conscious lyrics.

Stevie Wonder of the Apollo, ca. 1963

Aretha Franklin and Roy C. Hill, early 1970s

Etta James, mid-1970s

Tina Turner at the Apollo, ca. 1966

Gladys Knight and the Pips in Apollo lobby, ca. 1968

Sam Cooke at the Apollo, ca. 1958

The Supremes backstage at the Apollo: Mary Wilson, Florence Ballard, Diana Ross, 1965

The Gospel Caravan

Joyce Marie Jackson

Mahalia Jackson, Sister Rosetta Tharpe, Ernestine Washington, and promoter Thurman Ruth, 1960s. Ruth organized the Gospel Caravans that brought gospel to the Apollo stage.

From the time it opened its doors in 1934, the Apollo Theater was home to all of the most popular forms of African American entertainment. Yet it wasn't until the mid-1950s that one of the most popular musical styles—gospel—was featured at the Apollo. Thanks initially to promoter Thurman Ruth, gospel revues became regular and popular attractions at the theater from the '50s through the '70s. To understand how gospel music came to the Apollo, it is important to consider the issues surrounding the slow movement of gospel into African American popular culture.

African American sacred musical forms were originally performed in churches or at appropriate churchlike settings such as at revival meetings. However, a new form of popular gospel music emerged during the '30s and '40s. During the Great Depression, gospel music provided escape, encouragement, and hope to disillusioned and destitute blacks through its danceable rhythms and vernacular lyrics proclaiming good news in bad times. New and vital performers emerged, including Sister Rosetta Tharpe, Sallie Martin, Mahalia Jackson, the Dixie Hummingbirds, Willie Mae Ford Smith, the Fairfield Four, Clara Ward, the Selah Jubilee Singers, and the Golden Gate Quartet, to name only a few. This new music spread gradually through radio broadcasts, personal appearance tours, and recordings.

World War II and its aftermath accelerated the growth of the new gospel music. Following the war, massive groups of primarily rural, southern African Americans moved to northern industrial cities, where they were exposed to the emerging R & B sounds. The increased prosperity and new forms of consciousness among African Americans combined to intensify the growth of popular sacred music. Powered by growing incomes and an emerging youth market, both small and major recording labels released a wide variety of black musical expression. Old forms evolved and acquired new labels that seemed to better reflect the African American emerging realities. Spirituals, Dr. Watts hymns, and other congregational songs combined to become a polished and dynamic urban gospel. The older styles did not totally vanish,

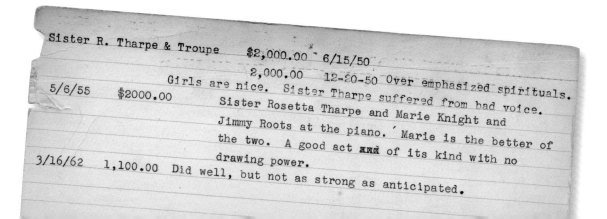

Sister R. Tharpe & Troupe $2,000.00   6/15/50
                             2,000.00   12-20-50 Over emphasized spirituals.
5/6/55 $2000.00   Girls are nice. Sister Tharpe suffered from bad voice.
                    Sister Rosetta Tharpe and Marie Knight and
                 Jimmy Roots at the piano. Marie is the better of
                the two. A good act and of its kind with no
                         drawing power.
3/16/62   1,100.00 Did well, but not as strong as anticipated.

but they became less prominent in many churches. Pioneer composers and performers such as Charles A. Tindley, Thomas A. Dorsey, and Roberta Martin helped create many of these new innovations, as well as entire repertoires of new songs.

The Sacred/Secular Dichotomy

Since gospel music was fresh, innovative, and a musical type that Apollo audiences would flock to see, why were these early gospel artists not booked on the shows? It was not for a lack of trying by owner Frank Schiffman.

Mahalia Jackson was approached several times. Frank's son Jack recalled, "We spent hours, almost days, trying to convince [Mahalia Jackson] that an Apollo appearance would be good for her, good for the audiences, possibly even good for the churches as well. But she remained deeply convinced that a theatrical appearance was somehow sacrilegious, and we finally had to abandon our dream of presenting her to our audiences."

The reason why many sacred music performers would not play the Apollo was the dichotomy between sacred music and secular performance spaces. This dichotomy has been a primary

Clara Ward (center) and her Singers at the Apollo, 1959. One of the pioneers of modern gospel singing, Ward was especially popular with Apollo audiences.

The Staple Singers on the Apollo stage, 1969. Roebuck "Pops" Staples leads on guitar, with his children Cleotha, Pervis, and Mavis Staples (far right) on vocals.

factor in determining the image and identity of the sacred music performer within the African American community. Jackson and many other gospel performers felt that it was wrong to perform gospel music in a secular setting.

Not all agreed, however, with such a strict position. Some secular music was performed by sacred groups (such as popular tunes and folk songs), and some sacred music was performed within secular contexts. A few gospel pioneers took the radical step of accepting bookings in popular clubs and halls

at a very early stage. For instance, the Dixie Hummingbirds took a flexible view of playing nightclubs. One member recalled, "We played our first night club at Number 2 Sheridan Square in New York in 1939." The Hummingbirds believed that different formats and contexts could be used to entertain as long as you "never get off the spiritual track." Larry Bell, of the later First Revolution Singers gospel quartet, said it well: "From reading the scripture…when Jesus visited Matthew at his home. The words came out that folks that are not sick don't need the doctor.

So I can't work on a patient if he is already well." (First Revolution performed in New Orleans on Bourbon Street in the French Quarter, in Jackson Square [a park], and in the Storyville Jazz Hall [a nightclub].) Other performers who made this radical move in the early years included Clara Ward and the Clara Ward Singers, Sister Rosetta Tharpe, and later the Staple Singers. Even the "Father of Gospel Music," Thomas A. Dorsey, was a composer of risqué blues and vaudeville star Ma Rainey's accompanist in the '20s before crossing over to the gospel music genre in the '30s.

Despite the general feeling that gospel didn't belong in secular spaces, a few performances of gospel music occurred at the Apollo during the '30s and '40s, although not in special gospel shows. Sister Rosetta Tharpe appeared on the Apollo stage in the '30s, performing with popular big bands led by Cab Calloway and Lucky Millinder, whose styles dovetailed with gospel. Tharpe had already appeared in popular venues, having been a featured performer at the Cotton Club and the Paramount. Later Tharpe, sometimes assisted by Marie Knight, graced the stage at the Apollo in the '40s and early '50s. She did not, however, sing exclusively gospel; she would perform a variety of songs including blues and ballads. Similarly, blues singer Josh White and a few other secular singers would intersperse an occasional spiritual into their Apollo acts. The Deep River Boys, the Golden Gate Quartet, and the Charioteers were also featured at the Apollo. Although these performers "went over" well, they were never top moneymakers.

The Gospel Caravan

Thurman Ruth, the leader of Brooklyn's legendary Selah Jubilee Singers and a well-known New York disc jockey on WOV, was the initial force who facilitated Frank Schiffman's booking of gospel performers. Even though gospel was moving out of the church community into the recording studios, auditoriums, and convention halls around the country, few of the

The Dixie Hummingbirds at the Apollo, 1965. A smooth vocal harmony group, the Hummingbirds brought gospel music to new audiences starting in the late '30s.

FRED BARR AND DOC WHEELER
Headline Apollo Show

3rd Gospel Caravan At Apollo On Friday

Starting Friday, the Apollo will present its third Gospel and Spiritual Caravan. Spurred by the phenomenal success of its two previous efforts and by countless requests and inquiries, the Apollo has decided that a Spiritual show is acceptable at anytime through the year.

WWRL's disk jockeys, Doc Wheeler and Fred Barr, are sponsoring the show and will act as masters of ceremonies.

Several of the groups in the show which will begin at the Apollo on Friday are new to Harlem audiences. Some of them appeared at the Apollo in its previous shows. All come with stirring Pro

Singe
first
them
excit
to b
rent
"Oh
them
Gosp

Th
sipp
as
Spi
hav
Chu
pel
gro
stir
pos
C
Fa
are
Go
r
pri
pe

happiness. This group specializes in the sweet type of Spiritual music.

Their recording "Let God Abide" has been a big sucess. Theatregoers will especially enjoy their rendition of the "Lord's Prayer."

The local contribution to this program is Prof. Herman Stevens' Singers, who are perhaps the most popular of all of the local groups. Their recording "Deliver Me O

Once promoter Thurman Ruth's first gospel caravan proved successful, many more shows followed. Lower: The Caravans at the Apollo, 1965, featured strong lead vocals by Albertina Walker (third from left).

leading performers would consider playing the Apollo. The theater had a "sin and devil's house" stigma for sacred performers and their audiences. Ruth eventually developed an idea that would turn this thinking and stigma around. He convinced Schiffman to program the gospel performers in a format similar to a rhythm-and-blues revue and call it "the Gospel Caravan." Because the Apollo was losing money in the mid-'50s, audiences were losing interest, and other integrated clubs were opening in the city, Schiffman had a strong incentive to try something new.

He agreed because he wanted to move in a direction still "untouched by white entrepreneurs," but the main obstacle was still to convince the "gospel performers that playing the Apollo Theater would be appropriate and morally correct." Ruth and Schiffman had conversations with the clergy of various churches, members of their congregations, and some of the performers, attempting to persuade them to perform at the Apollo. In their deliberations they offered some guarantees that helped them persuade these groups. The performers were guaranteed a churchlike atmosphere; a beautiful stage, great lighting, and acoustics; a paycheck, whether the show was a flop or not (unlike church programs); and the freedom to perform all types of sacred music: gospels, jubilees, and spirituals.

The first Gospel Caravan at the Apollo made its debut on December 15, 1955. The initial performers were the Pilgrim Travelers, the Mississippi Blind Boys, the Caravans with Albertina Walker (and James Cleveland on piano), Brother Joe May, the Sensational Nightingales, and the Humming Four. The format was critical for the success of the show, and it proved to be the key that held the entire performance together for many successful runs. Thurman Ruth later gave an account of the format:

> *We liked to open with a bang—give a nice fast opening. I learned that from my disc-jockey days. Give a good balance; but first of all, we'd get a nice song that everyone*

The Five Blind Boys of Mississippi at the Apollo, 1965. They were among the performers in the first Gospel Caravan show presented by Thurman Ruth in 1955.

could sing together when the curtains opened....All the groups would come onstage. We had chairs out on the stage with that church atmosphere. Everybody would be singing that opening song, "Glory Hallelujah" or "Since I Laid My Burden Down" or whatever. After that they introduced me as the master of ceremonies, and I'd bring the first act on. Each group used to push one another. If one group was singing, the other group was clapping or they would help you amen or something to help you out. This was cooperative. Everybody wanted to see everybody go big.

This was essentially a church format, with the lead singers taking on the role of the preacher when it was their time to perform.

The Apollo's gospel shows epitomized the same energy, ability, and emotion as the popular R & B revues, combining earthiness and exuberance with a sheer expression of spiritual reverence. In the midst of these shows there was momentarily a releasing of earthly problems to bathe in an aura of hope and joy. They successfully transformed the Apollo Theater into an extension of the black church.

The Gospel Caravan did four shows a day and an added one on Saturdays at midnight. Performers perfected their styles and materials, learning from the competition and just by being there.

Another important aspect of the format was the participatory element of involving everyone. This is a strong African

A later lineup of the Soul Stirrers, ca. 1963, with new lead singer Jimmy Outler (far right). This popular gospel group was the training ground for Sam Cooke.

practice that continues to be highly significant in the African American community. Throughout the '60s and into the '70s, groups such as the Pilgrim Jubilees played the gospel extravaganza, "stirring up the house" with much audience participation. The shows featured the top gospel acts; the Pilgrim Jubilees were the headliners only once, "but we were there in the show— we must have worked the Apollo for ten years," recalls baritone Major Roberson. From a low point in their career, the group reclaimed their position in the gospel world through their performances at the Apollo and a hit gospel tune called "I'm Too Close to Heaven and I Can't Turn Around." Many groups' careers were launched or rekindled by their Apollo performances.

Gospel singers encountered some special challenges at the Apollo. There were four shows scheduled each day, and it is not possible to time the Holy Spirit. Alex Bradford, one of the most exceptional gospel singers, asked Leonard Reed, the production manager, a question concerning the presence of the Holy Spirit. Bradford said, "Mr. Reed, what do you do if the Holy Spirit arrives?" Reed replied, "Make sure He leaves by the end of the record, that's all." Well, that happened some of the time, with Thurman Ruth's prodding. The majority of the time, however, the Holy Spirit overstayed, and the shows were behind schedule. If it was the last show, the stagehands had to be paid overtime.

Catalyst for Soul Music

The Apollo Theater was a common ground where gospel and rhythm-and-blues performers met and congregated. They learned from each other, but most performers will admit that soul music developed from gospel. Gospel performers at the Apollo had the opportunity to experience the reactions of a popular audience. This encouraged many to move to performing R & B and soul. Among the gospel artists who crossed over were Sam Cooke from the Highway QCs and the Soul Stirrers, Johnny Taylor, also from the Soul Stirrers, and Lou Rawls from the Pilgrim Travelers.

In several cases entire quartets who started out in gospel music crossed over to the secular arena intact. Another group from New Orleans that performed in the first Gospel Caravan at the Apollo, the Humming Four, had been singing quartet music for about twenty years. For a period of time the quartet worked "both sides of the fence." They sang sacred music as the Humming Four and secular music as the Hawks. This lasted for a while until on one show the promoter ask them to do both, which did not go over well with the local audience, and they were banned from the gospel world in New Orleans. Similarly, when Cooke left the Soul Stirrers and landed some hit records in the soul genre, he tried to make a comeback in gospel and do both, but audiences would not accept him in both musical realms. This crossover from sacred to secular often came as a result of prompting by record promoters and recording company personnel, who were always sitting in the audience or lurking in the wings of the Apollo. In addition, there were always other incentives and attractions of greater financial gain and popularity.

In the postwar years the Apollo Theater nurtured both the growth of gospel and the development of new popular forms, including R & B and soul. The theater was instrumental in organizing a cultural space, institutional framework, and market

Lou Rawls with the Pilgrim Travelers at the Apollo, 1965. The Travelers were part of Ruth's first Gospel Caravan at the Apollo.

opportunities for African American performers. Later this role began to collapse because of the increased opportunities for black performers in the broader entertainment world, thanks to the growth of integration. Most performers who have played the Apollo for one night or many nights, however, acknowledge the magnitude of the theater's impact on their personal lives and subsequently on their careers. For gospel performers, this impact led to greater exposure for them and their music, and helped introduce elements of gospel style into popular music.

Dionne Warwick: Working

Many great stars developed meaningful relationships with the Apollo. Dionne Warwick is one with particularly deep personal and professional ties to the theater, from her teenage days right up to the present. Warwick was just a sweet-faced teenager from East Orange, New Jersey, when she first played the Apollo as part of the Gospelaires, a group she had started with her sister Dee Dee and friends in 1958. Dionne grew up in the world of gospel music. Her mother, Lee, was a member of the Drinkard Sisters gospel group, along with Warwick's aunt, Cissy Houston (Whitney Houston's mother). Dionne sometimes accompanied her mother when they played the Apollo.

Many who witnessed the gospel shows at the Apollo feel that they were the most stimulating and exciting shows ever seen at the theater. "People would get overwhelmed, they'd fall out of the balconies." Warwick remembered. "It's not like a rock show. This goes a step further because you're emotionally involved in the spirit of God....There were people who fainted. I personally cry—dance for God. There are people who wring themselves about....The Apollo had nurses to bring you around with smelling salts."

On one of her visits with her mother's group during one of the theater's weeklong all-gospel shows, Dionne made her Apollo debut on Amateur Night. "Amateur Night was no different when they had the gospel shows there," she said. "But it was for gospel singers only. Our group decided to go up there and get the $50 prize and also an appearance at the Apollo for the next gospel show. And we did. We won first prize." The Gospelaires never made that return engagement, however. Instead, in a backstage encounter at the Apollo, they were asked to sing on a recording session for Sam "The Man" Taylor. After that, Dionne became a popular background singer for many R & B acts.

"I began doing background work and demo sessions in New York," she said. Warwick, who had never really been exposed to contemporary rhythm and blues at home, also began making the scene at the Apollo with her friends from New Jersey. "We went over as a group. There had to be at least thirty of us getting on the number 118 bus to go over to New York City and have a big time. We took the subway uptown and stood in line like everybody else, and I remember it cost something like a dollar which was very expensive after paying 35 cents to get over here and another 15 cents to get up there. I didn't have enough money to buy popcorn."

Her professional solo career began when the songwriting team of Burt Bacharach and Hal David were impressed by her singing on a Drifters recording and convinced Scepter Records to sign her. "Don't Make Me Over," her first solo release, came out in November 1962, the first of a string of thirty hit singles with Bacharach and David.

"The first time I had a [solo] performance at the Apollo was with a Scepter Records package: the Shirelles, Chuck Jackson, Tommy Hunt, Maxine Brown, the Isley Brothers, and me," she recalled. "I opened the show. I was the baby in the business, the new kid on the block, and they really protected me. There were a lot of 'elements' there."

The naive young star-to-be got an eye-opening lesson in the ways of the world at the Apollo. "One time this guy came up to my room," she said. "He came in with a brown paper bag and said 'I've got some really great stuff here.' My mind said diamonds, emeralds, and rubies and all kinds of goodies. I stuck my hand in this bag and pulled up all this ugly stuff that looked like tobacco, and I said, 'Oh, this is tobacco.' It would have been priceless if I had gotten a photograph of that man's face. The man ran down the steps and stopped at every dressing room and told them what

the Apollo

Dionne Warwick backstage, 1970. In her teens she, her sister Dee Dee, and two high school friends won first prize at a 1958 Apollo Amateur Night as the Gospelaires.

Warwick onstage, 1970. Her association with songwriters Hal David and Burt Bacharach made her a premier crossover artist in the '60s.

happened up on the third floor. Do you know for almost three years after that I had no idea what that man had brought me....I was the tobacco kid."

Warwick grew and matured at the Apollo as a person and as an artist. When she spoke at the Apollo's seventy-fifth anniversary season announcement and press conference in January 2009, she read excerpts from one of her prized possessions: the original index card of owner Frank Schiffman's fastidious notes of her every performance. In Schiffman's initial appraisal of the singer, he called her "pretty good" but "inclined to talk too much." Soon, though, he graded her "great" and "poised" and noted her "every song is a vocal treat."

On the other hand, Warwick had a complicated, love/hate relationship with the people who ran the Apollo. "Forget the old man," she told me, referring to Frank Schiffman. His son Bobby, she said, "was the buffer. Old man Schiffman was too busy counting his dollars in that cruddy old office." Theater manager Honi Coles, she said, "was the buffer between Bobby and us because Bobby represented the white man. Honi was the black guy that was in a management capacity, so when we had any real complaints we would say, 'Hey Honi,...' and he would say, 'Bobby,...' and by the time it got to Old Man Schiffman it was another story all together. Old Man Schiffman was a gruff, arrogant, but shrewd businessman who cared primarily first about the Apollo structure, then the entertainers. Bobby showed more compassion for the entertainers. He is one of the nicest people I've known."

Warwick saw Frank Schiffman as a strict and distant father figure and Bobby as the older brother of what she felt was a family of fellow artists, staff, and management. "We loved each other," she said. "That feeling was always there. If you did something to hurt me, you hurt everybody.

And if you hurt somebody, you hurt me. I really enjoyed that. I felt like I was with my family at all times. Performers didn't look forward to the five shows a day or the filthy dressing rooms....The theater was terrible: drafty, dirty, smelly, awful—and we loved every minute of it."

As Warwick found great success in the white pop world, she brought new friends into the family and introduced white stars such as Tom Jones and even Marlene Dietrich to the Apollo. When she first appeared at the theater, though, Bobby Schiffman and others were skeptical that her smooth, sophisticated style would be accepted at the Apollo. "I never had any problem relating to the people at the Apollo because that was my heritage," she told me. "When *Funny Girl* was just opening on Broadway, I was doing the song 'People' in my repertoire at the Copa. I just took my show up and did the same show at the Apollo. But Bobby Schiffman said to me at the rehearsal in the basement, 'You cannot sing this song here. They'll boo you off the stage. They won't understand it.' I said, 'Bobby, I want you to stand in the wings tonight.' That particular evening, especially, I think because I was so angry with him, even Streisand could have just packed the song away. She would never have topped that evening. It was the first standing ovation that he had seen in that theater since he was a kid. I turned around and looked in the wings and said, 'I can't sing this song here?' And I told the audience, 'The man who runs this theater told me I can't sing this song here. I'll sing it anywhere. I'm bringing downtown uptown.'"

As the Apollo ran into operating trouble in the 1970s, Warwick was one of the first African American superstars who went out of their way to come back and play the theater long after they no longer needed to, just to support the Apollo and help keep its doors open as long as possible. "I practically paid money to go in and do it the way

I wanted to do it," she said of her gala return engagement in October 1970. "I put a lot of money into my show. And they made an awful lot of money. They were getting ready to close the Apollo the year I went back in there. I said, 'You will never close the Apollo. Not as long as I live.' It was a wonderful, wonderful week, and it gave them the leverage that they needed. After I closed, Lou Rawls went back in, and Nancy Wilson, and the Temptations. I brought everybody back to the Apollo!"

Bobby Schiffman Remembers

Ted Fox

I had the pleasure of spending many hours listening to Bobby Schiffman regale me about his family's experiences running the Apollo Theater for my book, *Showtime at the Apollo*. "Write about the way the Apollo really was," he told me, "the good and the bad." Bobby is a great show business promoter and raconteur, and a gregarious, voluble personality. Ladies and gentlemen, Bobby Schiffman remembers:

I never thought that the bubble of the Apollo would burst. I thought it would go on forever. I placed a great deal of faith in the social rapport we developed with performers. We did everything to make them comfortable. I and the key people in my management regime—Honi Coles and Peter Long—talked and kidded and socialized with them. Smokey Robinson and I used to play golf together, and Marvin Gaye and I were very good friends. We used to go out together. Redd Foxx and I were extremely friendly. Nancy Wilson and I. Eartha Kitt. There were dozens of them.

With some acts our rapport was based on the fact that I used to do seven or eight acts on every show. The three or four acts at the top of the show were the ones that sold the tickets. The ones at the bottom were the ones whom we were giving a showcase. They could, for dollar return, nurture their talents and their popularity. And they owed us. The first time I played Gladys Knight and the Pips in the theater I paid them $800 for thirty-one shows over seven days. The last time I played them, I paid them $80,000 for sixteen shows. Now there was no way, based upon a long-standing personal relationship, that I could go to Gladys and she could say "no" to me if I said "I need you." Because I was involved in incubating her career.

When I first came to the Apollo to work as a professional in 1951 [at age twenty-two], the Apollo was open every day from ten in the morning till midnight. I worked with a half a day off every other week. My father paid me the grand sum of $35 a week, and he made me learn every facet of that business. I stayed at night and helped clean up with the porters. I worked as an air-conditioning engineer, a doorman, in the projection booth. I hung around backstage with the stagehands. My dad made sure that I was exposed—as was my brother, Jack—to every facet of that

business so that in years to come, when I took over the responsibility for the whole operation, there was no job that I hadn't performed at one time or another. I would not ask an employee to do a job that I didn't know how to do.

At that time the Apollo was into old-time show business: a well-balanced show that started off with a big band, a tap dancer, a comic, a trampoline act or a dog act, a vocal group, and maybe a headliner. [In the early 1950s,] with the cooperation of a disc jockey on WWRL named Doctor Jive—his real name was Tommy Smalls—we [realized] that people weren't coming to see the dog act and the trampoline act and the tap dancer. They were coming to see the vocal act, the act that had the hit record that was being played on the radio. So we spawned the idea of eliminating the tap dancer, the trampoline, and the dog act, and putting in other acts with hit records. That became known as an R & B revue….That turned the whole theater around financially, because the people loved it.

It was much more expensive to produce those shows, but the proceeds were much greater. During that era the theater was operating at capacity more than anytime else. We were doing five, six, seven shows a day; that's unheard of. I was doing seven shows on Saturday and Sunday.

My brother, Jack, was older than I and had been on the job for four or five years when I started. I used to listen with my mouth open to the manner in which they dealt with some of the performers they were booking. Because I was the third man on the block, I was relegated to a job that had nothing to do with the booking. We couldn't all do it. So they used to have me deal with personnel, maintenance, supplies, payroll, and all the other garbage that was a very important part of the operation. About four years later, my brother had the opportunity to go into another business, and he left. I became my father's fair-haired boy, and we got along famously.

My father had created a great legend. He was a fantastic theater operator....He was godlike as far as I was concerned. He guided the theater until 1961. I had been there ten years by then, and I went in and said, "Hey Dad, I think it's time we changed chairs. You be my assistant. Let me run the theater." He deserved more rest. And I felt that I could do it better because I was more contemporary. He told me, "I've been waiting for you to tell me that. I'll be glad to do that."

I was the young one, the contemporary one. I was into Smokey Robinson, Gladys Knight, James Brown, Little Willie John, Sam Cooke, and all of those young people who were the happening people in black show business. My father was into Ella Fitzgerald, Sarah Vaughan, tap dancers, and comics. Well, in order to stay competitive, you have to be where the people are, and the people are into young people's music. As a matter of fact, especially with black people, they are not interested in what happened yesterday. They want to know what's going to happen tomorrow.

I ran the Apollo from 1961 to 1976—the most productive period financially that the theater ever had. I knew what the people in the street were thinking and what they liked and what

Dancer Sandman Sims enjoys a moment with Bobby Schiffman at an Apollo reunion in 1985.

they didn't like, because I made it my business to find out. I would go into the bars and listen to the jukeboxes. I would go to the record companies and find out what was selling. Fortunately for me, the legend of the Apollo was already there. I felt that I was important, but the reason that the Apollo succeeded was the people of that community—the Joe on the street who came in and plunked down his money. The people of Harlem referred to the theater as "our theater." It never was the white man's theater or Frank Schiffman's theater. The Apollo belonged to the people, and the management just ran it for the people.

With the advent of Malcolm X and the growth of nationalistic pride in the black community, which was a very valid and worthwhile force, there came the feeling that the black community should own and operate their own institutions. For years the aim of the management of the Apollo was to sell it to a black entrepreneur. We had several offers that we turned down from white businessmen who wanted to buy the Apollo. We were waiting for a black organization to come along that had the knowledge, wisdom, and the money to buy the Apollo.

If one took a completely intellectual view of what happened to the Apollo, the walls of discrimination broke down, so black acts who heretofore had no place to play other than black areas were suddenly welcomed with great enthusiasm in the so-called downtown markets of the country. Places like the Apollo were destined to close because they couldn't provide the comfort, the money, the luxury, and all of the other ancillary things that downtown places of entertainment had the ability to provide because they had bigger capacities.

Towards the end in the '70s, 125th Street turned into a very deprived street. Dirty. Crime was rampant. The discomfort in coming to the theater multiplied. After the riots of '67 and the rioting in the early '70s, all the storekeepers put in those steel doors which closed over the windows. So the street looked like the Alamo after 7 p.m. The city of New York fell very short in its obligations to provide customer services, as it did in other areas of the city. Geographically, 125th Street is in a very favorable situation. All of the major highways cross there. All the major subway and bus lines. It should have developed. But obviously the city fathers took the position that there are just black folks up there. We'll do them last.

The Apollo and Civil Rights

Herb Boyd

Lead Belly, 1937. The blues singer's troubled life story was used initially as a sensational way to promote him to urban audiences.

The Apollo Theater was officially two years old in 1936 when Frank Schiffman invited folksinger and twelve-string guitarist Huddie Ledbetter to perform. Ledbetter, better known as Lead Belly, was on his second national concert tour after literally singing his way to freedom. Convicted of murder, though many claimed he had acted in self-defense, Lead Belly had been languishing in the Louisiana State Penitentiary when he was discovered by the folklorist John Lomax and his son Alan. They recorded him for the Library of Congress after he had successfully won a pardon from the governor by composing and then singing a song as a tribute to him.

In 1935 the Lomaxes brought Lead Belly to New York City for performances at various clubs, attracting national attention with his protest songs about race relations, world politics, and prison reform. "The first time I heard him sing was on the stage of the Apollo," Frank Schiffman told his son Jack. "We had constructed a prison scene in which Monty Hawley [who was so light-skinned

he could pass for white] played the part of the governor and Leadbelly sang before him. When he started to sing, I thought I'd die. I never heard such awful wailing. But even though I didn't like him, the audience did....Maybe they were right."

Right indeed. Lead Belly completed a highly successful tour, winning thousands of fans with his finesse on the guitar and such instant favorites as his composition "Goodnight, Irene." During World War II, Lead Belly became even more outspoken about the rise of fascism, composing and often performing his "Mr. Hitler" to standing-room-only audiences. Listeners were particularly appreciative of Lead Belly's lyrics about "tearing Mr. Hitler down someday."

One year later, on August 20, 1937, the Apollo Theater became more directly involved in civil rights, opening its doors and offering the stage to victims whose rights had been abused and violated. Sharing top billing that evening was bandleader Blanche Calloway, the inimitable Cab Calloway's sister, and her revue, and master drummer Chick Webb and his orchestra, featuring vocalist Ella Fitzgerald. But many had attended to see four of the nine Scottsboro Boys, who were out on bail. Ever since they had been wrongfully accused, tried, and convicted of raping two white women while riding a train from northern Alabama to Memphis in 1931, the boys' plight had become an international cause célèbre. Groups as disparate as the NAACP and the Communist Party had waged a futile defense for the boys. When four of them appeared at the Apollo, it was to raise funds for their appeals, which had dragged on for years without resolution.

Decades later, other young black and white Americans, fortunate not to have to hop trains in search of work like the Scottsboro Boys, dedicated their lives to the civil rights movement, and many of them were beaten and arrested. On August 11, 1962, with the civil rights movement formally in its seventh year, the Apollo hosted a benefit show to assist the Southern Student Freedom Fund. Among the notable performers were singer Tony Bennett, pianist/composer Thelonious Monk, percussionists Chico

Hamilton, Art Blakey, and Max Roach, pianist/educator Billy Taylor, and comedian Moms Mabley, an Apollo showstopper. The United States National Student Association, in conjunction with Progressive Talent, produced the show and promised to use all the proceeds for the southern students who had been expelled from school or had been jailed because of their participation in civil rights activities.

A year later, on August 23, the Apollo's stage was reserved for a fund-raiser to help finance the historic March on Washington, scheduled to take place five days later in the nation's capital. The redoubtable A. Philip Randolph, the march's chief coordinator, told the press that the cost of the march would exceed $65,000, including the cost of transportation for unemployed persons. Thus far, he said, they had raised $20,000 in contributions. It was not reported how much was raised at the event, but it must

have been substantial, because thousands were able to attend the march, thanks to funds donated at the Apollo and at other events across the nation.

In 1964 the Congress of Racial Equality (CORE) was the beneficiary after the theater distributed "passes for equality," permitting one free admission to any patron donating $2.50 to CORE. From 1966 to 1971, according to the theater's public relations director, the Apollo "presented twenty to twenty-five 'community activities' such as educational programs and local Theatre productions."

Dr. Martin Luther King Jr. waves to the crowd following his "I Have a Dream" speech from the steps of the Lincoln Memorial in Washington, D.C., on August 28, 1963.

In 1965 the Apollo, along with radio station WWRL, announced a "Freedom Week," with all the profits earmarked for civil rights organizations. Popular singers Clyde McPhatter and Betty Everett were among the featured acts to raise funds for the NAACP, New York CORE, and for a foundation established for James Chaney, Michael Schwerner, and Andrew Goodman, three civil rights workers slain in Mississippi.

But easily the most memorable evidence of the Apollo Theater's connection to the civil rights movement was a letter of appreciation that Dr. Martin Luther King Jr. sent to Frank Schiffman in September 1965. In that letter, which hung for many years in Schiffman's office, Dr. King expressed his gratitude to Schiffman, Dr. and Mrs. Arthur Logan, and Mr. and Mrs. Jackie Robinson for their generous donation of $5,500. The donation was presented to Dr. King and the Southern Christian Leadership

Conference (SCLC) to help launch the "Martin Luther King Freedom Fleet." "Needless to say," Dr. King wrote, "your great contribution will go a long, long way in helping us to carry out the herculean task ahead to double the number of Negro registered voters in the South." Apparently the money was raised from a tribute to Schiffman by his friends, and Schiffman chose to donate the funds to SCLC. "Your bigness of heart in giving the funds for such an important cause will never be forgotten," Dr. King concluded.

This was not the first or last demonstration of the magnanimity of Schiffman and his family. When Schiffman died in 1974, hundreds of Harlemites mourned his passing, not only remembering his great eye for talent, his determination to keep the Apollo's doors open no matter the economic climate, and his dedication to equal rights. As his obituary in the *Amsterdam News* observed: "Frank Schiffman kept the faith."

Ironically, the Apollo, which had played such a prominent role in the civil rights movement that dramatically altered the nation's social and political consciousness, would eventually be a victim of its commitment, because it helped to open other venues for African American entertainers. In effect, the Apollo, which had been a sanctuary for black entertainers unable to find opportunities elsewhere, had provided the wedge for these same entertainers to capitalize their talents on other stages no longer confined by segregation. A number of institutions, organizations, and businesses that had thrived because of discrimination watched their enterprises collapse. The Apollo, to some extent, was a casualty of its own dedication to human and civil rights.

Even so, change is inevitable, and by the 1990s the Apollo had resumed its involvement with civil rights by extending that important legacy to the educational arena. Recently programs have been developed to teach primary, middle, and high school students about African American music and culture, and the Apollo's relation to the civil rights movement. Showing young people how famous entertainers and noted activists came together for a common cause can be a useful conduit in broadening their understanding of the interplay between culture and politics. The world needs to know the interrelationship between such significant humanitarians as Dr. King, A. Philip Randolph, Max Roach, and Frank Schiffman.

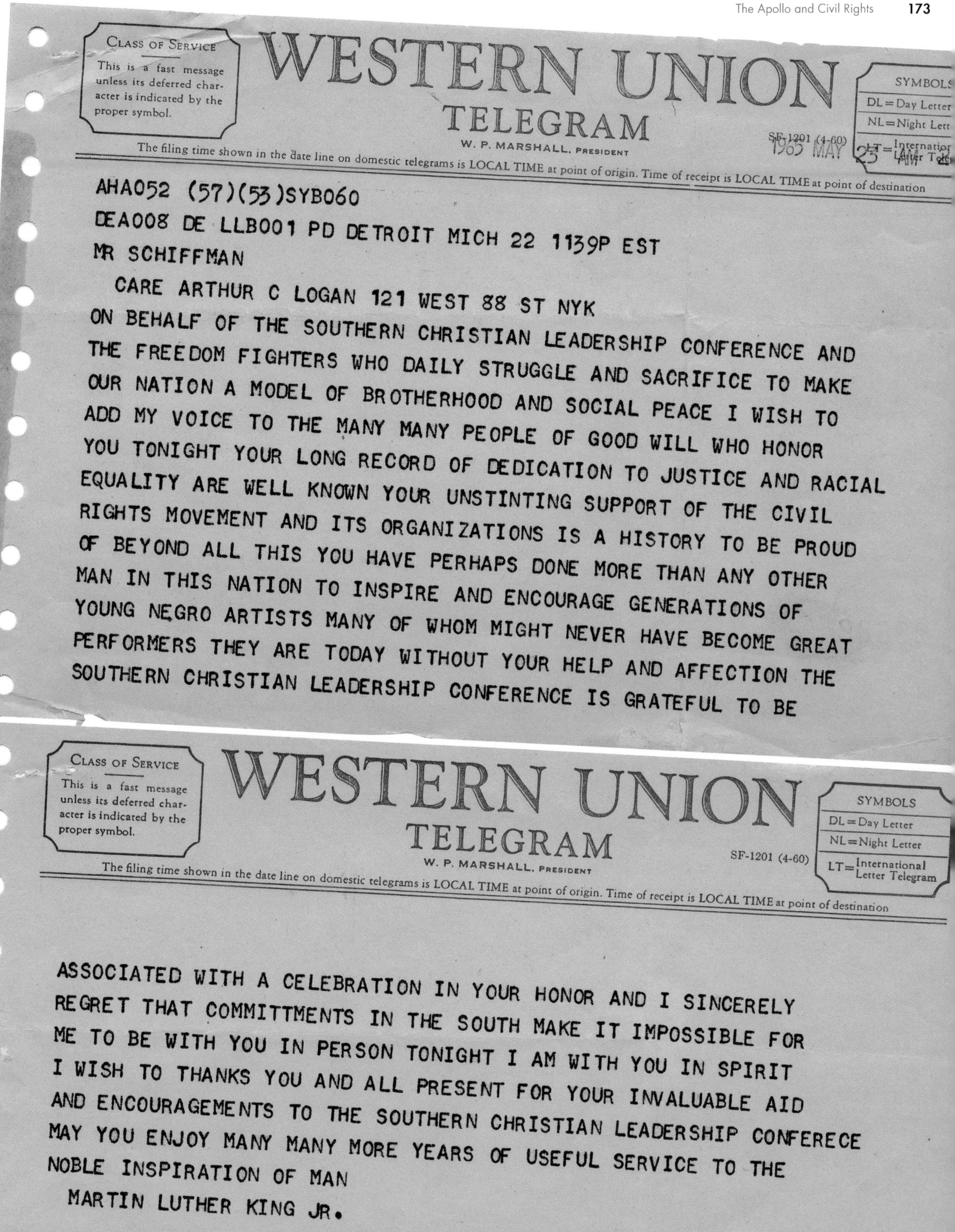

CLASS OF SERVICE
This is a fast message unless its deferred character is indicated by the proper symbol.

WESTERN UNION
TELEGRAM
W. P. MARSHALL, PRESIDENT

SYMBOLS
DL=Day Letter
NL=Night Lett
LT=Internatior Letter Te

SF-1201 (4-60)
1965 MAY 23 AM

The filing time shown in the date line on domestic telegrams is LOCAL TIME at point of origin. Time of receipt is LOCAL TIME at point of destination

AHA052 (57)(53)SYB060
DEA008 DE LLB001 PD DETROIT MICH 22 1139P EST
MR SCHIFFMAN
CARE ARTHUR C LOGAN 121 WEST 88 ST NYK
ON BEHALF OF THE SOUTHERN CHRISTIAN LEADERSHIP CONFERENCE AND THE FREEDOM FIGHTERS WHO DAILY STRUGGLE AND SACRIFICE TO MAKE OUR NATION A MODEL OF BROTHERHOOD AND SOCIAL PEACE I WISH TO ADD MY VOICE TO THE MANY MANY PEOPLE OF GOOD WILL WHO HONOR YOU TONIGHT YOUR LONG RECORD OF DEDICATION TO JUSTICE AND RACIAL EQUALITY ARE WELL KNOWN YOUR UNSTINTING SUPPORT OF THE CIVIL RIGHTS MOVEMENT AND ITS ORGANIZATIONS IS A HISTORY TO BE PROUD OF BEYOND ALL THIS YOU HAVE PERHAPS DONE MORE THAN ANY OTHER MAN IN THIS NATION TO INSPIRE AND ENCOURAGE GENERATIONS OF YOUNG NEGRO ARTISTS MANY OF WHOM MIGHT NEVER HAVE BECOME GREAT PERFORMERS THEY ARE TODAY WITHOUT YOUR HELP AND AFFECTION THE SOUTHERN CHRISTIAN LEADERSHIP CONFERENCE IS GRATEFUL TO BE

CLASS OF SERVICE
This is a fast message unless its deferred character is indicated by the proper symbol.

WESTERN UNION
TELEGRAM
W. P. MARSHALL, PRESIDENT

SYMBOLS
DL=Day Letter
NL=Night Letter
LT=International Letter Telegram

SF-1201 (4-60)

The filing time shown in the date line on domestic telegrams is LOCAL TIME at point of origin. Time of receipt is LOCAL TIME at point of destination

ASSOCIATED WITH A CELEBRATION IN YOUR HONOR AND I SINCERELY REGRET THAT COMMITTMENTS IN THE SOUTH MAKE IT IMPOSSIBLE FOR ME TO BE WITH YOU IN PERSON TONIGHT I AM WITH YOU IN SPIRIT I WISH TO THANKS YOU AND ALL PRESENT FOR YOUR INVALUABLE AID AND ENCOURAGEMENTS TO THE SOUTHERN CHRISTIAN LEADERSHIP CONFERECE MAY YOU ENJOY MANY MANY MORE YEARS OF USEFUL SERVICE TO THE NOBLE INSPIRATION OF MAN
MARTIN LUTHER KING JR.

Frank Schiffman kept this prized 1965 telegram that he received from King on the evening of a special Apollo benefit celebrating Schiffman's long commitment to civil rights.

Harlem, Black Creativity, and

Amiri Baraka

If you've ever been to Amsterdam, the capital of the Netherlands, you can see how closely it resembles the capital of that other "Netherlands," Harlem, New York, which was once called New Amsterdam—at least in the style of a lot of its older housing. In fact Harlem, New York, was named after Haarlem, Netherlands. This was the period of Dutch rule over the area, from 1624 until 1664, when the English took control and changed the name from Nieuw Haarlem to Harlem. The community actually remained independent from the rest of New Amsterdam and New York until 1873, when it became part of the borough of Manhattan.

the white real estate companies could no longer interest white renters to move there. Black people were drawn from the older black neighborhoods in New York: Greenwich Village, the first black community in New York (where black Shakespearean actor Ira Aldridge performed at the African Grove Theatre and where pianist-vocalist Fats Waller was born in 1904); Black Bohemia and the Tenderloin; and San Juan Hill (where Lincoln Center is now and where black people moved when run out of the Village during the antiblack Draft Riots of the Civil War, and where later jazz saxophone player/bandleader Benny Carter was born and pianist/composer Thelonious Monk was raised).

Amsterdam, Netherlands, 1991

Harlem, ca. 1920s

In the 1880s black people had come up from the South into the area around what is now West 125th Street ("Negro Tenements"). They began to arrive en masse in the early part of the twentieth century as a result of the mass migration out of the South to escape the remnants of slavery and the destruction of Reconstruction, as well as the "Black Codes" enacted in order to return to the era of outright chattel slavery. In 1904, according to *Time Lines of African American History*, there were eighty-three "reported lynchings."

That same year a black realty company taking advantage of a real estate crash began to bring blacks to Harlem, because

By 1928 Harlem was becoming the largest black community in the country, but both the Apollo's audience and the entertainers remained white! It was not until 1934 that owner Sidney Cohen and his manager Morris Sussman opened the doors to black audiences, a policy continued by Leo Brecher and Frank Schiffman when they took over a year later.

The forces that led to the Apollo becoming a "black venue" included the arrival of hundreds of thousands of blacks into Harlem. According to the U.S. Census, by 1920 32 percent of central Harlem's residents were black, and by 1930 70 percent were black.

Black Consciousness

There was also the interruption of the flow of cheap labor from Europe caused by World War I, hence the demand for an alternative, which would be answered by the flood of cheap labor migrating from the South.

As a result of this historic influx, the Harlem Renaissance was born, created by the gathering in Harlem of some of the most creative minds of Afro-America (including Africa and the Caribbean). The Renaissance was possible

Marcus Garvey (center), 1924

Silent march led by W. E. B. Du Bois, 1917

because of the changed demographics of time, place, and condition, the changed mindset of Afro-America just fifty years after the end of chattel slavery, inspired in part by the publication of W. E. B. Du Bois's *The Souls of Black Folk* in 1903. (Langston Hughes, one of the most prominent artists of the Harlem Renaissance, said he read *Souls* five times!) Du Bois followed with the founding of the Niagara Movement in 1905, with its call for "Free speech, Manhood suffrage, abolition of caste distinction," which caused a national stir and led to the founding of the NAACP five years later. Du Bois moved to New York in 1910 as the organization's "director of publications and research." It was from this post that Du Bois generated the spirit of what was to be called "the New Negro" as expressed in the anthology edited by Alain Locke fifteen years later.

Marcus Garvey arrived in New York from Jamaica in 1916, so that to Du Bois's message of true self-consciousness, equal citizenship rights, and the end of racism was added Garvey's most important and influential messages of self-determination even unto an independent black nation and black economic development. In 1917, in response to the lynch-murders of at least one hundred black people in East St. Louis, Illinois, Du Bois led a "silent march" of 10,000 black people down New York's Fifth Avenue. It is very important to note that both Du Bois and Garvey would be identified as well, in one way or another, depending on the identifier, with Pan-Africanism. It was this "new" ideological and philosophical passion that was sweeping through Harlem, and most people there, including the owners of the white-only establishments such as the Apollo and Cotton Club, had to know it. The beloved "outlaw" Bumpy Johnson—who ran Harlem's numbers operation—helped at the Cotton Club by periodically running the white patrons out with stink bombs.

After purchasing the Apollo, Cohen and Sussman's first presentation, on the black hand side, was a "colored revue" called *Jazz a la Carte*, with emcee Ralph Cooper, saxophonist

Benny Carter and his orchestra, and "16 Gorgeous Hot Steppers." In character for this kind of operation, the proceeds for the first show were donated to the Harlem Children's Fresh Air Fund. The Apollo's owners were responding to the change not only of the nationality of their environs but also to the tone of the discourse that was going on around them. It was around the same period that Bumpy Johnson ran Dutch Schultz out of the Harlem numbers racket and out of Harlem. The black-run numbers game provided an extensive

Adam Clayton Powell Jr. and John F. Kennedy, 1960

Rev. Martin Luther King Jr. and Malcolm X, 1964

support to the Harlem Renaissance and made a considerable contribution to Adam Clayton Powell's election to Congress.

From 1934 until the mid-'60s the Apollo was, without question, the most famous venue for presenting black entertainment in the world. A black entertainer had to play the Apollo to exist at all. Billie Holiday, James Brown, Duke Ellington, Lionel Hampton, Marvin Gaye, the Jackson Five, Diana Ross and the Supremes, Aretha Franklin, Stevie Wonder, Sarah Vaughan. The old-timey vaudeville-type shows were a staple of the Apollo as well. I saw comedians Stepin Fechit, Pigmeat Markham (in "Open the Door, Richard!"), and Moms Mabley with my parents at the Apollo. Despite these popular entertainers and performances, the Apollo Theater's relevance was called into question in the '60's as

a result of the shifting social mores, in Harlem and across the United States, brought about by the Civil Rights and Black Power movements.

The Dr. King–led "Civil Rights Movement" and the Malcolm X–inspired "Black Liberation Movement" constituted an objective united front, in that there were similar concerns voiced from each, which taken together had a powerful force. That force fighting through the centuries of black life under slavery and national oppression was so powerful and dynamic that only 145 years after the formal end of chattel slavery an Afro-American president could be elected.

The thrust of the Civil Rights Movement was inclusion and desegregation, echoing the calls of leaders such as Du Bois. Malcolm X used these calls as both a launching pad and as a method of criticizing the Civil Rights Movement for merely wanting to be included in "the Devil's" peck. Malcolm—first as a spokesperson for Elijah Muhammad and then as he evolved a more religious-free political line—advocated that black people embrace Black Nationalism in order to control the politics and economies of their communities. This would be heard not just in Temple No. 7 in Harlem but in "Black Muslim" mosques across the country.

In addition, Malcolm spoke frequently in the very streets of Harlem, in the tradition of sidewalk political orators, from a ladder draped with a flag (either "American" or red, black, and green), like Sufi or the less well-known Edward "Pork Chop" Davis and other Black Nationalists and Pan-Africanists, from the right or left.

Sun Ra, ca. 1970

Black Power rally, Harlem, early 1970s

In 1965 avant-garde jazz musician Sun Ra led his Arkestra in a march across West 125th Street, carrying the flag of a newer Harlem Renaissance (the Black Arts Movement) and the Black Arts Repertory Theater School. Malcolm X had been slain a month or so before, and his words were burning through a whole generation's psyche, lit up by Ossie Davis's gallant eulogy, "Malcolm was our manhood…Our Black shining Prince!" There was a veritable torrent of invective against white-owned anything in Harlem and in black communities across the country. As an example, on the night of the Northeast blackout in November 1965, some young black militants drove throughout central Harlem

with a loudspeaker on a truck urging Harlem residents to break the windows of the white-owned businesses and take what they needed. They were quickly arrested and even threatened by white policemen, who were soon surrounded by black people in the area. Ironically, when taken to the 135th precinct, they were saved by a black police commander, Eldridge Waithe, who had been appointed that same year.

The term "Black Power" had not yet become popular; that would happen when Stokely Carmichael and Willie Ricks of SNCC proclaimed it while marching with Dr. King in Alabama in 1966.

Later Carmichael explained that the slogan meant "Black people coming together to form a political force…which actually buttressed Malcolm X's call for 'The Ballot or The Bullet!'" Richard Wright had published a book, *Black Power*, in 1954, which focused on his trip to Ghana just before it became formally independent, meditating on the event and possibility of an actual black political power. It is ironic in the sense that Du Bois, Garvey, and Malcolm X also included an independent Africa in their political visions, but also because Kwame Nkrumah, the first prime minister of independent Ghana, was clear in his demand for a Pan-Africanism that meant a unified socialist Africa. This was the reason the West overthrew him and sent him into exile into Guinea, under Ahmed Sékou Touré, the only former French colony to demand independence.

D.C., in May 1966. The next Black Power conference, in Newark, was held just days after the 1967 rebellion in which twenty-six people (including two policemen and one firefighter) were killed. There were Black Power conferences in Philadelphia in 1968 and in Bermuda in 1969, from which this writer and activist Sonny Carson were banned. In 1970 the Black Power conference in Atlanta was the site for the formation of the Congress of African People, attended by some 3,000 people, including representatives from Africa, the Caribbean, and Australia. The Black Panther

Rev. Jesse Jackson, National Black Political Convention, 1972

Rioters in Newark, 1967

Party held its constitutional convention in Washington, D.C., the same weekend, which some 2,000 people attended. The most concrete project coming from the Congress of African People conference (actually the last Black Power conference) was the planning and beginning of organization for the 1972 National Black Political Convention in Gary, Indiana, which brought 8,000 black people together from all fifty states to try to concretize black political power.

Because the Apollo was a white-owned theater in Harlem with almost exclusively black entertainers and audiences in a time when the growing philosophy was that black people should control the economics of their communities, the Black Power

But Black Power came into focus in the movement when Adam Clayton Powell called for black people to seek "audacious power," initiating the first Black Power conference in Washington,

explosion made it difficult for someone like Schiffman to continue. It was standard street rap uptown, in the '60s and '70s, to talk bad about the Apollo's owners. There were various words on the street about people having talked to Schiffman, asking or more likely demanding more access to the Apollo for the grassroots arts that existed. "Access" was the kindest word used; most dreamed of some kind of takeover. At the Black Arts Repertory

IF YOU CAN JAIL A REVOLUTIONARY BUT YOU CAN'T JAIL THE REVOLUTION YOU CAN RUN A FREEDOM FIGHTER AROUND THE COUNTRY BUT YOU CAN'T RUN FREEDOM FIGHTING AROUND THE COUNTRY. YOU CAN MURDER A LIBERATOR BUT YOU CAN'T MURDER LIBERATION. MURDER

Fred Hampton Deputy Chairman Illinois Chapter Black Panther Party Born August 30, 1948 Murdered By Fascist Pigs Dec. 4, 1969

Poster by Emory Douglas of slain Black Panther Fred Hampton, 1970

Theater School, each night throughout the summer of 1965, as part of HARYOU-ACT's Operation Bootstrap, we put four trucks in the street. One carried easels to set up young black artists' works on the streets, directed by painters Betty Blayton and Selwyn Goldbourne; the others carried stages made of banquet tables, held together by vises designed by painter Joe Overstreet. The Black Arts flag was designed by painter William White. On these portable stages we performed drama (plays by this author, Charles Paterson, and others) and music featuring the most exciting

Afro-American musicians, including Sun Ra and Albert Ayler, organized by pianist Andrew Hill. I reached out for the most important young black poets of the period—Larry Neal, Sonia Sanchez, and Askia Touré (Roland Snellings)—who gave

AJASS members and Grandassa models, 1968

readings in parks, vacant lots, streets, and parking lots. A whole generation of actors, musicians, and poets came out of this effort at self-determination and self-development.

These efforts initiated and forwarded the Black Arts Movement, and in a few months Black Arts theaters emerged all over the country: in Detroit, Woodie King and Ron Milner's Black Arts Midwest, and in San Francisco–Oakland, Black Arts West, led by playwrights Marvin X and Ed Bullins, with new works by Dorothy Ahmad, Sonia Sanchez, Ben Caldwell, and Jimmy Garrett. The work there was in collaboration with the Black Student Union of San Francisco State and the Black Communications Project headed by LeRoi Jones, which brought black theater up and down the West Coast. Artist Emory Douglas, who was later the "revolutionary artist" for the Black Panther newspapers, and actor Danny Glover were active members of this project. In the South, John O'Neal's Free Southern Theater began at Tugaloo, Mississippi, in 1963, and in New Orleans, Kalamu ya Salaam established BLKARTSOUTH.

Similar theaters were created all over the country, including Spirit House in Newark and the New Lafayette in Harlem, modeled after the West Coast Communications Project. There were also well-funded "Negro" theaters such as the Negro Ensemble

Esther Rolle (third from left) and the Negro Ensemble Company, 1969

Company in New York, which developed because corporations and foundations saw that there was a need for a more liberal Afro-American theater than what the "extremists" were offering through the Black Arts Movement.

During this period, the Apollo lost much of its audience. The alternative force of a Black Arts Movement, not just in Harlem but across the country, gave black people the ideas that they didn't need the white-owned Apollos in their communities, and that they could produce their own art at venues they chose. Further, that these community spaces would allow the most advanced black art to penetrate into the black community.

What the Black Arts Movement showed nationally was that there was a deep wellspring of grassroots and professional art within the black community itself that only had to be developed and given venues and distribution within that community to find further expression nationally and internationally. Rap was a

Bronx-generated local phenomenon that has hip-hopped across the world. This is the kind of phenomenon that must be replicated with whatever genre for the people's own culture to develop, so that it is not just entertainment for the many and profit for the few, but is educational (inner attainment) as well as providing economic stability for the community, including training and jobs.

The paradigm of the Apollo has been, in a sense, like the story of African people themselves, stolen from their homeland as captives and then made chattel slaves, seen and used as "raw materials" for the conscienceless jaws of American development.

What does this all mean, in the spirit of the Akan idea, *Sankofa*, to go back in the past in order to understand the future? As I have said about black music, it is "the changing same." Like

Bill Clinton, ca. 2000

oil beneath the soil that will not be dug because they don't dig it. The greatest future for the Apollo will be as the venue and developer for its longtime indigenous Harlem residents. Though we should know that at this very moment, much of what we knew of Harlem has already disappeared in a great gentrification campaign. Former president Bill Clinton's "arrival" has seemed to be the gunshot that announced that old Harlem was something in a book or a song or in an old person's mind.

But say this to understand what is necessary and indeed possible: the Apollo must one day reflect the explosive creativity

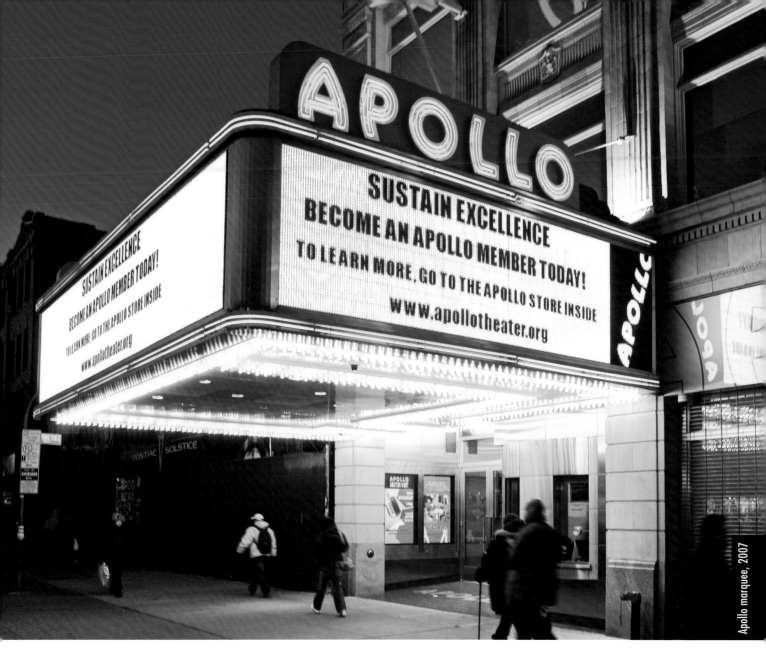

of that still disappearing-resistant majority. The paradigm of revolutionary determination to bring the highest self-consciousness that great art possesses must be the goal of any who would raise *the people* of that community, whoever that is who can finally be addressed as such. And if the Apollo still stands and can reflect that truth, then it will be a place that the indigenous people around it, and those from wherever who come to embrace that excellence, will raise to its highest historical significance.

What the Obama vision of a "post-racial" society, in relation to the Apollo, would mean is that the theater and black people generally would no longer function merely as "raw materials" for somebody else's development and wealth, but would be a self-conscious generator of equality and self-determination. This is the hope and the work to be done.

The absence of the most important developments and innovations of a people's culture removes the positive paradigms of actual community role models, as well as the education and employment and business development that would go with it. The struggle today and into the future will be to rebuild communities like Harlem in which the Apollo could be a flagship of recovery as well as to rebuild indigenous cultural flagships that would seed the development of many grassroots-engendered arts and cultural projects in benighted black communities such as Newark, Detroit, and South Central Los Angeles. This is the real challenge for the Apollo's future, to step beyond the "box" of merely "big-time" entertainment and begin projects that would raise a dozen grassroots community-driven Apollos.

Popular African American Dance of the 1950s and '60s

Thomas F. DeFrantz

The Supremes' first Apollo appearance, 1962. Mary Wilson, Florence Ballard, and Diana Ross perform as part of one of the Motortown Revues.

The return of African American soldiers from World War II inspired a huge acceleration in civil rights activism among Harlemites. As politicians and entrepreneurs worked to advance possibilities for African Americans in social status and business, entertainers followed suit with songs and dances that demonstrated both cool, assimilationist styles and fierce black pride. Popular music and dance styles of the 1950s and '60s sought to express complex African American identities that responded to the commercial marketplace as well as to the need for black Americans to resist racism and social oppression.

By the '50s new media technologies ensured that African American musicians could reach huge audiences of teenaged consumers. The expansive recording industry, abetted by a rise in television programming, catapulted black modes of expression into the global mainstream of popular culture more quickly than ever before. Of course, some artists tempered the vital energy of their Apollo Theater performances to suit mass markets less familiar with the ecstatic exchange of energy that African American audiences preferred. In the '50s, this meant the rise of refined "class acts" that offered elegantly dressed performers moving with subtle clarity. Dance teams such as Coles and Atkins perfected the art of understated, polished excellence.

Charles "Honi" Coles and Charles "Cholly" Atkins began performing together in 1946 and within a decade had achieved successes that included appearances on television, Broadway, and in films. Their distinctive style of tap dance and soft shoe combined popular social dances from earlier eras with relaxed, mature personas that suggested African American cool of the highest order. Moving in a relaxed but precise unison in many of their dance routines, Coles and Atkins set a standard emulated by many mainstream Hollywood artists, who engaged a similar noticeably cool physicality.

In the mid-'50s, Atkins began to branch out as a choreographer for younger singing groups, sharing his passion for perfection with an array of emerging talents. His precise choreography for the Cadillacs earned them a spot on the *Alan Freed Christmas Show* in 1955 that wowed audiences with its synchronization of singing and movement: dazzling struts, slides, turns, drops to splits, and seemingly impossible returns to unison dancing. Atkins became the principal choreographer for Motown Records in 1965. In this role, his influence over popular culture greatly increased. He coached many groups to develop movement sequences that suited their distinctive personalities, directing rehearsals to amplify quirky movements that distinguished their energy and style. The Supremes, the Temptations, the Four Tops, and Gladys Knight and the Pips all benefitted from the Atkins touch. The routines that Motown artists brought to the Apollo stage were tightly coordinated demonstrations of his subtle, effective choreography. It could be easily argued that the synchronized group choreography that Atkins developed to define Motown style in the '60s led to the development of popular dancing singers of the MTV era, including Michael Jackson, Janet Jackson, and Beyoncé.

The crossover appeal of African American artists coached by Atkins at Motown suited founder Berry Gordy Jr.'s

The Four Tops practice a dance routine in the Apollo basement with legendary dancer Cholly Atkins, 1964. Atkins helped provide several Motown groups with sophisticated choreography.

ambition to reach the largest possible audiences. Black artists had learned about white appropriation of African American music the hard way: Elvis Presley famously adapted African American song and dance styles to his own commercial ends, spearheading the rise of rock and roll. Some white promoters tried to define rock as distinct from the obvious African American rhythm-and-blues forms that inspired it, but performers including Little Richard and Chuck Berry kept black presence in the emerging rock idiom alive. These artists brought the ferocious energy of gospel revival–style performance to the stage, encouraging audiences to cut loose in free-form, ecstatic dance.

The rise of rock and roll also coincided with the emergence of teenagers as a prime marketing demographic, which had profound effects on generational affiliations in African American communities. Social dances that would have been practiced by young and old alike in previous generations were displaced by dances designed only for the young. Buoyed by

As popular entertainers became increasingly specialized in their stage dancing, the distance between dances performed onstage and dances done by audiences grew. But the dance that Chubby Checker popularized in a 1960 recording became the most widely circulated social dance of this era. The twist paid obvious homage to earlier African American social dances, including the mess around and the ballin' the jack of the 1910s. It elaborated on the improvisatory, breakaway section of partnered forms including the Charleston and the Lindy hop. In its basic movement, dancers swiveled their hips by twisting

The Temptations form a kick line, ca. 1964. They were known for their tailored suits, coordinated dance steps, and hits such as "My Girl."

television and radio programs that catered to the new youth culture, line dances, including the stroll and the madison, became popular among teens of all ethnicities. These dances allowed teenagers to socialize across racial identities, but typically without intergenerational participation.

Other teen social dances popular in Harlem were also popular all over the country. Simple social dances like the mashed potato, the Freddie, the frug, the hitchhike, the dog, and the Watusi—to name just a few among dozens—matched movements to the regular pulse of rock and pop music. The emergent soul idiom—epitomized by the spectacular abilities of James Brown— encouraged dancers to get funky with expressive, individualized dances that reimagined movements from earlier social dances. For example, the good foot of the '60s was a fast, soulful interpretation of the twisting foot movements of the nineteenth-century slow drag and the '20s Charleston. The good foot was like the mashed potato in its swiveling gestures, but unabashedly funky in its accent on the unexpected rhythmic upbeat that James Brown's band preferred.

both their feet as if putting out a cigarette on the floor, while bobbing up and down and leaning forward and back. Performed individually, the twist became the first mainstream noncontact partner dance practiced by an international audience.

The twist also numbers among the first African American dance forms significantly influenced by technologies of mass distribution. The dance first attracted national attention when Hank Ballard and the Midnighters, who recorded the song "The Twist" in 1958, performed it in Baltimore. Black youth gave the dance form, and white youth quickly copied its contents on the Philadelphia-based television program *American Bandstand*. In 1959 Cameo-Parkway Records hired Chubby Checker to rerecord the song in a family-friendly version, and this sanitized recording debuted August 6, 1960, on the nationally televised *American Bandstand*. The song became a top seller and inspired a merchandising industry that included innumerable sequel songs, low-budget films, and fashion items. As the dance gained international popularity in regions as distant as China and Russia, many considered its hip movements provocative, and it was banned by authorities in Cairo and Damascus, among other places. The twist founded a rock and roll dance culture that led directly to the establishment of the first discotheques in New York City.

The sounds and dances of this era had huge global impact. Leaders of recently independent African nations proclaimed their love for African American popular music; teenagers in Bahia, Brazil, and Japan sought out the emergent rock and soul dance styles. Entertainers who played the Apollo Theater in this era helped to define a youth culture that valued the unabashed vitality and endless energetic innovation of the young, one that continues to be a wellspring for global popular cultures.

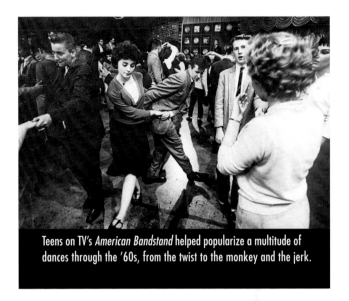

Teens on TV's *American Bandstand* helped popularize a multitude of dances through the '60s, from the twist to the monkey and the jerk.

A young Gladys Knight performs with her backup singers/dancers, the Pips, 1960. Left to right: William Guest, Edward Patten, and Merald "Bubba" Knight.

Stand-up Comedy

Mel Watkins

Moms Mabley, 1950s. Even as she transitioned from situational comedies to monologues, her classic costume of house dress, old hat, and oversized shoes remained a constant.

By the 1950s, African American stage humor was undergoing a major face-lift. The sketch style of comedy that had been developed on the black theatrical circuit during the first half of the century was changing dramatically. Influenced by the civil rights movement and its escalating push for racial equality, as well as mainstream acceptance of the irreverent, antiestablishment satire of such comedians as Mort Sahl and Lenny Bruce, black audiences were primed for more outspoken, dissident voices.

Satirical commentary critical of America's Jim Crow social arrangements was not new to African American folklore or street humor. But, owing to the minstrel show origins of black stage comedy and the prohibitions enforced by most white theater owners, it was rarely seen in public performances. Moms Mabley was among the pioneers of its use at the Apollo during the '40s. One of her popular stories involved an encounter with a southern policeman after running a red light:

> *"Hey, woman, don't you know you went through a red light?"*
>
> *I say, "Yeah, I know I went through a red light."*
>
> *"Well, what did you do that for?"*
>
> *I said, "'Cause I seen all you white folks goin' on the green light....I thought the red light was for us!"*

Mabley was one of several old-school comics who contributed to the transition from situational sketches to monologues and social commentary. Another notable was Timmie Rogers, a veteran of the vaudeville and TOBA circuits. In the mid-'40s he boldly abandoned his clownish stage costume and began appearing in a tuxedo, lacing his comic song and dance routines with social satire. At his first booking, Rogers recalled, he was told that he "was doing a white man's act" and fired on the spot. He persisted, however, and by 1957 had earned top billing at the Apollo.

Nipsey Russell was another of the early converts to stand-up comedy and social commentary. He graduated from the University of Cincinnati in 1946 and by the '50s was appearing at

Comedian Redd Foxx, 1956. His tendency to perform blue material led Jack Schiffman to note that Foxx was "funny but dirty."

Harlem's Baby Grand. Wearing discreet business attire topped by a raffish porkpie hat, he developed an articulate comic approach that featured catchy rhymes and witty aphorisms. His routines were never strictly focused on racial material, but they included satiric quips on topical issues such as integration: "A seat on the top deck don't mean a thing if the ship is sinking." Booked at the Apollo as an emcee and featured comic, he was an immediate

hit. Those appearances led to guest spots on Jack Paar's *Tonight Show* in 1959. During the '60s and '70s Russell became a fixture as a panelist on several TV game shows, but he regularly returned to the Apollo.

Slappy White and Redd Foxx were also among the early black-circuit comics who shifted their acts to include social commentary in the '50s. During the '40s they had worked at the Apollo as a team called Foxx and White. Their act featured traditional black-circuit song, dance, and gags, but the team broke up in the early '50s.

White, who would become known as the "father of the integrated joke," subsequently worked in duos and as a solo performer at the Apollo and many other venues By decade's end, his stand-up routines regularly included topical material. During an Apollo appearance, he quipped, "Mayor Daley did a nice thing to elevate the dignity of a black family in Chicago. He moved them from a $100-a-month apartment to one that rented for $300 so they could be closer to the welfare office." In another bit, he wore one white glove and one black glove and, with his clasped hands spotlighted, delivered a monologue about equality among men. During his '60s appearances at the Apollo, it was one of his most popular routines.

Foxx would ultimately be more successful than White, but his career took a highly circuitous path. As a single act, he also turned to monologue humor and often vitriolic social commentary. Because his routine was laced with profanity and racy gags, he usually appeared at black-circuit venues where blue humor was expected. Many of those performances were recorded and released as X-rated party records. When he was booked at the Apollo, where obscenity was frowned upon, his act was often restricted. When Jack and Bobby Schiffman assumed control in the '50s, some strictures were relaxed, but Foxx's double entendres and risqué one-liners still rankled them. For instance, a biting parody of Arkansas Governor Orval Faubus, which imagined the governor being felled by poison darts, might be followed by the rhetorical question: "What's the difference between a peeping Tom and a pickpocket?—A pickpocket snatches watches." In his notes about Foxx, Jack Schiffman wrote, "Funny but dirty."

Foxx's reputation as a blue comic ensured that he did not receive the type of mainstream acceptance accorded Russell, Rogers, and a handful of younger black comics in the '60s. It was not until 1972, when he debuted as the irascible but lovable

An early publicity photo of Dick Gregory, one of the most active social commentators of his generation, as well as a comedian.

junk dealer Fred Sanford on the TV sitcom *Sanford and Son*, that he received wide mainstream recognition. Two years later he appeared at the Apollo with top billing; at the time, according to Jack Schiffman, that show was one of the biggest money earners in the theater's history. Foxx remained an Apollo favorite throughout his career.

The early efforts of Mabley, Rogers, Russell, White, and Foxx in advancing African American comedy's shift from ragged attire, slapstick gags, and burlesque sketches to monologue humor featuring witty social commentary set the stage for the emergence of the most influential black comedian of his era: Dick Gregory. Gregory began his career doing monologue humor and, by the time he appeared at the Apollo in the mid-'60s, was one of America's stand-up comic icons. When he left Southern Illinois University in 1956 and took to the stage, he realized that traditional, racy, baggy-pants black stage humor was quickly becoming obsolete, and he began fashioning a different strategy. "I've got to be a colored funny man, not a funny colored man," Gregory calculated. "I've got to make jokes about myself before I can make jokes about them and their society."

Gregory tested that strategy when he appeared at Chicago's Playboy Club before a convention of white southerners in January 1961. He began with jokes aimed at himself: "They asked me to buy a lifetime membership in the NAACP, but I told them I'd pay a little bit at a time. Hell of a thing to buy a lifetime membership, then wake up one morning and find out the country's been integrated." Then he confidently segued into one of his signature routines:

Last time I was down South, I walked into this restaurant, and this white waitress came up to me and said, "We don't serve colored people here."

I said, "That's all right, I don't eat colored people. Bring me a whole fried chicken."

About that time these three cousins come in, you know the ones I mean, Ku, Kluck, and Klan, and

they say, "Boy, we're givin' you fair warnin.' Anything you do to that chicken, we're gonna do to you."

About then the waitress brought me my chicken.

"Remember, boy, anything you do to that chicken, we're gonna do to you," they reminded me.

So I put down my knife and fork, and I picked up that chicken, and I kissed it.

Gregory won over the hostile crowd. Within a year, he was featured in a *Time* magazine article. Offers for bookings on network TV shows and the best comedy rooms followed. In December 1962 a *Newsweek* story proclaimed, "From the moment [Gregory] was booked into the Playboy Club…Jim Crow was dead in the joke world." Gregory had vaulted ahead of the large field of more experienced comedians to become the first black mainstream superstar comic since Bert Williams and Stepin Fetchit had won national acclaim early in the century.

During the early '60s Gregory headlined on several occasions at the Apollo. His hip, coolly detached posture and poised, self-assured delivery of biting witticisms about racial inequity were quickly embraced by an audience that hungered for entertainment reflecting the black community's more aggressive attitude. In the mid-'60s, however, at the height of his popularity, Gregory began curtailing his stage career. Increased involvement in civil rights protests took precedence. By 1967 he had become more of a human rights advocate than a comedian. Eventually he resumed his stage career in the '90s, and in 2000 he made a memorable appearance at the Apollo with Paul Mooney, one of the new breed of satiric stand-up comics who had benefited from his groundbreaking work.

Gregory's rapid rise to fame had an enormous impact on African American comedy, opening doors for veteran black comedians as well as for a group of younger performers who waited anxiously in the wings. Among those who appeared frequently at the Apollo were George Kirby, Scoey Mitchell, and Godfrey Cambridge. The group also included three of the most popular and

Bill Cosby emcees *Motown Returns to the Apollo*, 1985. Cosby played the Apollo in a 1968 engagement that started slowly but eventually attracted enthusiastic, full houses.

influential comedians ever to appear at the Apollo or any other American theater: Bill Cosby, Flip Wilson, and Richard Pryor.

Cosby was the first to gain national recognition. He left Temple University in 1962 to work coffeehouses and comedy clubs in New York; the following year he appeared on the *Tonight Show*, where he became a regular guest. Early on it was clear that his stand-up act was unique. Unlike his contemporaries, Cosby brashly excised all racial identity from his biblical tales and whimsical stories about children and the frustrations of daily life. "I don't think you can bring the races together by joking about the differences between them," he explained. "I'd rather talk about the similarities, about what's universal in their experience." His comedy career soared, and characters such as Fat Albert and Weird Harold, created for his stage routines, became household names. Still, when first booked into the Apollo in 1968, he drew only a dismal opening-night crowd. But word got around that the costar of *I Spy* was appearing, and the next evening patrons "were standing in the aisles." "Cosby had come into the Apollo as a 'Who's that?' headliner," Jack Schiffman recalled. "At the end of a single week, he left about as close to a 'beloved figure' as it was possible to be."

During Cosby's meteoric rise to fame in the '60s, Clerow "Flip" Wilson was gaining an enthusiastic following as a featured comic and emcee on the Apollo stage. Unlike Cosby, Wilson had cut his teeth in small black clubs on the so-called chitlin circuit, and his comedy reflected the tenor and spirit of those lively, down-to-earth venues. His stand-up routines displayed an uninhibited celebration of black life that was in direct contrast to Gregory and Cosby's measured, more sophisticated approaches. In one sense it was a throwback to the raucous comedy of the Negro stage clown. But it was presented with a fresh, more overtly intelligent and confident attitude.

"I decided to enjoy myself—be myself," he said of his stage act. "What I try to express is real. It's what I know. I'm not tricking anybody. This is the way we are as people, we have desires, the

Flip Wilson's stand-up routines displayed an uninhibited celebration of black life that was in direct contrast to Gregory and Cosby's measured, more sophisticated approaches.

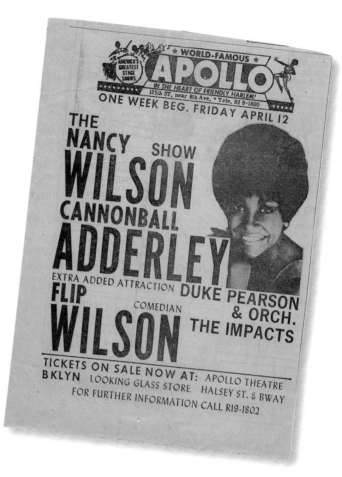

urge to conquer, to hunt, to survive. That's what I do on stage now. I hunt hearts!"

His joyful expressions of typical black attitudes and his flamboyant use of the timbre and resonances of street language gave his routines a distinctly black voice at a time when most comedians were abandoning it. That approach was reflected in such characters as the irrepressible Geraldine ("What you see is what you get") and with Wilson's imposition of black perspectives

on historical events and characters in his popular "Christopher Columbus" routine. Typical examples were Queen Isabella Johnson's excitement at the prospect of Columbus finding Ray Charles ("Chris goin' to America; he goin' find Ray Charles… what you say?") and an American Indian girl's reaction when Chris reaches the shore ("We don't wanna be discovered! You can't discover nobody if they don't want to be discovered. You better discover your ass away from here!"). He also laced his historical tales with casual asides that never failed to get belly laughs. "You couldn't get a bet on the Christians in the arena," he quipped during a bit about Julius Caesar. "Christians had a great coach, but the team was shaky."

"I'd bring different facets of black culture to the act, trying to expand consciousness," Wilson said. "I was telling an American story, and I think people understood it." Apparently, they did. When the *Flip Wilson Show* debuted on NBC in 1970,

it quickly became the number-one variety show on TV. By 1974 Wilson had become America's most popular comedian. He continued appearing at the Apollo and, with the possible exception of Moms Mabley, remained the most beloved comic to have performed there. Richard Pryor once told him: "You're the only performer that I've ever seen who goes on stage and the audience hopes that *you* like *them*."

Pryor, who would succeed Wilson as the nation's leading funnyman, had left the black theatrical circuit and arrived in New York City in 1963. Touted as the next Bill Cosby, his ascent was rapid. By 1964 he had appeared on national television, and his Apollo appearances during the mid-'60s drew rave reviews. But by 1967, tiring of what he called "white-bread" humor and of comparisons to Cosby, he began experimenting with edgier material. Introducing street types he had met growing up in Peoria, he depicted them in character-based vignettes that candidly echoed their rough language and style.

Initially, the response was not encouraging. White audiences were embarrassed. Even hip black audiences were puzzled by the new approach and offended by his insistent use of the word "nigger." Frustrated, Pryor cancelled bookings and dropped out; in 1970 he moved to Berkeley to work on his material. When he returned to Los Angeles in 1971, his act had been transformed. "I was in the audience when Richard took on a whole new persona—his own," Bill Cosby said. "Richard killed the Cosby in his act...then he worked on the audience, doing pure Pryor, and it was the most astonishing metamorphosis I have ever seen. He was magnificent."

During the '70s Pryor refined his approach, amplifying the voices of the hustlers and street folk and dicing his routines with clever social commentary. On the judicial system, he quipped, "You go down there looking for justice, that's what you find, *just us!*" With an incredible array of dramatic and comic skills— mime, impersonation, unerring timing—he was able to incorporate the gritty, often blasphemous, humor of the most unassimilated portion of the black community into his distinctive stand-up routines. When he appeared at the Apollo in 1974 before sold-out crowds, Bobby Schiffman noted: "Dirty! But funny! I have never seen an audience react with such laughter. They were absolutely hysterical."

Perhaps the greatest tribute to Pryor is that most stand-up comics and nearly every prominent African American comic who emerged during or after the '80s cite him as their most influential predecessor. That list includes Eddie Murphy, Bernie Mac, Martin Lawrence, Steve Harvey, D. L. Hughley, Chris Rock, and Dave Chappelle, all of whom have become part of the legacy of remarkable comedians who have appeared at the Apollo.

Richard Pryor in performance, ca. 1977. He incorporated gritty, often blasphemous street humor into his stand-up routines laced with social commentary.

Modern Jazz at the Apollo

Willard Jenkins

When the Apollo Theater opened the doors for its inaugural show on January 26, 1934, the trendsetting variety bill included the great jazzman Benny Carter and his orchestra. The big band or so-called swing era was in full flower, and these swinging seventeen-piece behemoths, spark plugs of the happy-feet crowd at historic Harlem haunts such as the Savoy Ballroom, soon found a welcoming home at the Apollo. Such great big bands as those of Duke Ellington, Chick Webb, Fletcher Henderson, Cab Calloway, Benny Goodman, Lionel Hampton, and many others were a core element of the Apollo's salad days in the 1930s and '40s. They paved the way toward the Apollo's accommodation of the succeeding years' modern jazz combos. It was in those wonderful big bands that so many of the original vanguard of the modern jazz movement prepped.

The early '40s protobebop Earl Hines Orchestra was a classic example. That band was a veritable academy for modernists, including two of the pacesetters of small group jazz: trumpeter Dizzy Gillespie and alto saxophonist Charlie "Yardbird" Parker. As Ted Fox recounts in his book *Showtime at the Apollo*, "The Apollo led the way to exposing bebop to a larger audience. It was Frank Schiffman who first booked the experimental bop band of Earl Hines early in 1943—with Dizzy Gillespie, Charlie Parker, and [trumpeter] Little Benny Harris." Significantly, that Hines band featured the voices of Billy Eckstine and Sarah Vaughan, who also doubled as the band's second pianist.

In 1944, when Eckstine formed his own band— one that took further steps into the modern era—he not only took Vaughan (who at eighteen had won the Apollo's famed Amateur Night) with him but also opened up his trumpet section to Gillespie, Fats Navarro, and younger fire-breathers such as Kenny Dorham and Miles Davis. The saxophone section was equally prodigious, including Bird, Leo Parker, Gene Ammons, Dexter Gordon, and Lucky Thompson. The rhythm section included bassist Tommy Potter, drummer Art Blakey, and pianist John Malachi.

Apollo Theater impresario and major domo Frank Schiffman was no moldy fig (as the conservative fans of swing and Dixieland jazz were known); he was said to be quite supportive of the new, modern jazz sound. This new sound developed almost out of rebellion against the strictures of big band playing, in favor of a sound that afforded freer flights of improvisation, plus more intricate rhythms and a broader harmonic universe. Although bebop grew out of the jazz atmosphere that encouraged social dancing, its various advancements limited dancing to only the most skilled terpsichorean hipsters. It was only natural that this music, which seemingly required more of a listening commitment on the part of its audience, would find a place on the Apollo stage.

The two Harlem haunts that served as the most famous modern jazz laboratories were Minton's Playhouse at 210 West 118th Street and Monroe's Uptown House at 198 West 134th Street, with the Apollo roughly equidistant between them. At Minton's the man later dubbed the "high priest of bebop," pianist Thelonious Monk, held court at the nightly jam sessions with drummer Kenny "Klook" Clarke, trumpeter Joe Guy, and bassist Nick Fenton. Those sessions, conducted on the downlow beyond the prying eyes of musicians' union officials who had banned jam sessions, were particularly combustible on Monday nights. Bandleader Teddy Hill, the Minton's manager who controlled the music policy, hosted Monday night buffet dinners for Apollo performers on their nights off. This savvy move ensured that the cream of the crop would show up on Mondays to jam.

As Dizzy Gillespie remarked in his memoirs, *To Be or Not to Bop*, "On Monday nights we used to have a ball. Everybody from the Apollo on Monday nights was a guest at Minton's, the whole band. We had a big jam session. There was always some food there for you. I was with the [big] bands at the time, and I would come in and out of town. When I was in the city, we were appearing at the Apollo....After the last show we'd go to Minton's and sit and listen to some of the guys play." Gillespie met his wife, Lorraine, at the Apollo, where she was a dancer in the chorus line.

Drummer Art Blakey, 1950s. The first great bebop drummer, he led the famous Jazz Messengers for decades.

Pianist Earl "Fatha" Hines backstage at the Apollo, 1947. His exuberant "trumpet style" of playing made him a standout among jazz artists.

Thelonious Monk at the Apollo, 1969. His angular, brooding compositions and percussive piano style made him legendary.

Gillespie, who, unlike so many of his bop cohorts, still had a lingering taste for the big band format, brought his pioneering bebop orchestra into the Apollo on several occasions, most notably in January 1947 and for two stints in 1949. Performances from these gigs were captured for the film *Jivin' in Bebop*. Charlie Parker's dream was his series of *Bird with Strings* sessions, which for him were efforts at engaging the classical atmosphere he relished. The week of August 17, 1950, Parker's peerless alto sax was bathed in strings onstage at the Apollo, which also included a live radio broadcast. The record shows, however, that these Parker efforts on the "legit" side came up short of the ever-demanding Apollo audience expectations and were met with a lukewarm response.

Ever the iconoclast, Monk brought a different vision to 125th Street. According to Fox in *Showtime at the Apollo*, "when the continually inventive pianist and one of the jazz world's great eccentrics played the Apollo in the late fifties he wore a pink sequined necktie—his one concession to the demands of show business." Experiencing Monk onstage at the Apollo amid comics and dancers must have been quite a vision. Accessing Frank Schiffman's meticulous five-by-eight-inch typed artist ratings index cards in the Smithsonian collection reveals the following Monk notation: "3/13/59 Very exciting jazz group." Later that year: "6/5/59 Not nearly as good as first time. No box office."

Trumpeter Dizzy Gillespie, c. 1950. His charismatic performance style—one part Cab Calloway, one part bebop hipster—made him a popular performer and bandleader for five decades.

The following year Thelonious's new band apparently righted the ship: "7/22/60 With quintet…very well received."

As the '40s evolved into the '50s and '60s, jazz made further stylistic advancements. These developments were more frequently featured on the stage of the Apollo than bebop, particularly in the early '60s. By this time, bebop had evolved into post- or hard bop, a sound characterized by more extended lines imbued with bluesy qualities that were labeled as "funk" or "soul jazz" as the next generation of jazz musicians expanded on the examples of Monk, Gillespie, Parker, and their cohorts.

The Schiffmans continued to feature more jazz attractions. The more song-oriented and the bluesiest of the hard boppers who had that sanctified sound were the most frequent modern jazzers then booked into the Apollo: Horace Silver, Art

Miles Davis at the Apollo, 1970. He was an early champion of "cool jazz," a cerebral, more restrained style in comparison with bebop.

Blakey's Jazz Messengers, Cannonball Adderley, Jimmy Smith, and the like. Popular white jazz artists of the day who also found a welcome included Dave Brubeck, Stan Getz, Buddy Rich, and Maynard Ferguson. Singers were an essential element of these shows, particularly to balance out the more innovative types such as Miles Davis, Monk, and John Coltrane. According to Lionel Hampton: "I saw Coltrane play the Apollo one time.

John Coltrane, ca. 1960. His technical virtuosity and harmonic sophistication made him one of the all-time jazz greats.

Charlie Parker, 1949. His astonishing technique has challenged generations of saxophonists.

Jazz vocalist Nancy Wilson, 1960s. She combined outstanding musicality with an ability to keep up with the fastest-paced boppers.

The place was packed when he went in there. When he left, there wasn't but a handful of people in there. He was playing his piece 'My Favorite Things' [his 1960 hit recording], and he played that piece for about half an hour."

This was also a period when the Apollo featured various radio DJ-produced extravaganzas. On the jazz side such radio show hosts as Symphony Sid Torin ("the all-night, all-frantic one") and Mort Fega brought shows to the Harlem stage. On March 30, 1962, Symphony Sid hosted a power-packed lineup featuring Coltrane, Herbie Mann, and Betty Carter. It was the Apollo stage that engaged Sid's growing taste in Latin sounds as well; witness his June 22, 1962, show featuring Tito Puente, Monk, Mongo Santamaría, Arthur Prysock, Tommy Rey and his Caribe Steel Band, and dancers. This show was clearly in keeping with the Apollo policy of mixing genres, as with another 1962 show mixing Horace Silver, Aretha Franklin, singer Tito Rodríguez, comic Timmie Rogers, Nigerian drummer Babatunde Olatunji, and Mann, which was successful enough that Schiffman noted on his index card: "may keep [this show] 10 days." The week of September 6, 1963, Mort Fega hosted Art Blakey's Jazz Messengers ("Cooperative and probably the finest jazz group in the country," according to Schiffman's rating card, "individually & collectively—but worn a bit thin in this house [attraction-wise]"), singer Teri Thornton, organist Jimmy McGriff, comedian Flip Wilson, and pianist Oscar Peterson. Symphony Sid's "Afro Jazz" brought Blakey (with guest Montego Joe), three dancers, Prysock, Santamaría, Eddie Palmieri, and Wilson to the theater.

One notes a common thread through all of these jazz-laden shows: the presence of at least one singer and usually a comedian as well. Singers in particular were included because Schiffman, despite his support of and appreciation of modern jazz, always believed that his shows needed at least one singer to ensure box office success. One of the great singers who came to prominence in the '60s was Nancy Wilson. Her longtime manager John Levy, former bassist and pioneering African American artist personal manager, produced several shows at the Apollo with the Schiffmans' blessings. "I had a great working relationship with the Schiffmans, both Bobby and the old man [Frank]," Levy, ninety-seven years young and sharp as a tack, exclaimed during a recent conversation.

The week of March 6, 1964, the Apollo hosted "John Levy Presents Free Sounds of '64," featuring Wilson, Cannonball Adderley, Ramsey Lewis, and comic Slappy White. A high point of the show came when Nancy sang her big hit of the day, "Guess Who I Saw Today," and as she sang the big finish, "I saw YOU," she gestured stage left and the spotlight shone on a big white chair with Oscar Brown Jr. sitting with his back to the audience. Brown then rose to the audience's delight, intoning the signature line from one of his own hits, "But I was cool!"

Unlike jazz festival shows of today, these shows were not a matter of one full set following another. According to Levy, the entire cast would come on together to open the show, the duration of which was typically ninety minutes. "One act introduced the other act," says Levy. Then, in typical Apollo fashion, after a thirty-minute break they'd do it all over again. Showtime at the Apollo—on a jazz tip. "We got a great response, we sold the houses out… and I made money," Levy remembers happily.

Carter, Betty
10/2/52 $250.00   Excellent bee-bop singer.
2/19/53 $250.00   Good voice, nice personality, registered well.
4/17/53   Called in FRIDAY NIGHT to help KING PLEASURE. Did very well with him and in her own spot. Had trouble with the police.
2/12/54   Lionel Hampton Revue. Same unattractive oddly dressed girl with a fine bee-bop style which registered very well.
11/15/57   250.00   Registered nicely.
4/22/60   450.00   Very exciting.
7/22/60   450.00   Used as closing act and held her spot very well. A good buy at this price. Excellent performer.
9/30/60   550.00   Well known to us. Excellent singer, no box office value.
6/16-23/61 $750.00
9/1/61 $750.00   still very good singer but no box office value.

4

A Changing Harlem, a Changing Apollo: The Apollo Theater in the 1970s and 1980s

1970
October
Dionne Warwick's gala return engagement.

1971
Week of June 7
Aretha Franklin's shows are major cultural events. Apollo bill says: "She's Home."

December 17
Attica benefit concert features **John Lennon and Yoko Ono**, Aretha Franklin, and local politicians in the wake of the Attica prison riots.

1972
April 4
Jesse Jackson speaks at a special event honoring Martin Luther King Jr. on the fourth anniversary of the death of the civil rights leader.

1973
July 2
Producer George Wein presents his Newport Jazz Festival at the Apollo over seven nights.

1974
January 16
Frank Schiffman dies.

April 24
B. B. King gives a blues concert for Harlem schoolchildren.

1975
Teddy Pendergrass leaves **Harold Melvin and the Blue Notes** during their Apollo engagement.

December 7
A man is shot and killed and another wounded at 12:15 a.m. during a Smokey Robinson show.

1976
January
Bobby Schiffman reluctantly closes the Apollo.

1978

May 5
Theater briefly reopens
under new management
with shows by Ralph
MacDonald, War, the
T-Connection, Sister Sledge,
and James Brown.

1979

October 10
**George Clinton and
Parliament/Funkadelic**
open a ten-night run at
the Apollo; the theater is
only half-full on opening
night, but concerts are sold
out by the end of the run.

October 25–28
Bob Marley makes his
Apollo debut.

November
IRS closes theater for failure
to pay payroll taxes.

1981

Percy Sutton's Inner City
Broadcasting Corporation
and investors purchase the
Apollo Theater.

1983

The Apollo receives
national, state, and city
landmark status as Harlem's
oldest active theater.

1985

The Apollo celebrates its
Fiftieth Anniversary with the
television special, *Motown
Salutes the Apollo*.

Amateur Night is relaunched
on Christmas Eve.

1987

Showtime at the Apollo
debuts on national
television. In its nearly
twenty-year run, numerous
celebrity comedians hosted
the show, including Rick
Aviles, **Steve Harvey**,
Whoopie Goldberg,
Mo'nique, and Sinbad.

The Apollo Adapts to a Changing World

David Hinckley

DJ Grandmaster Flash, 1982.
He was among the first celebrity
turntable artists, helping to
set the style for future rap groups.

The main thoroughfare of urban America, New York's 125th Street has always moved to the rhythm of the day's popular music, and in 1982 that was just starting to mean what the kids called rap. Like jazz and rock and roll before it, rap was an intruder, a different musical animal that gave its fans an exhilarating new touchstone and gave fans of more established popular music a headache. Their unease over rap was not soothed that year when Edward Fletcher and Melvin Glover, on a twelve-inch single released as "Grandmaster Flash and the Furious Five," broke from rap's standard theme of party all night to release a dark warning about the state of urban America. It was called "The Message." "It's like a jungle sometimes," went its simple, chilling chorus. "It makes me wonder / How I keep from goin' under."

Inside the Apollo Theater, the most famous building on 125th Street and even in darkness the most famous 1,500 seats in the entertainment world, that question didn't startle anyone. They'd been asking it about the Apollo for years. Even in its glory decades, from the 1930s to the early '60s, the Apollo was a much more fragile operation than legend might suggest. Weekly rotation of multiact shows meant rolling the dice every Friday, without much margin for miscalculation. The issue was income. Unlike the Metropolitan Opera or Carnegie Hall, the Apollo had no rich angels to cushion its bottom line. It had only the box office, where for years patrons paid just fifty cents to see Charlie Parker, Duke Ellington, the Orioles, Bojangles Robinson, or Billie Holiday. In an era that long predated "golden circle" premium seating, the first person through the door with one of those fifty-cent tickets could grab front row center and sit there all day, late morning to midnight.

Even when the tickets went up to a couple of bucks, each week was a gamble for the theater, and more so for the Apollo than the downtown theaters, because if it raised prices in a community where personal entertainment budgets were measured in pennies and nickels, a lot of those seats would sit empty. This financial reality trickled up and dictated what the Apollo could pay its artists, which led to an unspoken but unavoidable truth: for decades the theater survived by hiring filet mignon talent at chopped steak prices. Fortunately for the Apollo, if not so fortunately for the artists, that was simply the way it was on the whole black theater circuit. Washington's Howard, Baltimore's Royal, Philadelphia's Uptown, and others had evolved from the old Theatre Owners Booking Association, whose acronym was known among performers as "Tough on Black Asses."

When Sammy Davis Jr. was young he'd play a week at the Apollo, thirty-one shows, and get $900. Asked about it years later, when his price was considerably and justifiably higher, Davis had the same reaction as most of his peers: "Hey, we were just happy to be working." It was a cost structure that kept the Apollo profitable and operational for decades, and even into the early days of rock and roll every star below the level of Elvis Presley still dutifully did his or her live performances in low-budget package shows.

Today, looking over the lineup of Motortown Revue shows that played the Apollo in the early '60s is like reading a Hall of Fame roster: the Temptations, the Supremes, Smokey Robinson, Stevie Wonder, Marvin Gaye. Back then they were a bunch of kids who piled onto the bus after the engagement, rode to the next town, and might have been taking home less money than their driver. When the Temptations played the Apollo in the Motortown Revue in August 1963, they split that same $900 for their week's work.

But by the time the '70s rolled around, the old economic system had imploded, and it was rapidly taking the Apollo with it. The theater was by then facing multiple threats, some of which had been simmering for years, and none of which the Apollo could control. A sign of changing times came in 1965 with the "Harlem riots," which greatly affected 125th Street and the community. Businesses closed, tensions grew. A few years earlier, 125th Street had stayed open almost around the clock. Radio stations did midnight shows from storefront windows, just to comment on the passing nightlife. Now the people on the street after dark were hurrying home, not heading for the Apollo.

Beyond these social changes, the concert business had exploded in the late '60s and early '70s, in the process undergoing a seismic shift. As popular music became big business with the Beatles, Motown, soul music, and the rest, individual performers suddenly had unprecedented appeal, power, and leverage. By June 1969 the same Temptations who had earned $900 in 1963 were getting $22,500—and not doing thirty-one shows anymore. The Apollo still made money from the Temptations, even though the theater had to sell fewer seats at higher prices, because the Temps were stars at their peak. But there weren't enough Temptations to fill a year's bookings and, even if there were, higher-priced tickets threatened to make an Apollo show an occasional luxury rather than a weekly ritual for many longtime patrons. At the same time, the multiact package show that had been the foundation of Apollo bookings since it took the handoff from vaudeville in the '30s was fading away. Younger patrons didn't want to see three musical acts, two dance acts, a comedian, and a juggler. They wanted the headliner they'd paid all that money to see.

The breaking down of color barriers in other major venues gave the Apollo new competition for their most popular acts. As popular music became more popular, downtown theaters such as Radio City that wouldn't have touched 95 percent of the Apollo's roster in the '50s began reconsidering. In 1963 Marvin Gaye played the Apollo; in 1983 he played Radio City. The Apollo would have been ecstatic to have him, but those 1,500 seats didn't enable the Apollo to offer him enough money to compete with Radio City, which had 6,000. Artists such as James Brown still periodically returned to the Apollo. But he also played Radio City, the Palladium, and other downtown spots that could offer more money.

Popular music was splintering, and so was its audience. Until rhythm and blues and rock and roll came along in the '50s, popular music had remained a grownup sport. Artists such as Duke Ellington, Count Basie, Ella Fitzgerald, or the Ink Spots appealed to a wide spectrum of adult fans, leaving kids largely on their own. But R & B, rock and roll, and later offshoots such as rap changed all that, because the kids now had music of their own, and it often wasn't anything close to what their parents liked. Then each group further subdivided within itself, meaning that theaters such as the Apollo now had to program their new, more expensive shows for a narrower potential audience.

Not helping, either, was the quiet move by mainstream radio in the '70s to resegregate much of its programming. In the mid-'60s, Top 40 radio might follow the perky pop of Herman's Hermits with the hard-core soul of Wilson Pickett, an eclectic blend that provided broad exposure for black music. A decade later, artists as popular as the Temptations or Freddie Jackson were largely relegated to black radio. That still gave them plenty of exposure, particularly along 125th Street, but the lack of Top 40 play dried up a large pool of potential fans—even though the idea that white audiences don't want to hear black music is refuted by every stage of American popular music history.

Beginning in the '60s and accelerating in the '70s, the ethnicity of uptown was changing, with Hispanics moving in alongside the long-established black population. In 1960 the U.S. Census Bureau didn't even have a "Hispanic" category. In 1971 Herman Badillo became the city's first Hispanic congressman. By

William "Poogie" Hart and Wilbert Hart of the Delfonics stand under the Apollo marquee advertising their performances there in May 1970.

1980 almost 10 percent of the city was Hispanic. Much
of this growth was centered uptown, and Dominican and
Puerto Rican immigrants had their own music.

To make it even harder for the Apollo
and the Harlem community, the whole city was in trouble.
By 1976 New York City was close to bankruptcy,
which meant both public and private money tightened.
Harlem—the last place to attract city dollars and
downtown investors—was the first to suffer.

Bobby Schiffman, who ran the Apollo with
his father, Frank, and then solo for many years, would
later acknowledge that the Apollo had quietly been up
for sale since the mid-'60s, when he reluctantly saw ever
harder times ahead for a theater of the Apollo's size.
Black community leaders, who had always regarded
the Apollo as an anchor for 125th Street, started talking
with Schiffman. By 1974, he later told *Showtime at the
Apollo* author Ted Fox, a plan had been mapped out to

Wilson Pickett pours it on in the '70s.
He was one of the top stars of
the Stax/Memphis sound, with hits
such as "In the Midnight Hour"
and "Mustang Sally."

reinvent the Apollo for survival into the next century: A group of black businessmen
led by Clarence Jones, owner of the *Amsterdam News*, Harlem's most successful
newspaper, would buy the theater. This group was to include Percy Sutton's Inner City
Broadcasting Corporation, the new owner of WBLS and WLIB. They would then tear
the Apollo down and replace it on the same spot with a complex that included a more
economically viable 3,000-seat theater, the two radio stations, the *Amsterdam News*,
and a 400-room hotel. But the deal died, said Schiffman, when interest rates spiked.
A year later he ran newspaper ads offering the Apollo, plus an office building, for
a price the *New York Times* pegged at $2 million. There was interest, but in the end
there were no takers. In January 1976 Schiffman shut the doors.

The next few years were the darkest, literally and metaphorically, in Apollo
history. While efforts to find a buyer continued, the theater suffered the same fate
as many shuttered buildings. One cold night the pipes froze and burst, ruining the
stage. The seats and other interior appointments, never assiduously maintained,
deteriorated further.

After more than two years with only the occasional one-shot show, a
mysterious group named the 253 Realty Corporation announced in March 1978 that
it was buying the theater. Sure enough, it reopened in May 1978 and brought
a few big names back, including James Brown, Sister Sledge, and War. But booker
Sparkie Martin told Fox that many artists were wary. The O'Jays turned down
$40,000 because they could do better elsewhere, said Martin. Teddy Pendergrass

Former Manhattan borough president, Apollo owner, and chairman of Inner City Broadcasting Corporation Percy Sutton (center) stands under the Apollo marquee in 1982 with Donald Cogsville (left) and Rev. William Marceus James (right).

considered the Apollo, then decided to play Jones Beach. Persistent rumors about the shadowy nature of 253 Realty also created uncertainty, and it was later reported that the only principal ever identified, Elmer T. Morris, had been arrested on charges related to a large-scale drug conspiracy. On May 6, 1981, 253 Realty filed for bankruptcy, citing the same cash-flow problems that had plagued the Schiffmans.

There was talk by then that the Apollo might simply be demolished. But at least two bidders promised to save it: a local church and Percy Sutton's Inner City Broadcasting. Inner City won it for $220,000, a giveaway price that clearly reflected that this was no longer prime real estate. Sutton himself said the purchase price would be the cheapest part of bringing the Apollo back. But he believed that resurrection was essential, if only because the Apollo meant so much to so many. Sutton often told the story of how, on the day he proposed to his wife, he stopped at the Apollo to watch the show, take a deep breath, and consider the rest of his life. The Apollo had been and could again be, he said, a centerpiece for a bruised community. "A vibrant Apollo," he said, "makes all of 125th Street more vibrant."

The tricky part was getting to "vibrant," and Sutton's plan was to make the Apollo serve the future by drawing on its past, which meant drawing full value from the fact it was a brand with international recognition. While a 1,500-seat theater would probably never be viable on live shows alone, Sutton saw the Apollo as advantageously positioned to create supplemental revenue streams, most prominently from television. TV and video material with the Apollo name, Sutton suggested, could create the same kind of distinctive brand appeal as an HBO. It could also offer state-of-the-art production facilities for the music community at large.

Over many months of slow negotiations and presentations, Sutton finally sold his vision to enough public and private backers to assemble a $20 million package of grants and loans. That money would overhaul the theater, from seats to stage to dressing rooms to bathrooms, and fund the high-tech production facilities. Sutton envisioned Apollo television shows, an Apollo record label, an Apollo Hall of Fame, and a general push to monetize the Apollo brand with everything from T-shirts to tours—all of which was still, he admitted, a gamble. Convincing music producers to journey uptown would take work. So would rebuilding the Apollo's concert reputation. The long-term plan incorporated several short-term years of red ink.

"We're sure we can make it work," he explained. "But from the failures we have seen before, we also know that, realistically, we will probably need closer to $40 million than $20 million." Sutton's speculation would prove prophetic.

In late 1982, as Sutton was envisioning the Apollo's long-term place in the world, a man with an even bigger personal stake in the immediate Apollo was reflecting about life on the inside. Whether the Apollo had a show or not, eighty-nine-year-old Francis "Doll" Thomas was there every day. It was habit, really, he said. He was there the day it opened its doors on January 26, 1934, and almost fifty years later, he'd never left except to go home at night to the apartment that Bobby Schiffman had found for him next door.

"I started as an electrician," he recalled. "I was one of the first licensed colored electricians in the city. I don't do much electrical work now. They won't listen to me. But when they can't find something, or don't know something, they ask me. I know where everything is."

He also figured he knew what the Apollo meant. "Before 1934, colored patrons at theaters were treated very poorly or not wanted at all," he said. "When the Apollo opened, it was the beginning of an era. This used to be a different community when the Apollo was going. The theater would bring people back at night, and they'd go shopping and so forth. After 7 o'clock now, the street looks like an armed

The daughter of well-known backup vocalist Cissy Houston and a cousin of Dionne Warwick, Whitney Houston shot her "Greatest Love of All" video in the Apollo production studio in 1986.

camp. All shuttered up. It will be a great thing for this community to open up again. It will start rebuilding the whole street."

Thomas also figured it would help the artistic community: "There's a lot of talent in the street now, but no place to do anything with it." A new generation of performers, he added as an afterthought, might even be more grateful than the current ones. "When performers got more independent, some of them got more unreliable," he said. "You'd have the crowd all set to start the show, and the performer wouldn't come out until he was good and ready. You can't explain that kind of temperament to the public. It got to the point where the tail was wagging the dog."

As Doll Thomas walked around the Apollo in 1982, he offered a running narrative on its pending renovation. "See the face of the balconies up there, that's original," he said. "But there are signs here and there that somebody did this or that. The second balcony boxes still have their original facing." He stopped when he got to the back door, the one where performers could step outside between shows. They'd mostly chat or have a smoke, but they could also walk a few steps to 126th Street, where some of the town's shadier entrepreneurs would offer things that weren't part of the official hospitality package. "Back here, it was dead," Thomas recalled. "Like a graveyard, nothing but grief." Ironically, he mused, fighting that kind of poison "is what theaters were for. You could go inside for a little while and forget your troubles. That's why, when they close, it's the worst thing in the world."

The Apollo reopened in late 1983, with a Christmas Eve edition of the signature Amateur Night. The renovation wasn't finished, but Sutton believed it was important to make the statement that the Apollo was back. On May 5, 1985, the theater hosted *Motown Salutes the Apollo*, a national television special featuring stars such as Patti LaBelle, Diana Ross, and Stevie Wonder. It had great ratings and won multiple awards. The production studio drew artists such as Whitney Houston, who shot her "Greatest Love of All" video there. Barbra Streisand did a video, Prince filmed a VH1 concert, James Brown and Bill Cosby came back. But the numbers never added up the way Sutton had hoped. While *Showtime at the Apollo* made money as a syndicated TV series, the day-to-day ink stayed red.

It was widely estimated that Sutton's Apollo Theater Investment Group ended up underwriting about $2 million a year in losses through the '80s. With a $2.4 million loss in 1990 and $2.1 million projected for 1991, Sutton reluctantly endorsed what he now called the inevitable: reorganizing the Apollo as a nonprofit (which, some wryly noted, it already was). Formal nonprofit incorporation would happen in 1992. It would not end the Apollo's perils. But the fact the theater had made it to yet another handoff did say it had survived the two worst decades of its life. Considering that few of its compatriots on the old TOBA circuit or even the mainstream theater circuit were even standing, never mind functioning, simple survival was a powerful testament to the Apollo's stature among America's theaters.

In the theater's most difficult days, a young singer named Luther Vandross kept coming back to Amateur Night until he won—because, he would later say, that was a stamp he wanted his embryonic career to have. It's also true that, by the end of the '80s, 125th Street had visibly revived, and while that wasn't all the Apollo's doing, the Apollo didn't hurt.

"You know," Doll Thomas reflected, "this theater has never looked as big as it is. It's got that big lip on the stage and then it goes up two balconies. You get a lot more audience here than you think—and without the audience, you've got no show. We always kept it pretty simple here. You bought your ticket, you walked in. The wall of pictures was on the left, popcorn was on the right."

And straight ahead, sometimes through the hardest times of trouble, remained a tenacious outpost of the American dream.

Would-be stars gather in front of the Apollo for the revived Amateur Night in the mid-'80s.

The Queen of Soul

Herb Boyd

Aretha Franklin in the early '70s. When Atlantic Records signed her in the mid-'60s, they guided her transformation from a jazz-pop balladeer to a mighty soul singer.

It may come as a surprise to many of her fans, but Aretha Franklin's first appearances at the Apollo in the early 1960s were not to perform. She was there to catch the Four Tops or one of the other fabulous Motown acts. "I myself couldn't play the Apollo because I didn't have any hits," she told David Ritz, who helped write her autobiography. "My show was tailored to jazz clubs and one-night venues. I felt it important to sing songs people knew and could sing along with."

Although she had already established herself among the divas of soul singers, it was not until the 1967 release of her debut Atlantic album, *I Never Loved a Man the Way I Love You*, that Franklin had the tunes the world could sing along with and also the hits she needed to get her name on the Apollo's marquee.

Of her early appearances as a performer at the Apollo, most Franklin aficionados recall her date there in the summer of 1971. Along with her previous hits at that time, including "Baby I Love You," "I Never Loved a Man," and Otis Redding's "Respect"—all selling more than a million copies—Aretha brought the house down with a stirring rendition of Simon and Garfunkel's "Bridge over Troubled Water." Complementing Franklin's memorable performance that evening were such showstoppers as King Curtis and the Kingpins, the Sweethearts of Soul, the LaRocque Bey Dancers, and comedian Stu Gilliam.

In 1974 Queen Aretha was once more on her throne at the Apollo, this time for an extended stay of six days. Opening day was typical of the nearly weeklong engagement as she serenaded her legion of admirers with a list of favorites, beginning with "Rock Steady" and "Day Dreaming." Arrayed in a long, white mink coat and having shed more than thirty pounds, Lady Soul now looked as captivating as she sounded. "It's really nice to be back in the Apollo," she said, before easing into a bluesy version of "Dr. Feelgood."

Franklin, 1967. Her late '60s stage outfits recalled the heyday of Bessie Smith.

She closed the set with "Spirit in the Dark," which left her fans pleading for more after they snapped out of the trance she had induced. It was vintage Franklin, and this was just the first night.

Later, outside the Apollo, fans were still exuberant, eager to share their impressions with reporters. "'Retha," one fan exuded to Gerald Fraser of the *New York Times*, "has the genius of combining all forms of black culture into music; the way black people approach the totality rather than an isolated aspect. Her voice and style have the totality of the experience of black people in this country. No matter how pained she is in the song, she is never the victim. She can deal with it. That's the way we are. We can deal with it." Those feelings were expressive of hundreds at this show and the succeeding shows during a triumphant week for "Soul Sister No. 1," among the sobriquets she had acquired in her march up the charts.

From this moment on, Franklin's appearances at the Apollo drew massive turnouts, with lines extending down 125th Street and around the corner. "People treated her like she was royalty," recalls Billy Mitchell, the Apollo's in-house historian, who in his more than forty years at the theater has seen a parade of Hall of Famers come and go. He isn't sure about the accuracy of one story Franklin has related during one stay at the Apollo, when she encountered the great Count Basie:

My fondest memory of the Apollo Theatre is one afternoon between shows; I was in the phone booth downstairs at the foot of the steps, and I was in there at the exact time that Count Basie liked to put his numbers in and play his horses. He almost beat the door of the phone booth off, yelling "Come on out of there now!" because I was talking to my boyfriend and there was no rushing me. He was in a panic on the other side of the door, and I did not know what was wrong with this man. I could not figure out why he was panicking the way he was until I heard later it was the time of day he played his numbers and his horses.

Basie's predilections were long forgotten by the time Franklin commanded the Apollo's stage again in 2006. Once again the comments from her fans offered the best barometers of her performance. "She was off the hook," was one effusive response on a blog. "I screamed for two hours. She opened with 'Respect' then 'Chain of Fools' and 'Dr. Feelgood' and she was incredible." Incredible is always the operative word when trying to describe the range and passion of Franklin's voice. As one devoted fan concluded after her most recent Apollo performance, "She was made for the Apollo, and the Apollo was made for her."

Aretha at the Apollo, 2006. Her appearances at the theater have always drawn legendary crowds.

Up South at the Apollo
Funk Takes Center Stage in the 1960s and '70s

Kandia Crazy Horse

George Clinton's Parliament performs in the '70s. One of his most popular stage props was a large spaceship that landed amid clouds of smoke.

Once upon a time in 1980, a giant egg landed on a ramp and cracked open to reveal a boogie child in a diaper and zebra-striped Afro, sucking on a bottle nipple. Amid the onstage glitter of an uptown Saturday night at the Apollo, mutant light lasers spidered a predominantly black audience awash in reefer madness. Members of the crowd were throwing devil horns, going wild as they awaited a ride upon some mythical entity called the Mothership. The intergalactic orchestra, fronted by a four-guitar army—in superhero garb straight from the wardrobes of Sun Ra, Liberace, and Screamin' Jay Hawkins—held down the beat on the One. And Dr. Funkenstein, in his long black

revolutionary son of the South and the Yankee territory known as "Up South." Yet his polemical, heavy funk was as fundamentally old school as it was futuristic, at core echoing the prewar sentiments of New Negro icon Paul Robeson, behind the horns' fanfare and tinselly garb: "I knew a Negro lawyer could only go so high, no matter how good he was. On the stage, it was different. Only the sky, I felt, could be my roof." Clinton and his carnivalesque cohorts did Robeson one better, tearing the roof off the sucker and aiming their sonic boom shots straight at the heart of the universe.

Heart of Darkness

Although Clinton, born in Kannapolis, North Carolina, was at the height of his personal sonic renaissance circa 1971, when his group released the incendiary "Wars of Armageddon," helming two bands simultaneously—the vocal-centric Parliament and the fuzzy freak show of Funkadelic— the sound at the heart of his projects was subtly on the wane, both at the Apollo and over America's airwaves. In retrospect, the Parliafunkadelicment Thang seems the end of the cycle officially kick-started by James Brown's inchoate innovation in a studio in Charlotte, North Carolina—the production of "Papa's Got a Brand New Bag" in 1965—rather than the genesis of a whole new thing (per Sly Stone's 1967 debut).

The star on funk at the Apollo had shone even earlier than the Mothership's final flight therein. Dixie "funk" was a term and sound already au courant in prewar New Orleans. Inasmuch as a large percentage of the black influx into Harlem in the early twentieth century derived from southeastern migrants, much of the rising talent and entertainment traditions on display at its nightspots could be said to stem from a southern, rootsy, and blues aesthetic—even as black Americans were ruthlessly modernizing, and these artists' hopes of crossover tempered any expressions of unfettered negritude.

In the years before Mr. Brown, the "Godfather of Soul," roared out of his Augusta, Georgia, base to permanently fix the funk at the Apollo in 1956 and in a universal cultural firmament, a cavalcade of stars with their roots in southern ecclesiastical

wig, exhorted his wonderfully deranged faithful to respond as an acid amen corner from beyond the exploding smudge pots, scream-singing: "ONE NATION, UNITED, UNDER A GROOVE!"

It's Nation Time

It is pure kismet that, just as America was undergoing its second revolution—its *only* true revolution, that is, the civil rights movement—in the 1960s, a sound powerful enough to reckon with the turbulence, changes, and newfound sense of black power would emerge, especially from the South. The Mothership's Lord of Misrule, George Clinton, was one such

and blues styles plied their trade on 125th Street: Sister Rosetta Tharpe, Big Mama Thornton, the Clara Ward Singers, and the Soul Stirrers featuring Sam Cooke (perhaps the last great benefactor of soul music, as he dazzlingly rode the line between the sacred and the profane in the '50s). Another significant development was the booking of all-star mambo shows at the Apollo, featuring such future legends as Tito Puente and Mongo Santamaría, highlighting the renaissance of African-derived rhythms, the Spanish tinge, and spirituality afoot in black and brown America.

Hail, Hail, Rock and Roll!

Some claim that when country and western (or hillbilly music) and rhythm and blues had a love child at the dawn of the '50s, they named it rock and roll. Others might not get tripped up in the nomenclature and merely focus on the new electric sensibility that pervaded most forms of black

Buddy Holly, ca. 1958. When Holly first played the Apollo, audience members (and management) were surprised to discover that he and his group, the Crickets, were white.

popular music after World War II. Yet the accelerated sounds *were* marred by an intransigent racial divide, one carried over from plantation days and the prewar "race records" industry, making it a provocative issue that Apollo honcho Frank Schiffman booked artists with hits, regardless of race, who had palpable appeal for his audience. So the stage was trod by the Four Aces, Bobby Darin, Jerry Lee Lewis, Jimmy Cavallo (the first white rocker to infiltrate the hall), and, rather famously—as recollected by Leslie Uggams and other Apollo denizens—Buddy Holly and the Crickets, during the era that cemented Mr. Brown's early stardom.

Holly's Apollo debut was salvaged during the band's third day of their week standby covering the sonic manifesto of Chicago boxer-turned-guitar-slinger Bo Diddley, born Ellas Otha Bates in McComb, Mississippi. Known for devising a trademark rectangular guitar, a Gretsch nicknamed "the Twang Machine," the late great Diddley was anointed as "the Originator" for his Promethean role in the transition of Delta blues and southern roots styles to rock and roll. Diddley's hard, protometal guitar sound was supplemented by a pulsating beat anchored to "hambone" and rumba rhythms (courtesy of ace Jerome Green's maracas). This made him a rock supernova well before the rise of Jimi Hendrix. Diddley enspelled Elvis Presley, when the so-called King of Rock and Roll caught his act at the Apollo in 1955, and he even surpassed comedienne Pearl Bailey's house record there. Then there's the little fact that Brother Bo and his legend provided a name for the dog Senator Ted Kennedy gave to the nation's first black president, Barack Obama, in 2009 amid the theater's seventy-fifth anniversary.

According to Ted Fox's *Showtime at the Apollo*, Bobby Schiffman said of the Originator:

> *Bo Diddley played jungle music....I remember the first time we had [Diddley] in the theatre, I thought we were gonna have an uprising. The music was so stimulating to everybody, including me, that it was whipping everybody into a frenzy. They never heard of anything like that. It was just a complete new, different style of singing. Rock and roll's main ingredient was the beat, and he was the leading*

```
BO DIDDLEY          Good blues singing guitarist.  Very well
6/10/55    Dr. Jive's Revue.    backed up by his own drummer.

8/19/55    Dr. Jive's Revue.    About the same routine.  Very low
                                down rhythm and exciting

4/11/55    Dr. Jive's Revue.    Same routine.  As exciting as usual

3/30/56    Dr. Jive's Revue     A quartette with an excellent guitarist
                                a poor drummer and a rather useless boy w
                                who plays the moroccos.  Reaction
                                indicates that we have had too much of
                                him.

8-24-56    1000.00    Registered better than previous show. Very
                      well received.

10/16/56   Dr. Jive's Revue. Same vein.

3/22/57    1000.00    Did opening number with violin.  Good.  Balance
                      same as heretofore.

8/30/57    $1,075.14.  Same

12/25/57   1,286.00   Not so exciting, but registered well.

10-17-58   1000.00    Popularity seems to have diminished to nothing
```

exponent of that. To him melody meant nothing, lyrics meant nothing, it was the beat that was infectious. That would drive you crazy. He really set the place on fire.

And yet, five decades later, the notion of black rock is anathema to young Wednesday Amateur Night audiences—based on this author's unscientific observations from the second balcony amid the choruses of boos and hip-hop patois heckling and banishing young black artists who would explore their inner blues-picker selves under that merciless spotlight. Of course, as Schiffman the younger once opined: "Black people don't care what happened yesterday, they want to know what's going to happen tomorrow." Back in the '50s and '60s—as now—crowds tended to be more comforted and reassured by straight shouters and male songbirds generating excitement through harmonic tension and release, often supported by chops-heavy but essentially faceless bands. The Coasters, Jackie Wilson, Hank Ballard and the Midnighters, Frankie Lymon, and the mentor Mr. Brown used to open for in his Apollo salad days, the tragic Little Willie John, more easily fit this category.

Bo Diddley on the Apollo stage, 1964. He was known for his famous "Bo Diddley beat," which often drove audience members to dance spontaneously in the aisles.

Screamin' Jay Hawkins rises from his casket, 1978. Famed for his kitschy stage routines, he was a talented R & B shouter who influenced performers from Little Richard to Alice Cooper and Marilyn Manson.

Star Time

One exception to the rules of who found favor at the Apollo was crucial: Funkadelica forefather Screamin' Jay Hawkins. The artist formerly known as Jalacy Hawkins, who once aspired to an operatic career in the vein of Paul Robeson, dropped his biggest smash, "I Put a Spell on You," in 1956, when Mr. Brown was establishing his star time at the Apollo.

Whereas Buddy Holly, early on considered to be black by unwitting listeners, won over the Apollo by channeling Diddley, Hawkins was too fearsome and eccentric to be mimicked until the rise of Alice Cooper, Black Sabbath, and such later shock rockers as Twisted Sister's Dee Snider and GWAR in the '70s, '80s and '90s. With a stage setup including a coffin, vampire cape, turban, a skull-topped stick dubbed "Henry," and other voodoo-reminiscent props, Hawkins was a clear trailblazer for what eventually made George Clinton's funk mob iconic, alongside Birmingham, Alabama—or is that Saturn?—native son Sonny Blount, aka Sun Ra, Kemetic rhythm scientist and leader of his intergalactic Arkestra.

Screamin' Jay, the wild orator of "Constipation Blues," showing years ahead of time that he could have held court with P-Funk's blitzed sybarites, fittingly told Ted Fox:

I used to love the Apollo. Directly across 126th Street there was a house where they sold white lightning, moonshine. They used to make it in the toilet. Used to get it in a little half-pint milk bottle. I used to wait until the last act before I was gonna go on, then I'd shoot across the street and get me some of that white lightning.… By the time I got in there, near the water fountain backstage at the Apollo, the bottle was empty.…The guy would call my name, and I'd ease out onstage. By then an explosion went off in my head. Those hot lights on me…

Then there was the little country colored boy from Macon, Georgia, who dominated the soul genre roughly between Mr. Brown and the Famous Flames' history-making album *Live at the Apollo* (1963) and the turn-of-the-'70s ascent of another Apollo habitué, Al Green: Otis Redding. A slow starter at Memphis's famed Stax label, Redding evolved a strain of particularly pathos-ridden deep soul, his gloriously gritty voice fearlessly exploring heartache, despair, and the hard times so familiar to black folks in a disintegrating Harlem and across the nation. Dig the September 1965 classic *Otis Blue* for an illustration—but first Redding had to follow Mr. Brown out of Macon's historic black vaudeville venue, the Douglass Theatre, to tackle the "black Vegas" of the Apollo. As Mr. Please Please "recalled" in his ghostwritten autobiography, *The Godfather of Soul,* Redding arrived to open there for the esteemed headliner sans charts for the Apollo house band. Mr. Brown directed his saxophonist and bandleader, St. Clair Pinckney, to pen the arrangements, which the former claimed were "the first ones [Redding] ever had, and I think they really helped him get over."

Get over, Otis "Mr. Pitiful" Redding did, in spades, with the vital aid of the Stax/Volt family, led by Booker T. Jones and his pioneering biracial southern band, the MGs, which supported Redding on wax and on tour until the singer's sad, untimely demise in 1967 (by plane disaster, like Buddy Holly). In the bold footsteps of Dr. King, and as his forebear Sam Cooke (deceased 1964) had evinced on "A Change Is Gonna Come," Redding and his generation of soul men preached a message to love in infinite ways before the Beatles were universally celebrated for it. They paved the sonic way for other Apollo favorites and major artists of the wider black world to follow in the '60s, such as Curtis Mayfield, Hendrix, Green, Sly Stone, and Motown titan Marvin Gaye—the Affrilachian song catcher who served as the polar opposite to the grit of Mr. Brown, Redding, and Joe Tex, yet still infused his hits and experiments with disembodied southern spirit and soul yodeling.

Redding's label mates Sam and Dave were also bold as love, albeit with a different bent: their 1966 monster hit, "Hold On, I'm Comin'," was banned by the FCC for six months because of its title, making future hip-hop censorship "battles" pale by comparison. Dave Prater, the duo's Georgian half—born in Ocilla, raised in Albany—remembered that they "had to sing the tune on every show at the Apollo. That was the 'in' thing, man, like they were really into it. I tell you what; it made a lot of babies that year."

If Redding's history-making embrace by the peace-and-love crowd at the 1967 Monterey Pop Festival rendered him a more ethereal soul man on a par with Dr. King, Sam and Dave extended the gutbucket styles of such fellow Atlantic Records mack daddies past and then current as Brother Ray Charles and the "Wicked" Wilson Pickett for mid-'60s uptown crowds punch-drunk on soul and Black Power allure. They obviously came across big time at the "black Grand Ole Opry," despite resurrecting a certain rustic air and dialects the venue's earlier smooth senders and militant comics eschewed. As Prater said, "In the Apollo it was like you were home."

Al Green at the Apollo in the '70s. He combined gospel fervor with smooth-voiced soul.

"Soul Men" Sam and Dave in their hit-making heyday, 1967. The duo helped define the Stax sound.

Otis Redding, 1967. He was second only to Sam Cooke in his impact on soul.

Uncle Jam Wants You

So, back to that giant flying egg!…

If cracked open, the cosmic egg of George Clinton's peculiar but legitimate crystallization of the black aesthetic would reveal not just all of the aforementioned cultural ancestors, but also the frustrations of Clinton's pilgrim's progress from early doo-wop days fronting the sharp-suited Parliaments from Plainfield, New Jersey—the quintet founded during Mr. Brown's first *anno mirabilis*, 1956—through the sprawling intergalactic big band's mid-'70s apotheosis with *Mothership Connection* and the attendant Earth Tour. Recording under assorted names, this psychedelic funk rock collective produced thirteen Top 10 hits in the American R & B music charts between 1967 and 1983 (including six number ones) and were inducted into the Rock and Roll Hall of Fame in 1997. Yet before these laurels and 1967's "(I Wanna) Testify / I Can Feel the Ice Melting" for

Revilot Records, the quintet struggled for acceptance and career sustenance, finally finding their fortunes turn with the rising tide of '60s sociopolitical turbulence and the Vietnam War. Clinton chose to move his backing group—Billy Bass Nelson (low-end theorist), Eddie Hazel (lead guitar), Tawl Ross (guitar), Tiki Fulwood (drums), and Mickey Atkins (keyboards)— to the forefront and dispense with the tight choreography and sartorial splendor that had served his Motown rivals such as the Temptations so well throughout the decade.

Supplicating his outfit before Mr. Brown's Rosetta stone of funk, Clinton also appears to have studied those other alternative and visionary acts that held sway at the Apollo during the '60s. These included the all-transvestite Jewel Box Revue booked every February; the classic quartet of North Carolina native John Coltrane, which took free jazz prophecy to the stage in 1962; the rhythmic incursions of breakout African stars Olatunji

Montage by Gordon "Doc" Anderson from the Jewel Box Revue's production, *25 Men and 1 Girl*. Female impersonators were a major draw at the Apollo in the '70s.

and Miriam Makeba in the late days of the decade; and, above all, the acid-drenched volume revolts and Afropean fusion of Jimi Hendrix—who won first place in an amateur musician contest at the Apollo in 1964, before his inner "Wild Man of Pop" erupted—and of Sly and the Family Stone.

Indeed, as the '60s faded into the bleaker '70s, Clinton drew from Sly Stone's wild creativity, studio wizardry, and will to never do the same thing twice—and then he ultimately made away like a bandit with various disgruntled giants of Mr. Brown's band, including Maceo Parker, Fred Wesley, and young brothers Catfish and Bootsy Collins, giving stoned soul and acid rock its last highlights. The purity and rigor of the fabled P-Funk horny horns was distilled from the Brown revue and the coruscating partnership between the Family Stone's Cynthia Robinson and Jerry Martini, permitting the roiling chaos of the guitar army led by Eddie "Jimi" Hazel to soar to unprecedented heights, while the rhythm section held it down securely enough to entice Apollo audiences to accept Funkadelic in the way post–chitlin circuit Hendrix never had been.

"What is soul?!" "I don't know!" goes the call-and-response kicking off 1970's *Funkadelic*, with Clinton and company's stance noncommittal as they flirted with many ideas in the mad swirl of the time, from in-studio fornication to the Jesus-and-Lucifer-worshipping Process Church. As then-rising Neo-HooDooist wordsmith/cultural critic Ishmael Reed proclaimed in his iconoclastic 1972 masterpiece, *Mumbo Jumbo*:

> *A new generation is coming on the scene. They will*
> *use terms like "nitty gritty," "for real," "where it's at,"*
> *and use words like "basic" and "really" with telling*
> *emphasis. They will extend the letter and the meaning*
> *of the word "bad."… they will have abandoned the*
> *other world they came here with and will have become*
> *mundanists pragmatists and concretists. They will*
> *shout loudly about soul because they will have lost it.*
> *And their protests will be a shriek. A panic sound.*
> *That's just the way it goes, brothers.*

George Clinton (in 1977, 2005, and at the Apollo in 2004) combines showmanship, a sense of stagecraft, and an ability to attract major talents to his groups.

This passage most accurately describes the social and cultural milieu into which Clinton interjected his own masterpieces, *Maggot Brain*, *America Eats Its Young*, and *Cosmic Slop*, teleporting the P-Funk brand of galactic gallows humor to the black college students, bewildered revolutionaries, and street kids who would throng his group's Apollo shows. Paternalism may be a contested charge where the Schiffman family is concerned, but Funkadelic took the empowering energy of the postsoul nu-black man to heart when they indicted famed West Coast venue owner and rock concert promoter Bill Graham with "Philmore," a space-age minstrel song about the group's lack of welcome in such hippie rock social arenas as the Fillmores.

To paraphrase Clinton, he pointedly conceived of P-Funk as a subgenre that whites and other nonblack artists could not co-opt in the ways Holly had covered Bo Diddley and Elvis Presley and many British Invasion rock stars of the '60s had trolled the Apollo in search of its black mystique. In the year of the Apollo's opening, the *New York Age* had declared: "Everything the Negro does on the stage or the screen is done with an idea of selling it to white people." Perhaps between "(I Wanna) Testify" and "Flash Light," Parliament-Funkadelic could not cross over, but they never really aspired to. They operated securely in their own potent, absurdist, ghetto sci-fi, floating dystopia, bringing vestigial messages of black nationalism and Shine-worthy signifyin' to cities from coast to coast and beyond, while the Movement foundered and "black is beautiful" again became a dirty phrase.

On another hallowed Apollo night in 2004, some time after the venerable old hall's grand splash return to active entertainment duty, this author was invited onstage to dance during "Atomic Dog," before a hooting, rapt P-Funk audience including a new generation of white jam band freaks and Dr. Henry Louis "Skip" Gates Jr., hopping around on his cane to defeat Sir Nose D'Voidoffunk and his dance-fearing allies. The group had ripped and roared all evening through twisted rockabilly, standards from mid-'70s concept albums featuring elaborate socio-sonic mythology and Pedro Bell's brilliant artwork, and gracefully incorporated the Dirty South crunk of Lil Jon into their own sacred/profane hot mess—*Au, skeet skeet skeet skeet!!*

That night they shored up the ideals of soul and black pride when a good deal was at stake, seamlessly reaching back to Cab Calloway hi-de-ho-ing through "Minnie the Moocher" and moonwalking fifty years before Michael Jackson, to Earl "Fatha" Hines's "Second Balcony Jump" ode to (unscathed) buzzard's roost leapers, to Bo Diddley surfing his Twang Machine past the stratosphere, to Screamin' Jay getting happy off a baby bottle of toilet liquor under the spots, to DJ Jocko Henderson of the 1280-on-the-dial "Rocket Ship Show" landing his craft onstage to announce acts, and to drummer/bandleader Chick Webb exiting an egg in 1937 to spur his orchestra to glory. Clinton the Funky President may have been temporarily supplanted by Obama, but he still shows no signs of slowing down, venturing inexorably forward in the new millennium like the Apollo to urge his people to keep on smilin' and shinin' under the sun, *under the sun, under the sun, under the sun, under the sun.*

The cover art of Funkadelic's 1973 album *Cosmic Slop* reflects Clinton's eclectic interests in Afro-Caribbean influences and his vision of a Pan-African universe.

Latin Music at the Apollo

Christopher Washburne

Reading histories of the Apollo Theater, one might think that Latin musicians rarely graced its hallowed stage. Nothing, however, could be farther from the truth. Though the numerous Latin bands and Latino musicians who regularly performed at the Apollo have been largely ignored in print, it can be argued that the Apollo was one of the most significant Latin American stages in the United States through the twentieth century.

Situated just blocks from one of the most vibrant Latin American neighborhoods in North America, Spanish Harlem or El Barrio, the Apollo was a nexus for intercultural exchange between African American and Latin musics, two musical lineages that have been inextricably linked for many years. Performances at the Apollo frequently paired those two traditions in innovative ways, popularized Latin music styles among African American audiences, and fostered new experimentation and stylistic mixing. Latin bands were often programmed as specialty acts within the variety show format favored by the Apollo's producers, Latino performers were featured as guest soloists with jazz and popular music groups, and a number of Latino musicians contributed and participated in the weekly performances of African American music.

Prior to the Apollo's inaugural show in 1934, Latin music was establishing a foothold in Harlem's theaters and clubs. As Latino populations grew in the mid-1920s, a number of Spanish Harlem venues such as the Golden Casino and the Park Palace's catering hall began programming daily performances in Spanish. As these productions became more professionalized, promoters sought established institutions outside of Spanish Harlem. Beginning in 1926, the theater known as the Apollo Burlesque became one of the principal venues featuring Sunday matinee all-Spanish productions. The Apollo Burlesque, owned by Sidney Cohen, was a small theater on 125th Street, located above the foyer of the Harlem Opera House (which happened to be partly owned by Frank Schiffman) and just down the street from the current theater. When Cohen acquired the present-day Apollo Theater in

1934, the Apollo Burlesque had just closed, so he borrowed the name in hopes of capitalizing on the smaller theater's past successes. The matinee shows at the Apollo Burlesque included zarzuelas (half-spoken, half-sung lyrical dramas) and their Cuban cousins known as *bufos cubanos*, along with the usual revues, musical numbers, and other vaudevillian entertainment. These shows helped launch the careers of many local Latin musicians and showcased a number of acclaimed bands from Cuba and Puerto Rico. For instance, the production on September 19, 1926, included the zarzuela *La fiesta de San Antón*, Vila Martínez and dancers, and the acclaimed Cuban band Sexteto Occidente, led by María Teresa Vera, which included Ignacio Piñeiro on bass (he would found the highly influential *son* group Sexteto Nacional in 1927).

By the time the new Apollo Theater opened its doors in 1934, the Cuban music that had graced the Apollo Burlesque's stage was having a significant impact beyond the confines of Harlem. Most notably, the Cuban *son*—which was misnamed in the United States as "rhumba"—had become the dance craze of the day. Because the new Apollo opted for a variety show format, rhumba bands and dancers were frequently programmed as specialty acts. These bookings provided high-profile exposure of the newest Latin dances to African American audiences and propelled Latin music groups, such as Alberto Socarras's band, to greater popularity.

At the same time, a number of Latino musicians regularly worked with the top black bands of the '30s that frequently appeared at the Apollo. For instance, Cuban trumpeter Mario Bauzá, who would later direct Machito's band, appeared a number of times at the Apollo as the lead trumpeter for Chick Webb, Noble Sissle, and Cab Calloway; Puerto Rican trombonist Juan Tizol performed with Duke Ellington; and Rafael "Ralph" Escudero played with Fletcher Henderson. All these bands had rhumbas and other Latin American styles in their repertoire and undoubtedly performed Latin music numbers at the Apollo. Latino musicians continued to perform in non-Latin music settings for many years. Panamanian saxophonist Walter Gene Jefferson, for example, played in the Apollo's house band throughout the '60s. Under the direction of saxophonist Reuben Phillips, the house band performed weekly, backing up every major star in black music.

During the post–World War II years, significant stylistic changes occurred in Latin music in New York, reflecting shifts in the social landscape, particularly concerning issues of race. An emboldened younger generation of innovative musicians began exploring their cultural roots through Pan-African explorations. A central figure in these newer trends was trumpeter Dizzy Gillespie, whose fascination with Cuban music spawned a new jazz hybrid in 1947 that he coined "Cubop." A major jazz innovator and popular bandleader, Gillespie performed at the Apollo for thirteen one-week engagements between the years of 1947 and 1953, introducing African American audiences to this new style. In fact, just days after he debuted Cubop at a Carnegie Hall appearance that featured Cuban percussionist Chano Pozo, he brought his band along with Pozo uptown to perform at the Apollo. Critic Dan Morgenstern documented how Pozo, a consummate performer and expert in Afro-Cuban religious practices, served as an impetus for a cultural shift in the jazz landscape through his staging of "African traditions." Morgenstern wrote that when Pozo, "a powerfully built black man stripped to the waist, bathed in purple light—lit an oil lamp and began to heat the skins of his congas, it was a tableau that created tremendous anticipation. And when he had finished his beautifully timed, unhurried, stately and dramatic preparations and began to play and chant, he gave everything the prelude had promised, and more." This respectful and informed display of

Trumpeter Mario Bauzá with bandleader Machito, 1940s. Machito led a popular Latin jazz band from the '30s to the '60s.

Graciela Grillo-Lopez and her brother, Machito, perform together on the Apollo stage. A featured singer in Machito's orchestra, Graciela was an early heroine of Afro-Cuban music.

Saxophonist James Moody, conga player Chano Pozo, and Dizzy Gillespie combine forces in the early '50s.

Famed disc jockey Symphony Sid, a pioneer in presenting Latin acts at the Apollo.

African traditions performed by a gifted Cuban musician singing in Yoruba diverged drastically from the "exotica" stagings of the '30s and resonated well with African American audiences at the Apollo. By conjuring a shared African heritage, Gillespie's Latin and jazz mixings sonically unified the two most prominent communities of Harlem and opened the doors for many other black and Latino collaborations at the Apollo.

Cuban bandleader Frank "Machito" Grillo and his Afro-Cubans, an important mambo group that featured both Latino and black musicians, was also central in creating this collaborative space. He appeared for thirteen one-week engagements at the Apollo from 1949 through 1962. These appearances were important in the popularization of the mambo throughout the black community

Cuban-born Latin jazz singer and bandleader Machito (Francisco Raúl Grillo) plays the maracas while leading his band, the Afro-Cubans, 1940.

and led to a high level of African American participation at
the famed Palladium Ballroom in midtown, one of the first truly
integrated dance floors in the United States.

A further boost to Latin music programming came in
March 1949, when prominent radio DJ and Latin music enthusiast
"Symphony Sid" Torin began producing weekly shows at the Apollo.
He teamed up with producer Monte Kay (from the Royal Roost jazz
club) to present the first "night club style stage show," a format
that would become a tradition at the Apollo. That first show
included Sid as the master of ceremonies, Machito and His Afro-
Cubans, the bop vocal team of Buddy Stewart and Dave Lambert,
singer Harry Belafonte, and trombonist Kai Winding and His
All-Stars. The initial success of this genre-mixing variety show
ensured future performances of Latin music at the Apollo, and Sid
continued to produce "theme-based" shows throughout the '60s.
His most audacious venture occurred in the first week of May 1954,
when he booked an unprecedented all-Latin show for his "Mambo-
Rhumba Festival." The week's engagement featured the mambo
bands of Joe Loco and Tito Puente, Cuban crooner Miguelito Valdés,
Cuban percussionist Candido Camero, Puerto Rican singer Myrta
Silva, Cuban singer Mercedes Valdés, Cuban bandleaders Arsenio
Rodríguez and Gilberto Valdés, and the Mambo Aces dancers.
Although the show was only moderately successful financially,
it set the stage for future Latin music presentations and introduced
a revue-style format that replaced the variety shows of the past.

In June 1960 Sid produced an "Afro-Jazz Revue" that
featured pianist and singer Hazel Scott, Bauzá and His Afro Jazz
Band (note the name change to better fit the theme!), jazz flutist
Herbie Mann and his Quintet, Nigerian percussionist Babatunde
Olantunji and his band, and jazz drummer Philly Joe Jones and
his Sextet, which included Cuban percussionists Carlos "Patato"
Valdés and José Mangual. In May 1964 Sid produced a "Latin
Americana" show that featured Cuban vocalist Celia Cruz
(her Apollo debut), Machito, Puerto Rican boogaloo artist Joe
Cuba, Latin jazz vibraphonist Cal Tjader, and singer Al Hibbler.
His "Afro-Latin Jazz" program in February 1964 featured mambo

Eddie Palmieri, 1987. He was a celebrated Latin jazz bandleader and showman, who helped popularize the music from Harlem's streets to around the world.

percussionist Tito Puente, Cuban percussionist Mongo Santamaría,
Cuban singer La Lupe, R & B singer Arthur Prysock, Joe Cuba,
and the Tommy Jonsen Dancers, along with the feature film
Lilies of the Field, starring Sidney Poitier. Throughout the '50s
and '60s Symphony Sid was responsible for bringing every major
Latin music act to the Apollo, ensuring wide exposure to the latest
Latin dances and maintaining the Apollo as one of New York's
preeminent Latin music venues.

Besides Sid's productions, the Amateur Night shows at
the Apollo also featured Latin music acts. A notable example
was pianist Eddie Palmieri, who first appeared at the Apollo in an
amateur show in 1950 as a sideman in a small Latin jazz combo.
Although the group did not win that evening, Palmieri returned
in 1964 for a week's engagement with his newly formed band,
called La Perfecta, which featured a distinctive instrumentation of

Tito Puente on the vibes, 1954. One of the most beloved bandleaders in New York's Latin jazz community, he won five Grammy Awards over a career that exceeded five decades.

two trombones, flute, and rhythm. This powerful, bluesy sound would revolutionize the sound of salsa within the next few years. With so many shows per day, Palmieri started to improvise a riff at the end of each set to serve as an impromptu theme song. Over the course of the week, trombonist Barry Rogers added melodic phrases to it, transforming the riff into a number that would later become one of the band's hits, "El Tema del Apollo."

With the rising popularity of soul and funk, the decline of mambo, and the emergence of salsa, the '70s saw a decline in Latin music at the Apollo. Early salsa stars such as Willie Colón, who performed his hit "Che Che Colé" on a soul revue show in April 1970, did not cross over well to Apollo audiences. Bobby Schiffman complained in his notes that Colón was "too Latin" and "did not fit." Salsa, a Latin music genre that was inspired by the civil rights movement, was forged by a young generation of Latino musicians attempting to assert Latino cultural pride through music. This culturally introspective musical expression did not easily translate to African American audiences. Colón's lack of success marked the end of the Apollo's service as a central meeting space for black and Latino culture in Harlem. The theater closed

TITO PUENTE & BAND
6/12/53 $2700.00   First appearance. Good Mamba band. PUENTE is a very co-operative person. No drawing power. (Contract Price $2750.00 plus $96.00 for two hour rehearsal).

1/29/54 $2846.00   A highly intelligent and capable musician. The band is excellent and it seems to be quite popular.

5/7/54   Mambo-Rhumba Festival. Played entire show for Mambo-Rhumba Festival. Good.
$3000.00

3/11/55   Sarah Vaughan Revue. Played show satisfactorily. Four specialty numbers all good. Band a very co-operative and worthwhile one.

Good performance. Some popularity. Was well paid at indicated price.

9/2/55 $3000.00   Katherine Dunham Revue. Played show very well.

1/27/56   3,250.00   Excellent show band. Opened show very well cooperative colorful. Well recieved. Tito later added girl to good

3/1/63

effect.

its doors in 1976, at the height of salsa's popularity, just as the music began appealing to more diverse audiences.

Since the theater reopened in 1983, Latin music has returned to the Apollo only for special events. In 1987 Tito Puente helped organized a tribute to Machito that was filmed and later televised. He hired a young dancer named Eddie Torres to choreograph several numbers, and Torres credits the televised show as the seminal moment for launching the mambo dance revival and for establishing his dance company. The Eddie Torres Dancers have been one of the most influential Latin dance groups in New York over the last twenty years, staging numerous mambo shows and offering dance instruction throughout the city. Celia Cruz and Puente returned on March 23, 1990, to take part in a performance staged in celebration of the recent release of Nelson Mandela, sharing the bill with South African singer Miriam Makeba. Two years later, the Second Annual Caribbean Music Awards were held at the Apollo, featuring a number of salsa groups including Puente, José Alberto, Ray Sepúlveda, Conjunto Imagen, and Johnny Ray. The most recent return of Latin music came on June 22, 2001, when a group of independent producers attempted to launch a "Latin Nites at the Apollo" series, booking Rubén Blades, Ednita Nazario, and Franco De Vita. I had the pleasure of performing with Blades that evening, and though we played to an enthusiastic and sold-out crowd, the series has yet to be continued. Hopefully it will be revived soon, to continue the Apollo's tradition of providing a special meeting place for Latin and African American musicians, bringing together the two most prominent communities of Harlem and fostering innovative musical exchange.

Bandleader/conga player Mongo Santamaría was famous for his composition "Afro Blue" and for his cover of Herbie Hancock's "Watermelon Man."

Young amateurs vie for the prize on Apollo's Amateur Night playing maracas, bongos, and conga drums, 1952.

Bandleader Joe Cuba on the congas, 1970. He moved from Latin jazz fusion to "Latin boogaloo" in the '60s.

Celia Cruz

Christopher Washburne

Celia Cruz dances in a typical colorful costume. Her vibrant stage shows wowed audiences from Las Vegas to the Apollo and around the world.

Celia Cruz, born Úrsula Hilaria Celia Caridad Cruz Alfonso, debuted at the Apollo Theater in a weeklong engagement that began on May 29, 1964. By that time, Celia was already a seasoned performer, having had an illustrious career in Cuba. In the 1950s she had been regularly featured on Cuban radio broadcasts, had headlined at Havana's premier Tropicana nightclub, and was the lead singer with Sonora Matancera, one of the island's most acclaimed bands. After immigrating in 1961, her popularity within the United States grew as she quickly established herself as the preeminent female vocalist in Latin music, evidenced by an invitation to debut at Carnegie Hall on September 27, 1963. So it's not surprising that Celia received top billing over some of Latin music's biggest stars when radio personality Symphony Sid Torin invited her to perform for the first time at the Apollo.

Sid had compiled a roster of performers that departed from his typical variety-show format, which favored a combination of music styles, dancers, singers, bands, circus acts, and comedians. Instead the week's bill mainly featured Latin music acts. This was a risky venture, since most previous all-Latin music bookings had proven financially disastrous for the theater. In an interview with the *Amsterdam News*, Bobby Schiffman lamented that all-Latin shows "just didn't seem to have a valid appeal in the Black community." Sid's decision to feature a generational blend of performers proved visionary, yielding one of the Apollo's most financially successful Latin shows to date.

Appearing with Celia that week was the mambo star Machito and his band, Apollo regular Al Hibbler, an African American vocalist and civil rights activist, and emerging young stars such as the innovative Latin jazz vibraphonist Cal Tjader, percussionist extraordinaire Willie Bobo, and boogaloo sensation Joe Cuba. Because all the other artists had previously appeared at the Apollo, Celia's presence was credited with providing the additional draw that made the week's engagement such a success. Frank Schiffman effusively wrote about Celia's debut in his personal notes: "A real Star. Looks like Jo Baker and sings and dances with great animation." Thus began Cruz's long and productive association with the Apollo, which would last for close to forty years. Throughout her career she returned to the Apollo stage, appearing with the best bands and musicians in Latin music, including Tito Puente, Johnny Pacheco, Ray Barretto, Sonora Matancera, and José Alberto, among others.

For Celia, an artist who was particularly attuned to and proud of her Afro-Cuban heritage and interested in exploring those roots through performance, appearing at the premier venue for African American music was particularly significant. In her autobiography, she expressed how honored she felt to perform on "the same stage where the greatest figures in African American entertainment had delighted crowds." Her energetic performance style, virtuosic vocal abilities, larger-than-life stage presence, and proud assertions of African pride resonated equally well with both Latino and African American audiences, regardless of the fact that many audience members attending Apollo performances could not understand Spanish.

In some ways, Cruz's presence transformed the Apollo into a truly transcultural space, bringing the two most prominent communities of Harlem, black and Latino, together through music. Promoters often included her in events that centered on themes of unity. On March 23, 1990, for example, she took part in a truly historic event, a performance staged in celebration of the recent release of Nelson Mandela. Celia shared the bill with South African singer Miriam Makeba, the Tito Puente Orchestra, and Forces of Nature, a New York–based dance troupe. Upon taking

Already a major star when she made her Apollo debut in 1964, Cruz was thrilled to work "the same stage where the greatest figures in African American entertainment had delighted crowds."

the stage, Celia sang a tribute to the Orisha Shango, a deity prominent in a number of neo-African religious traditions. Her blend of older African traditions with contemporary salsa sounds aptly captured the spirit of the emancipative celebration by symbolically sounding out the shared cultural heritage between Africa and Harlem, all of which compelled the elated crowd to transform the Apollo into a raucous Latin dance club.

Throughout her long and illustrious career, the historic stage of the Apollo Theater provided a special space for Celia to realize her greatest potential. She was a catalyst for bringing diverse communities together in musical celebration.

Cruz (center, front row) and members of Fania All-Stars, 1971. Her elaborate shows included musicians, backup singers, and dancers, as grand as a Vegas revue.

5

A New Apollo for a New Harlem: The Apollo Theater in the 1990s and 2000s

1991

The Apollo Theater Foundation, a nonprofit organization, is established to manage, fund, and program the Apollo Theater.

1992

Ray Chew & the Crew begin their tenure with the Apollo as house band for *Amateur Night* and later *Showtime at the Apollo.*

1993

Prince plays the Apollo in an exclusive VH1 concert.

1994

A tribute to Martin Luther King Jr. launches the Apollo Theater Foundation's first performance series.

1997

Tony Bennett sells out the Apollo in an engagement honoring Billie Holiday.

1999

Korn is the first rock band to perform at the Apollo. The concert is broadcast worldwide via satellite, Webcast, and radio.

Comedian **Chris Rock** records his HBO special, *Bigger and Blacker*, live at the theater.

2000

The Apollo Theater and Jazz at Lincoln Center partner to present Jazz for Young People concerts.

2001

The Apollo begins a major restoration and renovation of its facade and marquee.

Whoopi Goldberg launches her first tour in a decade at the Apollo.

Maxwell, David Byrne, and the Strokes make their Apollo debuts to sold-out audiences.

2002

George C. Wolfe's new musical, **Harlem Song**, opens to enthusiastic reviews and has a six-month run.

The Apollo Theater Academy is launched.

2003

Jonelle Procope becomes president and CEO of the Apollo Theater Foundation.

2004

The Apollo celebrates its
Seventieth Anniversary with
a gala hosted by Denzel
Washington and featuring
Ashanti, Patti LaBelle,
Savion Glover, Bob Dylan,
Gerald Levert, and
Brian McKnight.

2005

The Salon Series, an
incubation and performance
program for new artistic
works, is established.

The first phase of theater
restoration is completed with
the installation of more than
1,500 new house seats,
a restoration of the facade,
a **new marquee**, and a
new stage.

2006

The Apollo Legends
Hall of Fame is created.

Following his death,
James Brown's body lies in
state on the Apollo stage,
drawing tens of thousands
of mourners.

The Apollo Theater
Education and Community
Outreach program is
launched.

2007

Ashford and Simpson
star in the Apollo's Legends
Concert Series.

The Apollo's long-running
syndicated television show
Showtime at the Apollo
comes to an end.

The Performing Arts Series
begins on the main stage.

2008

Denzel and Pauletta
Washington receive the
Ruby Dee and Ossie Davis
Humanitarian Award.

Elvis Costello films a
Sundance Channel television
series on the Apollo stage.

Celebrating the release of
the group's first album in
over thirty years, **Labelle**
returns to the Apollo for a
special reunion concert.

2009

The Apollo Theater launches
its Seventy-fifth Anniversary
season.

June 25

A spontaneous tribute to
Michael Jackson grows
outside the theater following
his passing. A memorial
service is held at the theater
on June 30.

An Anchor in Harlem
Apollo, More Than a Theater

David J. Maurrasse

How appropriate that throngs of mourners and

revelers congregated outside the Apollo Theater in summer 2009 upon learning of the death of Michael Jackson. That energetic young man from Indiana and his brothers had once exploded across that stage, launching a colossal entertainment enterprise. It was just as fitting when Barack Obama took the theater's stage in November 2007, expressing his combination of lofty eloquence and street-rally community organizing oratory, along his historic and meteoric path to the U.S. presidency.

The Apollo's heart beats with the performing arts, especially that which emanates from the African American experience. Gaining the favor of a raucous and discriminating Apollo crowd evolved into a proverbial stamp of approval for the highest levels of entertainment that the black community could provide. To this day, "Showtime at the Apollo" displays the competitive spirit of hardworking performers hoping to become the next megastars or, at the very least, to finish their acts before succumbing to the collective rattle of displeasure. Just as much as an Apollo crowd could extinguish, so it could ignite; this bolstering ability is what so many would-be performers have coveted.

Imagine 125th Street without that historic neon sign at the center of its vibrant corridor. The street itself, which attracts visitors worldwide, benefits from the presence of its various assets, with the Apollo at its core. Despite the emergence of chain retail that could just as easily be on 34th Street, the presence of the Apollo and its historically preserved look and feel reminds us all of the distinctiveness of Harlem's rich culture and history. We know of the Apollo's historic significance, but what constitutes an Apollo for today and the future? How has the Apollo adapted to a changed world, and how will it adapt to a continually altering Harlem?

The Apollo, now on the National Register of Historic Places, remains a unique attraction that brings visitors and dollars to the surrounding community. Although many come simply to tour the facility or pay homage to its past, the Apollo continues to present special events (such as 2008's Labelle reunion concert, with its memorable acoustic performance by the trio during a storm-caused power failure) and ongoing educational and performance workshops. In addition to maintaining its historic role as a performing space, the Apollo has evolved into a

Democratic presidential candidate Barack Obama greets supporters at the Apollo Theater on November 29, 2007.

The restored Apollo theater marquee remembers the great singer/dancer Michael Jackson after his death in June 2009.

center of community life. Its meeting spaces have hosted many critical presentations and discussions relevant to the surrounding area. Its overall engagement with the community has expanded and diversified.

As Harlem reinvented itself in the 1990s, the Apollo underwent its own transformation. Harlem was in, then out, and then in again between the mid-'70s and the '90s. In its leaner years, the neighborhood saw capital fly away, but the Apollo, along with many of Harlem's historic sites, remained. There were of course many other institutions that weathered this tough period, including the Studio Museum in Harlem, the Dance Theatre of Harlem, Jazzmobile, The Harlem School of the Arts, National Black Theatre, Aaron Davis Hall, and the venerable Schomburg Center for Research in Black Culture. New institutions have also arisen, such as the National Jazz Museum and Harlem Stage, to preserve Harlem's rich cultural history while also

The Apollo's resident historian, Billy Mitchell (holding camera) photographs tourists as they gather around the Tree of Hope, now on the Apollo stage.

promoting emerging artists. But the Apollo has remained a particularly visible anchor institution through changing times. Despite its financial trials, someone has always identified enough value in the theater to keep it going.

The Apollo continues to be open to experimentation and innovation in trying to find the right mix of education and entertainment. Just as it segued from the old-time variety format to the R & B shows of the '60s, the Apollo in the '90s tried various different formats to bring new audiences to the theater. Perhaps the bravest and most innovative was the mounting of George C. Wolfe's 2002 production, *Harlem Song*, both an overview of the theater's—and community's—entertainment history and a statement of its continued vitality. The production was noteworthy not only for its live performances but for its incorporation of historic photographs and video interviews with many of the Apollo pioneers—from name performers to chorus girls. But the show was as much a challenge to the present as an ode to the past. As Wolfe himself wondered to a *New York Times* reporter at the time, "Will this piece bring about economic rejuvenation [to Harlem and the Apollo]?" Unfortunately, the costs of mounting such an ambitious project could not be sustained by the size of the audiences. But the show did stand as an important statement of the theater's intentions to continue producing new work relevant to its audience.

A nonprofit organization after it was acquired by the state of New York in 1991, the Apollo has expanded its mission, taking advantage of its history and its significance to the Harlem community. The Apollo Theater Foundation boasts a range of programs serving the community and complementing its historic role. For aspiring students of the arts, the Apollo Theater School offers a full curriculum in theater, music, and dance. For those in midcareer, the Apollo Salon Series gives access to Apollo resources to help create new material and produce two performances, followed by dialogue with audiences. The lively dialogue between audience and creators that made the Apollo's Amateur Night famous in its day continues in this modern version of give and take.

The Apollo's community engagement is reflected in many special programs that highlight African American history and culture. These activities for the community include health fairs, daily tours, and talent competitions for seniors and children.

Renovating the theater is another important mission for the current Apollo management. In 2005 a major $96 million restoration campaign began, the first phase of which included refurbishment of the facade, storefront, and box office. This phase produced a new marquee with LED visuals, newly high tech but also preserving the '40s design style and features. Even such a simple feature can provide a powerful message: the new marquee has become a highly photographed icon of the reborn Apollo. The second phase of renovations will address the interior and lobby, including an additional 4,000 square feet for community and education use.

Sightseeing tours on the Uptown Loop discuss Harlem's vibrant neighborhood and drive by the Apollo on 125th Street, 2007.

As 125th Street and the Harlem community as a whole continue to evolve, the significance of the arts to the neighborhood has remained evident. The rebirth of the Apollo in the midst of a range of residential, commercial, and demographic changes in the area delivers a strong statement about the unique culture that Harlem has brought to the nation and the world. Harlem as a neighborhood is more than a physical space; it is a compelling expression of the culture and experiences of African Americans and those of African descent worldwide. Harlem is perhaps the best-known neighborhood in the world, one that has become synonymous with African American culture and life. It is this tradition that attracts tourists from all over the world—a tradition epitomized by the Apollo.

The preservation and renovation of the Apollo reflect the broader recognition of the distinctive culture and history that have made Harlem more than a neighborhood. The Apollo has not only embraced the responsibility of upholding traditions that have made tremendous global contributions; it has also transcended its historic role and expectations, morphing into an even more direct partner with its community. The seventy-fifth anniversary has been a most appropriate time to reflect on the Apollo's many contributions over the years and to enhance the direction of an iconic institution on the rise. Indeed, the Apollo is a hallmark of Harlem's past, but it is poised to become a critical feature in the neighborhood's future.

Rap Music and Hip-Hop Culture

Mark Anthony Neal

At the very historical moment that chitlin circuit institutions such as the Apollo Theater began to lose prominence in black communities in the mid-1970s, a seemingly new form of urban expression began to emanate from street corners, parks, community centers, and apartment building vestibules throughout New York City. By the end of the twentieth century, rap music and hip-hop culture were pervasive in American and increasingly global culture, representing a multibillion-dollar economy in itself and becoming one of America's leading cultural exports. By-products in part of the emergence of the postindustrial city, rap music and hip-hop culture are also part of a generation of contemporary black expressive arts shaped by the sensibilities and processes that chitlin circuit institutions helped to foster decades earlier.

Rhythmic rhyming over music was not a new phenomenon when Clive Campbell (aka Kool Herc), often referred to as the "founding father of hip-hop," immigrated to the United States in 1967. Musicians and artists such as Cab Calloway ("Hi-De-Ho") and Dewey "Pigmeat" Markham ("Here Come de Judge") had performed popular precursors to rap music at the Apollo and elsewhere, and heavyweight boxing champion Muhammad Ali often engaged in rhyming banter aimed at demeaning his opponents. Additionally there was the example of the black arts movement of the '60s, which stimulated a renewed interest among African American youth in poetry and the spoken word, perhaps best exemplified by the poetry of Sonia Sanchez, Nikki Giovanni, Amiri Baraka (Leroi Jones), and Haki Madhubuti (Don. L. Lee), as well as the spoken-word recordings of the Last Poets, Gil Scott-Heron, and the Watts Prophets.

Campbell's immediate musical influences were the mobile DJ sound systems he was exposed to as a child in his native Jamaica. Campbell's family was part of a wave of immigrants who came to New York City in the aftermath of the Immigration and Nationality Act of 1965, which increased immigration from non-European countries. The influx of different cultural sensibilities from the Caribbean made New York City, and the Bronx in particular, fertile for the new cultural practices that hip-hop came to represent. Circulating largely in black and Latino enclaves in New York City, hip-hop culture developed as an underground phenomenon that encompassed four major elements: dance (b-boying/b-girling and break dancing), visual arts (graffiti), turntablism (DJing), and spoken word (MCing).

The culture begin to flourish within the context of an erosion of social services, diminished funding to public schools, high unemployment rates, and the general demise of the quality of life in New York, which was in the midst of a financial crisis in the mid-'70s. In the Bronx, many black and Latino communities were disrupted and displaced in the name of development with the building of the Cross Bronx Expressway in the 1960s under the auspices of Robert Moses, who then oversaw all public works projects in New York City. The aim of the Cross Bronx Expressway was to connect northern New Jersey with Queens and Long Island, making both commerce and leisure more efficient. Stable black, Latino, and working-class white communities in the Bronx were sacrificed in the process. The period also witnessed the transformation in some cities from an industrial-based economy to a service-based economy. Journalist and historian Jeff Chang describes the impact of the transition on the Bronx: "the South Bronx had lost 600,000 manufacturing jobs; 40 percent of the sector disappeared. By the mid-seventies, average per-capita dropped to $2,430, just half of the New York City average and 40 percent of the nationwide average."

Against this backdrop, in the early '70s Campbell and his sister Cindy began giving parties at a community center at 1520 Sedgwick Avenue in the Bronx, in an attempt to provide social alternatives to the rampant gang culture of the period. It was during one of these parties that Campbell, a DJ by trade, began to experiment with "break beats"—the highly rhythmic and percussive portions of records, or what Campbell called the "get-down part"—recognizing that his audiences would become

The Sugarhill Gang

Afrika Bambaataa

Kool Herc
Cold Crush Brothers

Grand Wizard Theodore
Kurtis Blow

Queen Latifah

Salt-n-Pepa

4

Run-DMC

animated during those portions of his set. James Brown recordings became early and lasting favorites among DJs, as Michael Holman writes: "James Brown created the ultimate dance music because it had unrelenting repetitive beats and rhythms that could make us dance forever." Brown's break beat in the song "Funky Drummer" was a particular favorite. But DJs also found break beats from more eclectic sources, as was the case with Afrika Bambaataa, one of Campbell's peers who also gave parties during the era in the Bronx River Housing Project. Bambaataa credits his mother with introducing him to "the Motown sounds, James Brown sounds, the Stax sounds, Isaac Hayes and all of them. As well as Edith Piaf, Barbra Streisand, the Beatles, the Who, Led Zepplin." Campbell's use of the break beat, later refined by Bambaataa, Joseph Saddler (Grandmaster Flash), and Theodore Livingston (Grand Wizard Theodore), became the foundation for contemporary rap music. Bambaataa, who was a member of the Black Spades, a notorious youth gang in the Bronx, also helped drive youth away from the gangs and into the emerging culture.

The subgenre's appeal began to grow beyond its origins when rap music was first formally recorded in the late '70s (cassettes tapes of live DJ and rapper sets at clubs and parks had long been commercially available). The Fatback Band's "King Tim III's Personality Rap" is generally regarded as the first commercially available rap single, though "Rapper's Delight, " recorded by the Sugarhill Gang in 1979, would prove the most influential. Released on Sylvia Robinson's Sugarhill Records, "Rapper's Delight" would break into the Top 40 pop charts and spark an interest in rap music, largely among independent labels. Unknown at the time of its release, some of the lyrics to "Rapper's Delight" were written by Curtis Fisher (Grandmaster Casanova Fly), who was never credited or compensated, despite the song's popularity. Fisher was a member of the Cold Crush Brothers, one of the many early influential groups that did not make the transition from hip-hop culture's informal economy to the more corporate-shaped rap music that began to appear in the early '80s. Other successful acts in this period were Spoonie Gee ("Love

Rap"), Kurtis Blow ("The Breaks"), and the Sequence ("Funk You Up"). The genre began to generate critical acclaim on the strength of Grand Master Flash and the Furious Five's social commentary "The Message," and Bambaataa's "Looking for the Perfect Beat" and "Planet Rock" emerged as two of the most popular singles of the first generation of artists.

Films such as Charlie Ahearn's *Wild Style* (1982) and the Tony Silver and Harry Chalfant's PBS documentary *Style Wars* (1983) were also instrumental in helping rap music and hip-hop culture reach a wider audience. *Wild Style* documented the increasing interest in graffiti art within the downtown art scene, where artists like Fred Braithwaite (Fab 5 Freddy), Keith Haring, Jean-Michel Basquiat, Sandra Fabara (Lady Pink), and Lee Quiñones made inroads. Photographer Martha Cooper's book *Subway Art* helped capture this particular moment in the development of hip-hop visual art. In the arena of dance, mainstream films such as *Breakin'* (1984) and *Beat Street* (1984) took advantage of the popularity of break dancing, which could regularly be witnessed on the streets of Manhattan, with the influential Rock Steady Crew appearing in the latter film. By the mid-'80s, rap music and hip-hop culture began to generate more crossover appeal, largely on the strength of Run-DMC (Joseph Simmons, Darryl McDaniels, and Jason Mizell), who successfully fused hip-hop rhythms with rock guitars on tracks like "Rock Box" (1984) and "King of Rock" (1985), which established them as the best-selling rap act of the era.

Run-DMC reached their commercial peak with the release of *Raising Hell* in 1986. The album was the genre's first platinum-status recording, selling more than three million copies. It included the group's seminal collaboration with the noted rock band Aerosmith on the track "Walk This Way." A cover of an earlier hit for Aerosmith, Run-DMC's version was instrumental in helping rap music break into regular rotation on the dominant music video channel, MTV. When that channel was launched in the summer of 1981, it had largely ignored the music of black artists. Although the late Michael Jackson was prominently featured on the channel in the mid-'80s, it was slow to embrace rap music. The crossover success of Run-DMC and the Beastie Boys convinced many entertainment entities that there were audiences for hip-hop culture beyond black and Latino youth. MTV debuted its first hip-hop–themed program, *Yo! MTV Raps*, in August 1988, and the program immediately generated some of the highest ratings on the network. A year later, Black Entertainment Television (BET) debuted its own rap music show, *Rap City*. It was also during this period that the Apollo Theater begin to regain national visibility via the *It's Showtime at the Apollo* television series; Run-DMC was prominently featured during the program's first season in 1987.

The commercial success of hip-hop culture in the late '80s intensified efforts by mainstream corporate labels to sign rap acts, distribute the music of independent rap labels, and create rap-themed boutique labels. Warner Brothers' relationship with the Cold Chillin' label, home to influential acts such as Big Daddy Kane, Biz Markie, MC Shan, Roxanne Shanté, and Kool G Rap, is one example of such a relationship. Cold Chillin' began its first national tour in November 1988—the Juice Crew All-Star Show—opening at the Apollo Theater in a show that *New York Times* critic Peter Watrous described as "intense and fevered." Ice Cube also came to the Apollo in July 1991 on a national tour that supported his solo album debut, *AmeriKKKa's Most Wanted*, while he was also promoting his first major film role in John Singleton's *Boyz in the Hood*. While many large arenas were fearful of booking rap artists during this era (because of several well-publicized acts of violence at rap shows), the Apollo Theater showed a willingness to open its doors to rap stars.

The period of 1987–92 is often referred to as the golden age of rap music, in part because it was an era that was largely defined by its inclusivity, with successful acts running a gamut of styles and lyrical content. Groups as diverse as Salt-n-Pepa, De La Soul, Queen Latifah, Special Ed, Boogie Down Productions (KRS-One), Eric B and Rakim, N.W.A., DJ Jazzy Jeff and the Fresh Prince, Public Enemy, Kool Moe Dee, Slick Rick, Doug E. Fresh, MC Lyte, and Whodini all found audiences. The period marked the

transition of the so-called old-school era of hip-hop, exemplified by acts such as Kurtis Blow and even Run-DMC, to a new generation of acts whose narratives touched on black nationalist politics, middle-class lifestyles, feminist issues, Five-Percent Nation ideology, the drug trade, and police brutality. Two milestones from this era spoke to the changing fortunes of rap music and hip-hop culture: DJ Jazzy Jeff and the Fresh Prince (Will Smith) won the first Grammy Award in the category of "Best Rap Performance," and N.W.A.'s release *efil4zaggin* became the first rap album to top the pop charts in June 1991. N.W.A.'s success, with virtually no radio airplay, was the direct by-product of the introduction of the Nielsen SoundScan system to compute record sales. With the use of the new system, rap music's prominence in the recording industry became solidified, with N.W.A.'s style of "gangsta rap" becoming one of the most popular styles. The popularity of gangsta rap also led to a heightened public scrutiny of the content of some rap music, exemplified in the obscenity charges against the Florida-based group 2 Live Crew and the controversy over Ice-T's "Cop Killer" recording.

Perhaps no figure better understood the shifting terrain that hip-hop stood on in the late '80s than Russell Simmons. Simmons, who managed Run-DMC and other rap acts through Rush Communications, was the cofounder with Rick Rubin of the influential Def Jam label, which included major stars such as the Beastie Boys, Public Enemy, EPMD, and LL Cool J on its roster. The Def Jam Label at various points in its history was distributed and co-owned by Sony, Polygram, and finally Universal—and itself distributed the Roc-A-Fella label. Simmons sold the label to Universal in the late '90s for a reported $100 million. He might be singularly responsible for the branding of hip-hop culture, which by the end of the twentieth century included not simply its original four elements but had extended into advertising, higher education, fashion, mobile communications, automobile detailing, television and film, stand-up comedy, the spoken word, and even cuisine.

Public Enemy

DJ Jazzy Jeff and the Fresh Prince

Doug E. Fresh

Savion Glover

Zita Allen

There was Savion Glover, onstage at the Apollo Theater in 2003, tapping his heart out during a tribute to his mentor, the late, great Gregory Hines. Savion's signature style dazzled the eye and boggled the mind. There he was: the bouncing dreadlocks, the billowing, baggy clothes, the tall, lanky frame hunched over, knees bent, in a zone as he nonchalantly laid down an explosive volley of taps that brought the audience to its feet.

In his foreword to *Savion! My Life in Tap*, Hines recalls his first time seeing Glover dance in 1985: "It was not enough for me that great living legends…had all raved to me about Savion's tap skills and stage presence. No, I had to see for myself if this twelve-year-old tap dancer was really something special." Seeing was believing. He was "doing Jimmy's [Slyde] slides, Ralph's [Brown] heel work, Lon's [Chaney] syncopations, and throwing Buster's [Brown] rhythms all around the stage." Praising Savion's hip-hop–influenced, funky style, Hines called him "the Michael Jordan of tap": "What he does is so amazing, I can't figure out how he can dance so fast and so clean."

Savion is the latest in a long line of legendary hoofers, masters of dance steps with such colorful names as "fallin' off a log," "buck and wing," "off to Buffalo," "over the top," "through the trenches," and more. Tap came out of a uniquely American cauldron that blended African and European cultures. Its history includes the shame of slavery, the mimicry of minstrelsy, and the exploitation first of vaudeville, then Broadway and Hollywood. Tap was a key draw at the Apollo, with legendary performers appearing from the beginning of its 1934 transformation into a center of African American entertainment. Bill "Bojangles" Robinson was a regular on its stage, as were the acrobatic Nicholas Brothers and the refined Honi Coles and Cholly Atkins. The young Sammy Davis Jr. amazed audiences with his hot tapping prowess. The heartbeat of the Apollo was the beat of tap shoes on its venerable stage.

Tap wizard Savion Glover sports green tap shoes in this routine photographed at the Apollo, 2008.

With tap's resurgence as an internationally popular art form, Savion has helped honor its innovators by reclaiming its integrity and not only evoking history but making it. When asked to describe his style, Savion says he's more concerned with "hitting," or laying down innovative combinations, than with deconstructing the process. He says his is a "meditative" approach to tap. "My approach to tap is to allow the audience inside the education surrounding my art form versus just the entertainment that they may get out of it. I lean more towards a journey that allows them to know, first, who my teachers are, second, what I learned from them, and, third, what I have become from that." He comes from a tradition that doesn't dance by counting beats but treats tap like the rhythmic reflection of a distinctive musical language. In his book Savion writes, "I wake up with rhythms in my head, like I've been dreaming about them, and I start making them right away with my mouth. Diggi-diddi diggi-diddi. Nothing complicated. Rudiments…. I think in rhythms, and I talk that way too."

A sketch of Savion's own history shows that his size 12EE shoes refuse to be easily labeled. When his mother, Yvette, arranged for tap lessons when he was seven

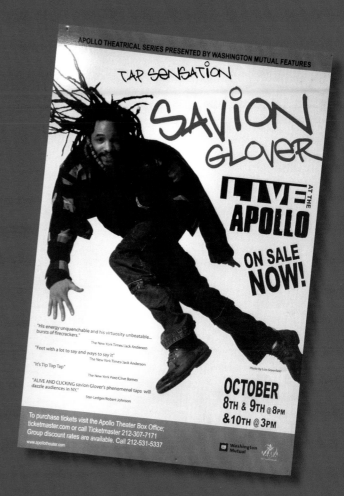

years old, he would practice endlessly, anywhere and everywhere—on the sidewalk, in stores, and at home. He was catapulted from the street to the stage in 1984, when at twelve he made his Broadway debut alongside Gregory Hines in *The Tap Dance Kid*. A Tony Award–nominated performance in *Black and Blue* followed, then a starring role as legendary jazz pianist Jelly Roll Morton in George C. Wolfe's brilliant musical *Jelly's Last Jam*. In 1996 *Bring in 'da Noise, Bring in 'da Funk* took his career to another level. His showstopping performance stole audiences' hearts, and the show won four Tony Awards.

Today Savion continues to lay down a cascade of clean, crisp steps and rhythms using the part-choreography, part-improvisation creative concoction that his mentor Gregory Hines dubbed "improvography." He dances with an inimitable ease and finesse that he says "is easy when you know how, but it takes a long time to learn," while insisting, humbly, "I'm just a work in progress."

Above: Savion Glover and Gregory Hines, c. 1990.
Top right: Poster for Glover's Apollo show *Improvography*.

Nightbirds at the Apollo
The Legendary Labelle Reunites in Splendor

Kandia Crazy Horse

Sarah Dash, Patti LaBelle, and Nona Hendryx during their historic
reunion show at the Apollo on December 19, 2008.

When Labelle's reunion concert came to the Apollo in December 2008, we showed up in finery and feathers for sonic revelation. There was something silver in the air beneath the hallowed theater's gilded proscenium arch at the long-awaited, sold-out show. Revelers strode ecstatically up 125th Street through a burgeoning snowstorm, arriving from around the block and as far away as Los Angeles and Japan, primed for siren songs, spectacle, space-age sartorial splendor, and spirit. Many had waited for this historic night, the return of the all-time greatest woman rock and soul trio—Nona Hendryx, Sarah Dash, and Patti LaBelle—that successfully

morphed from a begowned girl group, since they had called it quits in America's bicentennial year, when Apollo owner/manager Bobby Schiffman closed the theater.

Yet prior to their becoming universally loved "Space Children," the climax of Labelle's early career—as Patti LaBelle and the Bluebelles—derived from being anointed as "Sweethearts of the Apollo." Before they recorded a live album of the same name for Philadelphia's Newtown Records, the former quartet—once including latter-day Supreme Cindy Birdsong—began playing the top venues of the chitlin circuit in the wake of establishing themselves as the Ordettes in 1960. Hendryx and Dash of the Del

Capris joined Patricia "Patsy" Holte and Sandra Tucker (replaced by Birdsong) in what evolved into the Bluebelles—only to have their 1962 audition for the Philadelphia-based label undermined when the headman denigrated lead singer Holte as "too dark and too plain." This humiliation led Holte to change her name to Patti LaBelle after the group took off ("la belle" denoting "the beautiful" *en français*).

It was a zigzag ascent that earned the group the right to return to the Apollo over thirty-two years later, with fellow upstart/uppity diva Whoopi Goldberg introducing the icons seconds before they opened with their sensitive, nuanced rendition of "Miss Otis

Regrets," a lost track featuring the Who's late drummer Keith Moon and now rescued from the vaults. All was well and bated breath until, about twenty minutes into the concert, the amplifiers blew out during another vintage cut, "Candlelight" by Hendryx (intergalactically resplendent in a jeweled Chi Wara horned headdress)…but drama was obviously nothing new to Labelle.

From the start of the Bluebelles' long, hard slog through the segregated chitlin circuit in the mid-twentieth century, their collective experience was not all wigs, gowns, and glory. Behind their stunning vocal prowess and such sparse hits as "I Sold My Heart to the Junkman," "You'll Never Walk Alone," and "Danny Boy" (on Cameo-Parkway), and "All or Nothing" and "Over the Rainbow" (at Atlantic Records), was a lot of struggle, heartache, and professional frustration at a level most contemporary urban artists could scarcely understand. An instance of this comes to mind from 1985's *Motown Returns to the Apollo*, produced by benefactor Bill Cosby in the effort to spearhead the theater's restoration and reopening. A famous highlight of that televised program is when Patti LaBelle—bedecked in a glittery, hot red, fringed dress and the severely ironed Mohawk of her "New Attitude" period—appears to duet with English northern soul icon Joe Cocker on his early '70s hit "You Are So Beautiful," backed by the late California soul sessioneer Billy Preston. Cocker's footage at Woodstock had made his spastic stage tics renowned enough to be mocked by *Saturday Night Live*'s John Belushi a decade later, and ol' skool Apollo audiences were well acquainted with Miss Patti's floor rolling and revamp of the buck and wing. So, on site and at home before their sets, watchers sat on the edge of their seats in delight at this showstopping pairing, applauding their extraordinarily matched energy and the soaring heights of their vocal blues power.

Yet even before this amazing sequence prompted Cosby to entreat LaBelle and Cocker to return to the stage and let the cameras keep rolling overtime, LaBelle herself had another memorable moment. Alone, humbled, and vulnerable giving backstage reminiscences between commercials, she told candidly

Patti LaBelle, 1970s. Starting out with the Ordettes in 1959, she has been celebrated for five decades for her intensity, wide vocal range, and high-octave belting.

her former husband/manager, Armstead Edwards, her son, Zuri, her mother and sisters, and, of course, God, is well documented in the back pages of *Ebony*, *Essence*, and in such tomes as her memoir, *Don't Block the Blessings*. Above all, she has kept the circle unbroken by never breaking the bonds of fellowship with her honorary sisters Hendryx and Dash. This rare ability to sustain sisterhood over almost five decades of collaboration in such a cutthroat arena as showbiz is what distinguishes Labelle from the overcrowded field of girl groups past (the Ronettes, the Runaways) and recent (En Vogue, TLC, Destiny's Child) that could not keep their relationships and careers from crashing and burning.

Yes, Labelle lost Cindy Birdsong to the crystalline lure of Motown in the late '60s, but the fruits from their hiatus of career reconfiguration and spiritual rebirth instigated by former manager Vicki Wickham were surely recognized and rewarded by the Apollo audience when the newly minted trio returned to performance at the venue in 1971. After a six-month stay in London, this debut revealed that Hendryx, Dash, and LaBelle had not been idle through the turbulent end of the '60s by any means. Offstage they'd grown Afros, renewed vital friendships with the flagship groups of the British Invasion leading to tours with the Rolling Stones and the Who, gained fellow "Space Oddity" David Bowie as a voluble champion, and discovered kinship with Bronx songbird Laura Nyro—with whom their masterful partnership on *Gonna Take a Miracle* yielded a fresh sonic self-confidence for the trio.

And Labelle was obviously kick-starting the '70s with a historic assertion of black power and female pride even more inspiring than their morphing beat, denim-to-spacesuit glam look, and arresting gospel-eros fusion, which inserted a new genre into the decade's complicated sonic landscape of "sissy soul," jazz fusion, MOR (middle of the road) pop, disco, soul folk, SoCal singer-songwriter sounds, hard rock, and metal. Just a surface consideration of the female artists who graced the Apollo stage and its black music orbit—at least as far back as October 1942 Amateur Night winner Sarah Vaughan, who later

of her salad days performing at the Apollo, of being required to set hot dogs between the lightbulbs of the dressing room mirrors to keep them heated for her postshow dinners. This image has persisted for this writer and fan now for twenty-five years— as much as the fabled Cocker duet. It was a great illumination of both the very real toll of being a dreamer in Jim Crow America and of what it truly takes to achieve greatness beyond mere celebrity. The hardship *and* discipline, the big hair *and* the divine pipes all combined to crown the woman born Patricia Louise Holte as a supreme diva so iconic you got to declare her name twice: "Patti!! Patti!!"

However, what's so wonderful about Sister Patti is that she has never claimed to accomplish this alone. The support of her network, including longtime musical director Bud Ellison,

doubled as singer and second pianist for Earl Hines's bop outfit—underscores the virtual invisibility of female *musicians* in the postwar era. Labelle's new incarnation of modern rock had very few precedents—Vaughan, Vi Redd, and such Apollo habitués as Sister Rosetta Tharpe; those magnificent sisters trading guitar leads with Bo Diddley, Peggy "Lady Bo" Jones and the late great Norma-Jean Wofford; Sly Stone's aces Cynthia Robinson and Sister Rose Stewart—and most of those never lived and created in an "all-girl band." Like the recently "rediscovered" Betty Davis, Labelle distinguished itself in a period of extreme black macho (think the Black Panthers and *Shaft*) and a persistently male-dominated field by treating their voices as lead instruments and central conduits to expression instead of remaining in the shadows, underserved and unsung, as did members of the Raelettes, Ikettes, et al.

They say that in America there are no second acts. Yet Labelle, rising like the phoenix and transforming like the chameleon they sang of, has enjoyed not just a second but a third act as well, with the release of *Back to Now* in autumn 2008. Bravely, Hendryx dug deep as Labelle's primary composer/lyricist, penning both intimate epics such as the Janis Joplin paean "Nightbirds" (which served as reunion closer) and a stunning dig at their star-tripping former support player, (Sir) Elton John, "(Can I Speak To You Before You Go To) Hollywood?" (the midshow Hendryx-and-Dash set piece), always keeping at the core of her experimentation and daring how best to enshrine Sister Patti's voice. Never mistake Dash and Hendryx for mere backing vocalists, though; they functioned akin to the multiple guitarists in major rock bands, such as that of their friends the Rolling Stones.

This combination of strength and flexibility enabled the trio to reinvent the girl group model for explosion in the '70s stratosphere, leaving the Supremes and their former lead diva, Diana Ross, who had dominated the '60s, far behind, sucking their stardust. Only their unplugged fellow travelers Sweet Honey in the Rock were remotely able to hang tough with the African-and-sistah-centered audacity of Labelle's shared vision.

Labelle sold out its triumphal return to the Apollo because this vision was so hard-won. In David Nathan's '74 article in *Blues & Soul*, Patti LaBelle had confessed just how much: "I really fought the changes because I just didn't think we'd be accepted by anyone—especially our own fans—because we were going so far away from what we'd been doing before. It took a long time for me to agree to try it out, and I really found it hard to come to terms with singing songs like 'Morning Much Better' and [Cat Stevens/Yusuf Islam's] 'Moonshadow.' But I did—and although I still don't regret what we were doing before, I know that we're doing the right thing now."

Which brings us back to now, when the women of Labelle continue to do the right thing—a very public symbol of which was on display when the trio extended their Apollo reunion concert to a two-night stand owing to disaster. Their press statement summed up their class and consciousness after the international horde of spangle-bedecked fans had been outraged by the blizzard-triggered power outage and barely placated by the free drinks offered by Jonelle Procope and her staff during the hour-plus interval waiting for another backline to miraculously materialize:

We are very disappointed by the unforeseen problems with the power that occurred at the first show on our "Back to Now Tour" last night at the Apollo Theater. As a result of the winter storm, a power surge in the Harlem electric grid disabled the sound system. All parties involved put forth every effort to rectify the problem. It was an unfortunate situation and we sincerely apologize to all our fans who were in attendance. We are honored and touched that despite the setback, our fans were patient and even participated in our impromptu a cappella performance upon our return to the stage. We are pleased to announce that all tickets from last night's (December 19, 2008) performance will be honored for the rescheduled concert tonight—Saturday, December 20, 2008 at 8 PM.…

Sincerely,

Sarah Dash, Nona Hendryx and Patti LaBelle

That a cappella performance was one for the history books, in the elite cadre of Apollo events like Mr. Brown's lying in state the previous winter. Labelle—doubtless recalling the chitlin and cabaret days when mics were scarce at best—returned to the stage with just a piano and black-clad choir for accompaniment, performing the two singularly most appropriate songs for the occasion: "Hollywood" and the radical chic era's greatest polemic, "What Can I Do for You?"

Audience members were soul clapping, dancing, and going back to Africa by grace of the ancestors, ecstatic that the spirit metal of Labelle could trump any and all adversity—even a flood of snow from the firmament. The still-lit gilt and red velvet house served as a buffer zone against the storm, a rich semblance of heaven on earth swollen with transcendence emanating from three sexagenarian women in swathes of iridescent cloth, pheasant feathers straight out of *Ganja & Hess,* and blinged stilettos fit to rival their silver, thigh-high platforms of yore. If one was fortunate enough to have a hotel booking and no pressing job hours, this sense of euphoria carried you over to the Saturday evening restitution concert, introduced by a sly Paul Mooney. That evening was even more remarkable owing to Sister Patti's trouping despite almost lapsing into a diabetic coma, proving herself once and for all Mr. Brown's heir as the consummate show-woman. As a smiling Hendryx was moved to cry: "There is no lack of power when you have a voice like Patti LaBelle!" By the time the big-Afroed and skinny, black leather–clad Hendryx was balancing vaingloriously atop the bass drum during the encore, Labelle had once again spoken the truth of "Showtime at the Apollo" to power forever and ever, amen.

The triumphant trio—LaBelle, Dash, and Hendryx—
accepts the Apollo audience's love.

Postludes

Billie Holiday at the Apollo, 1937.

Acknowledgments

It was a fortuitous moment when the Apollo Theater Foundation approached us at the Smithsonian's National Museum of African American History and Culture (NMAAHC) to collaborate on an exhibition to commemorate the Apollo's seventy-fifth anniversary. This publication and the exhibition that it accompanies were both propelled by a mutual sense of purpose and commitment by our respective organizations. The early enthusiasm of NMAAHC director Lonnie Bunch gave the project a steadfast advocate and enthusiastic advisor. His foreword sets the tone for this volume and for our shared endeavor.

The late Caroline Newman recognized the power and possibility of a publication from the earliest days. This book is a tribute to her vision for this undertaking and to her work as a beloved Smithsonian colleague. Carolyn Gleason stepped in after Caroline's untimely passing and has been a stalwart beacon and guide overlooking all aspects of the publication from the overarching ideas to the smallest details. Her deft hand is evident throughout; we are all in her debt. My co-editor Richard Carlin was a valued partner who brought his considerable musical and publishing skills to an array of activities, from helping to identify potential authors, to editing text, writing captions, and reviewing photos – thereby greatly enriching the book. We also thank Marie Brown, editorial consultant to the Apollo for this publication. Her suggestions for authors were invaluable; in ways both large and small she also provided critical advice and insight. An enormous debt of gratitude is owed to Ted Fox whose book *Showtime at the Apollo: The Story of Harlem's World Famous Theater* was a rich resource for all involved and whose timeline provided a key framework for situating the history of the theater.

The book would not have been possible without the gifted authors whose essays animate the story of one of the most enduring and influential venues of American entertainment and culture. We extend thanks to them all. Smokey Robinson's very personal foreword provides us with intimate first-person insights from one of American music's most eloquent and influential songwriters and singers. Special thanks are due to the exhibition curators, Tuliza Fleming, NMAAHC museum curator, and musicologist Guthrie (Guy) Ramsey. In addition to contributing compelling essays, they provided research and scholarship essential to the book's development. We are also grateful to Guy for his role in shaping the approach to the overall project and to Tuliza for the identification of materials for the book.

A large note of gratitude is due to the full editorial and production team at Smithsonian Books, whose diligence and creativity made this publication possible: Christina Wiginton, project editor; Duke Johns, copy editor; Dennis Favello, book design; Kate McConnell, production and art direction; and Michelle Lecuyer, editorial assistant. Photo research was shared by Heather Hart for Smithsonian Books and Laura Kreiss for NMAAHC, who also worked on the exhibition team.

A very special thank you goes to colleagues on the staff of NMAAHC. Lynn Chase's early interest and encouragement were essential to both the exhibition and publication. Jacquelyn Serwer and Dwandalyn Reece played invaluable roles in reviewing the manuscript; Jackie also provided advice all through the process. The exhibition team headed by Marion Gill, and including James Deutch, Timothy Anne Burnside, Renee Anderson, Deirdre Cross, Bryan Sieling, and Shira Goldstein, enriched the publication with their ideas and advice. Media affairs specialist LaFleur Paysour brought her expertise at crucial moments. Other NMAAHC colleagues who provided an array of assistance were Adrienne Brooks, Rex Ellis, Esther Washington, Drew Talley, Leslie Casaya, Cynthia Smith, Lynn Ellington, James Gordon, Debora Scriber-Miller, Taima Smith, and Twanita Simpson.

And finally, we heartily thank our colleagues at the Apollo Theater Foundation. Apollo President and CEO Jonelle Procope's keen interest in our work provided encouragement that helped propel us forward. Dick Parsons, chair of the Apollo's board and co-chair of the NMAAHC Council is also due our thanks for his leadership and support of our mutual work. Mikki Shepard and former Apollo staffer Adrienne Edwards first suggested the overall exhibition project and worked closely with us as it took initial shape. Mikki was later joined by Laura Greer and Shirley C. Taylor, whose tireless work helped us create a publication worthy of the legacy of this great theater. In their roles as advisors to the Apollo's archive project, Billy Mitchell, Mary Marshall Clark, Jennella Young, Abimbola Cole, Chuck Jackson, Robert O'Meally, and Deborah Willis also deserve thanks.

On behalf of the Apollo, we extend thanks to supporters of the Apollo Theater Archive Project and the Apollo's Seventy-fifth Anniversary, both of which provided important underpinnings for the exhibition and book: the Edward and Leslye Phillips Family Foundation, Coca-Cola Company, the Rockefeller Foundation, JPMorgan Chase & Co., the Peter Jay Sharp Foundation, Bloomberg, the Neuberger Berman Foundation, American Express, the Booth Ferris Foundation, the William Randolph Hearst Foundation, and the New York Community Trust.

This publication would not have been possible without the extraordinary performers who graced the Apollo's stage over the past seventy-five years. In the end this book is a testament to their enduring contributions to American and global entertainment and culture.

Bibliography

Albertson, Chris. *Bessie*. Rev. and expanded ed. New Haven, Conn.: Yale University Press, 2003.

Atkins, Cholly, and Jacqui Malone. *Class Act: The Jazz Life of Choreographer Cholly Atkins*. New York: Columbia University Press, 2001.

Badger, Reid. *A Life in Ragtime: A Biography of James Reese Europe*. New York: Oxford University Press, 1995.

Baraka, Amiri. *Blues People: Negro Music in White America*. Westport, Conn.: Greenwood Press, 1980.

———. *Digging: The Afro-American Soul of American Classical Music*. Berkeley: University of California Press, 2009.

Bascom, Lionel C., ed. *A Renaissance in Harlem: Lost Voices of an American Community*. New York: Avon Books, 1999.

Bergman, Peter M. *The Chronological History of the Negro in America*. New York: Harper and Row, 1969.

Blesh, Rudi, and Harriet Janis. *They All Played Ragtime*. New York: Oak Publications, 1971.

Bowman, Rob. *Soulsville U.S.A.: The Story of Stax Records*. New York: Schirmer Books, ca. 1997.

Boyd, Herb, ed. *The Harlem Reader: A Celebration of New York's Most Famous Neighborhood, from the Renaissance Years to the Twenty-First Century*. New York: Three Rivers Press, 2003.

Brooks, Tim. *Lost Sounds: Blacks and the Birth of the Recording Industry, 1890–1919*. Urbana: University of Illinois Press, 2004.

Brown, Geoff. *Otis Redding: Try A Little Ten derness*. London: Canongate Books, 2003.

Brown, James. *James Brown: The Godfather of Soul*. New York: Da Capo Press, 2003.

Campbell, Mary Schmidt, ed. *Harlem Renaissance: Art of Black America*. New York: The Studio Museum in Harlem/Harry N. Abrams, 1987.

Charters, Ann. *Nobody: The Story of Bert Williams*. New York: Da Capo Press, 1983.

Chilton, John. *Let the Good Times Roll: The Story of Louis Jordan and His Music*. Ann Arbor: University of Michigan Press, 2000.

Chilton, Karen. *Hazel Scott: The Pioneering Journey of a Jazz Pianist from Café Society to Hollywood to HUAC*. Ann Arbor: University of Michigan Press, 2008.

Clarke, Donald. *Wishing on the Moon: The Life and Times of Billie Holiday*. New York: Viking Press, 1994.

Cooper, Ralph, with Steve Dougherty; *Amateur Night at the Apollo: Ralph Cooper Presents Five Decades of Great Entertainment*. New York: HarperCollins, 1990.

Crazy Horse, Kandia, ed. *Rip It Up: The Black Experience in Rock 'n' Roll*. New York: Palgrave Macmillan, 2004.

Davis, Angela. *Blues Legacies and Black Feminism: Gertrude "Ma" Rainey, Bessie Smith, and Billie Holiday*. New York: Pantheon Books, 1998.

DeFrantz, Thomas, ed.. *Dancing Many Drums: Excavations in African American Dance*. Madison: University of Wisconsin Press, 2002.

DeVeaux, Scott. *The Birth of Bebop: A Social and Musical History*. Berkeley: University of California Press, 1997.

Early, Gerald. *One Nation under a Groove: Motown and American Culture*. Rev. and updated ed. Ann Arbor: University of Michigan Press, 2004.

Egan, Bill. *Florence Mills: Harlem Jazz Queen*. Lanham, Md.: Scarecrow Press, 2004.

Ellison, Ralph. *The Collected Essays of Ralph Ellison*. Edited by John Callahan. New York: Modern Library, 1995.

Europe, James Reese. "A Negro Explains 'Jazz.'" *Literary Digest*, April 26, 1919, 28.

Fishgall, Gary. *Gonna Do Great Things: The Life of Sammy Davis, Jr.* New York: Scribner, 2003.

Floyd, Samuel A., Jr., ed. *Black Music in the Harlem Renaissance: A Collection of Essays*. Westport, Conn.: Greenwood Press, 1990.

Forman, Murray, and Mark Anthony Neal, eds. *That's the Joint: The Hip-Hop Studies Reader*. New York: Routledge, 2004.

Fox, Ted. *Showtime at the Apollo: The Story of Harlem's World Famous Theater*. Rev. ed. Rhinebeck, N.Y.: Mill Road Enterprises, 2003.

Franklin, Aretha, with David Ritz. *Aretha: From These Roots*. New York: Villard, 1999.

George, Nelson. *The Death of Rhythm & Blues*. New York: Pantheon Books, 1988.

———. *Where Did Our Love Go? The Rise and Fall of the Motown Sound*. New York: St. Martin's, 1985.

Glasser, Ruth. *My Music Is My Flag: Puerto Rican Musicians and Their New York Communities, 1917–1940*. Berkeley: University of California Press, 1997.

Gottschild, Brenda Dixon. *Waltzing in the Dark: African American Vaudeville and Race Politics in the Swing Era*. New York: Palgrave, 2000.

Gourse, Leslie. *Louis' Children: American Jazz Singers*. New York: Morrow, 1984.

———. *Sassy: The Life of Sarah Vaughan*. New York: Scribner, 1994.

Gregory, Dick, with Robert Lipsyte. *Nigger: An Autobiography*. New York: Washington Square Press, 1986.

Harris, Stephen L. *Harlem's Hell Fighters: The African-American 369th Infantry in World War I*. Washington, D.C.: Brassey's, 2003.

Hasse, John Edward. *Beyond Category: The Life and Genius of Duke Ellington*. New York: Simon & Schuster, 1993.

Heilbut, Anthony. *The Gospel Sound: Good News and Bad Times*. Updated and rev. ed. New York: Limelight Editions, 1985.

Hill, Constance Valis. *Brotherhood in Rhythm: The Jazz Tap Dancing of the Nicholas Brothers*. New York: Oxford University Press, 2000.

Hill, Errol G., and James V. Hatch. *A History of African American Theatre*. New York: Cambridge University Press, 2005.

Horne, Lena, with Richard Schickel. *Lena*. Garden City, N.Y.: Doubleday, 1965.

Howze, Margaret. "The NPR 100: St. Louis Blues." National Public Radio, January 16, 2000.

Jackson, Jerma A. *Singing in My Soul: Black Gospel Music in a Secular Age*. Chapel Hill: University of North Carolina Press, 2004.

Jackson, Joyce Marie. "The Cultural Evolution of the African American Sacred Quartet." In *Saints and Sinners: Religion, Blues and (D)evil in African American Music and Literature*, edited by Robert Sacré. Liège, Belgium: Société Liégeoise de Musicologie, 1996.
———. "Working Both Sides of the Fence: African American Quartets Enter the Realm of Popular Culture." In *Bridging Southern Cultures: An Interdisciplinary Approach*, edited by John Lowe. Baton Rouge: Louisiana State University Press, 2005.

Jackson, Mahalia, with Evan McLeod Wylie. *Movin' on Up*. New York: Hawthorn Books, 1966.

Jasen, David A., and Gene Jones. *Spreadin' Rhythm 'Round: Black Popular Songwriters, 1880–1930*. New York: Schirmer Books, 1998.

Jones, Hettie. *Big Star Fallin' Mama: Five Women in Black Music*. New York: Viking Press, 1974.

Jones, Max. *Louis: The Louis Armstrong Story, 1900–1971*. New York: Da Capo Press, 1988.

Kay, Jackie. *Bessie Smith*. Bath, England: Absolute, 1997.

Kimball, Robert, and William Bolcom. *Reminiscing with Sissle and Blake*. New York: Viking Press, 1973.

LaBelle, Patti, with Laura B. Randolph. *Don't Block the Blessings: Revelations of a Lifetime*. New York: Riverhead Books, 1996.

Levering Lewis, David. *When Harlem Was in Vogue*. New York: Penguin Books, 1997.

Lornell, Kip, ed. *From Jubilee to Hip Hop: Readings in African American Music*. Upper Saddle River, N.J.: Prentice Hall, 2010.

Magee, Jeffrey. *Fletcher Henderson and Big Band Jazz: The Uncrowned King of Swing*. New York: Oxford University Press, 2005.

Malone, Jacqui. *Steppin' on the Blues: The Visible Rhythms of African American Dance*. Urbana: University of Illinois Press, 1996.

Markham, "Pigmeat," and Bill Levinson. *Here Come the Judge!* New York: Popular Library, 1969.

Maurrasse, David J. *Listening to Harlem: Gentrification, Community and Business*. New York: Routledge, 2006.

Neal, Mark Anthony. *Songs in the Key of Black Life: A Rhythm and Blues Nation*. New York: Routledge, 2003.
———. *What the Music Said: Black Popular Music and Black Public Culture*. New York: Routledge, 1999.

Nicholson, Stuart. *Ella Fitzgerald: The Complete Biography*. New York: Routledge, 2004.

O'Meally, Robert. "Hitting a New Note." Review of *A Life in Ragtime: A Biography of James Reese Europe*, by Reid Badger. *Washington Post Book World*, February 19, 1995, 1, 14.
———, ed. *The Jazz Cadence of American Culture*. New York: Columbia University Press, 1998.
———. *Lady Day: The Many Faces of Billie Holiday*. New York: Arcade, 1991.

Perpener, John. *African-American Concert Dance: The Harlem Renaissance and Beyond*. Urbana: University of Illinois Press, 2001.

Ramsey, Guthrie P. *Race Music: Black Cultures from Bebop to Hip-Hop*. Berkeley: University of California Press, 2003.

Reed, Ishmael. *Mumbo Jumbo*. New York: Doubleday, 1972.

Ruth, Therman T., and Linda Saylor-Marchant. *Gospel: From the Church to the Apollo Theater*. Brooklyn, N.Y.: T. Ruth Publications, n.d.

Schiffman, Jack. *Harlem Heyday: A Pictorial History of Modern Black Show Business and the Apollo Theatre*. New York: Prometheus Books, 1984.
———. *Uptown: The Story of Harlem's Apollo Theatre*. New York: Cowles, 1971.

Shipton, Alyn. *Groovin' High: The Life of Dizzy Gillespie*. New York: Oxford University Press, 1999.

Simon, George. *The Big Bands*. 4th ed. New York: Schirmer Books, 1981.

Spellman, A. B., and Murray Horwitz. "Bessie: The Essential Bessie Smith." National Public Radio, June 10, 2005.

Stearns, Marshall and Jean. *Jazz Dance: The Story of American Vernacular Dance*. 2nd ed. New York: Da Capo Press, 1994.

Tucker, Sherrie. *Swing Shift: "All-Girl" Bands of the 1940s*. Durham, N.C.: Duke University Press, 2000.

Vincent, Rickey. *Funk: The Music, the People, and the Rhythm of the One*. New York: St. Martin's, 1996.

Washburne, Christopher. *Sounding Salsa: Performing Latin Music in New York*. Philadelphia: Temple University Press, 2008.

Watkins, Mel, ed. *African American Humor: The Best Black Comedy from Slavery to Today*. Chicago: Lawrence Hill Books, 2002.
———. *On the Real Side: A History of African American Comedy from Slavery to Chris Rock*. Chicago: Lawrence Hill Books, 1994.
———. *Stepin Fetchit: The Life and Times of Lincoln Perry*. New York: Pantheon Books, 2005.

Williams, Elsie A. *The Humor of Jackie Moms Mabley: An African American Comedic Tradition*. New York: Garland, 1995.

Wolk, Douglas. *Live at the Apollo*. New York: Continuum, 2004.

Young, Alan. *The Pilgrim Jubilees*. Jackson: University Press of Mississippi, 2001.

Zolten, Jerry. *Great God A' Mighty! The Dixie Hummingbirds*. New York: Oxford University Press, 2003.

Contributors

Robert L. Allen teaches African American studies and ethnic studies at the University of California, Berkeley. His books include *Black Awakening in Capitalist America, Honoring Sergeant Carter* (with Allene G. Carter), *Brotherman* (with Herb Boyd), and *The Port Chicago Mutiny*. He is coeditor with Robert Chrisman of *The Black Scholar* journal.

Zita Allen was the first African American dance critic for *Dance Magazine*, and she has written widely on dance for other major magazines and newspapers. She wrote and edited the Alvin Ailey American Dance Theater's twenty-fifth anniversary souvenir book and served as a consultant on the PBS/American Dance Festival documentary, *Free to Dance*. She holds a master's degree in dance history from New York University.

Amiri Baraka was born Everett LeRoi Jones in 1934 in Newark, New Jersey. In 1963 he published *Blues People: Negro Music in White America*, still regarded as the seminal work on Afro-American music and culture. In 1965 he moved to Harlem, where he founded the Black Arts Repertory Theatre/School. In 1966 he returned to Newark, with his new bride, Amina Baraka. Together they established Spirit House and the Spirit House Movers, which presented drama, music, and poetry from across the country. Amiri Baraka's numerous literary honors include fellowships from the Guggenheim Foundation and the National Endowment for the Arts, the PEN/Faulkner Award, the Rockefeller Foundation Award for Drama, and a lifetime achievement award from the Before Columbus Foundation. He was inducted into the American Academy of Arts and Letters in 1995. In 2002 he was named Poet Laureate of both New Jersey and the Newark Public Schools. His latest work is *Digging: The Afro-American Soul of American Classical Music.*

Herb Boyd is a journalist, activist, teacher, and author whose most recent book is *Baldwin's Harlem*, a biography of James Baldwin, which was a finalist for a 2009 NAACP Image Award. In 1995, with Robert Allen, he was a recipient of an American Book Award for *Brotherman: The Odyssey of Black Men in America*, an anthology. He teaches at the College of New Rochelle in the Bronx and at City College New York, and is also the managing editor of Our World Today, www.ourworldtoday.tv, an online news service.

Lonnie G. Bunch III is a historian, curator, educator, and the founding director of the Smithsonian's National Museum of African American History and Culture. A widely published author, he has written on topics ranging from the black military experience, the American presidency, and all-black towns in the American West to the history of African Americans in aviation and the impact of funding and politics on American museums. Prior to his 2005 appointment as a Smithsonian director, he served as president of the Chicago Historical Society.

Richard Carlin is a music writer and editor. He is the author of *Worlds of Sound: The Story of Smithsonian Folkways* and general editor of the *Facts on File Encyclopedia of American Popular Music*, among other works. He is currently executive editor for college music textbooks at Pearson/Prentice Hall.

Karen Chilton is the author of *Hazel Scott: The Pioneering Journey of a Jazz Pianist from Café Society to Hollywood to HUAC* (University of Michigan Press).

Kinshasha Holman Conwill is deputy director of the Smithsonian's National Museum of African American History and Culture. Previously she was director of the Studio Museum in Harlem, where she launched a major expansion and renovation of the facility and started the museum's sculpture garden. She also organized or co-organized more than forty major exhibitions, including "Contemporary African Artists: Changing Tradition," "Explorations in the City of Light: African-American Artists in Paris, 1945–1965," and an award-winning contemporary African art exhibition at the 1990 Venice Biennale.

Kandia Crazy Horse was the 2008–2009 Anschutz Distinguished Fellow in American Studies at Princeton University. As a rock critic for over a decade, the Washington, D.C., native has contributed to numerous publications, including the *Village Voice* and the *San Francisco Bay Guardian*. She supported Afrofuturism by editing *Rip It Up: The Black Experience in Rock 'n' Roll* (2004). Currently she is working on a multimedia project about the New South, and leading her "southern metal" band, Rebelle.

Thomas F. DeFrantz earned degrees from Yale University, City University of New York, and New York University. A performer, his research centers on African American performance. His books include *Dancing Many Drums: Excavations in African American Dance* and *Dancing Revelations: Alvin Ailey's Embodiment of African American Culture*. He directs SLIPPAGE: Performance | Culture | Technology in residence at MIT, where he is a professor of music and theater arts.

Tuliza Fleming, a museum curator for the Smithsonian's National Museum of African American History and Culture, is co-curating the museum's exhibition on the history and relevance of the Apollo Theater. Previously she was an associate curator of American art at the Dayton Art Institute in Ohio. In 2005 she guest curated the exhibition *Black Is a Color: African American Art from the Corcoran Gallery of Art* at the Taft Museum of Art in Cincinnati. She has written several articles and essays for various books and journals, including the National Portrait Gallery's exhibition catalogue *Breaking Racial Barriers: African Americans in the Harmon Foundation Collection.*

Ted Fox wrote *Showtime at the Apollo: The Story of Harlem's World Famous Theater*, the first and only full-scale history of the Apollo. Originally published by Holt, Rinehart and Winston in 1983, the book has since been released in a number of subsequent editions. Fox is also the author of *In the Groove*, a collection of interviews with the people who shaped the music industry. He coproduces and manages four-time Grammy nominee Buckwheat Zydeco.

John Edward Hasse is an author, curator, and speaker. Since 1984 he has served as curator of American music at the Smithsonian Institution's National Museum of American History, where he founded the Smithsonian Jazz Masterworks Orchestra and Jazz Appreciation Month. Hasse is the author of *Beyond Category: The Life and Genius of Duke Ellington*, the editor of *Jazz: The First Century*, and coproducer of *Jazz: The Smithsonian Anthology.*

James V. Hatch, theatre professor emeritus, City University of New York, is cofounder with his wife, Camille Billops, of the Hatch-Billops Collection, a research library. His books include *Black Theater USA* and, with Errol G. Hill, *A History of African American Theatre*. Hatch is a two-time Obie winner in theater and received a Grand Jury Prize from the Sundance Film Festival for the documentary *Finding Christa*.

David Hinckley discovered popular music in the late 1950s and couldn't believe his luck to find out that someone would pay him to listen to it. Sonny Til was the headliner on the first show he saw at the Apollo, and he also can't believe that years later he was able to stand on the same floor, in the same spot. He has covered popular culture for the *New York Daily News* since 1980.

Willard Jenkins is a Washington, D.C.–based writer and regular contributor to *JazzTimes* and *DownBeat* magazines. His book *African Rhythms*, the autobiography of NEA Jazz Master Randy Weston—composed by Weston, arranged by Jenkins—will be published by Duke University Press in 2010. He also has been a programmer for twenty years at WPFW 89.3 FM, Pacifica Radio, in Washington. He is artistic director of the Tri-C JazzFest Cleveland, the Tribeca Performing Arts Center jazz concert series, and the Mid-Atlantic Jazz Festival and has produced and consulted with other presenting organizations across the country. He can be found on the Web at www.openskyjazz.com, home of the Independent Ear, a blog.

Joyce Marie Jackson is an associate professor in the Department of Geography and Anthropology at Louisiana State University, Baton Rouge. She has been instrumental in the production of several documentary recordings and authored several interpretive liner-note booklets published by Smithsonian Folkways Recordings, Capitol Records, and the Louisiana Folklife Recording Series. She has also completed a book on traditional gospel music, *From These Roots: African American Sacred Quartet Performance as an Expression of Cultural Values and Aesthetics* (forthcoming).

David Levering Lewis is the Julius Silver University Professor and professor of history at New York University. Recipient of two Pulitzer Prizes for his two-volume biography of W. E. B. Du Bois, he is also the author of *When Harlem Was in Vogue* and numerous other books.

David J. Maurrasse is the president and founder of Marga Incorporated. Since 2000 he has also been on the faculty at Columbia University's School of International and Public Affairs. A leading author, speaker, and researcher on the relationship between major institutions and their surrounding communities, he has written *Listening to Harlem: Gentrification, Community and Business* (2006), *A Future for Everyone: Innovative Social Responsibility and Community Partnerships* (2004), and *Beyond the Campus: How Colleges and Universities Form Partnerships with Their Communities* (2001).

Mark Anthony Neal is professor of black popular culture in the Department of African and African American Studies at Duke University. He is the author of several books, including *What the Music Said: Black Popular Music and Black Public Culture*, *Soul Babies: Black Popular Culture and the Post-Soul Aesthetic*, and the recent *New Black Man: Rethinking Black Masculinity*.

Robert G. O'Meally is the Zora Neale Hurston Professor of English and Comparative Literature and founder and former director of the Center for Jazz Studies at Columbia University. He has written extensively on African American literature, music, and culture, including books on Billie Holiday and other classic jazz vocalists.

Guthrie P. Ramsey Jr. is professor of music and Africana studies at the University of Pennsylvania. He is the author of *Race Music: Black Cultures from Bebop to Hip-Hop* (2003) and *In Walked Bud: Earl "Bud" Powell and the Modern Jazz Challenge* (University of California Press, forthcoming). His Philadelphia-based band, Dr. Guy's MusiQologY, released a CD in 2007 titled *Y the Q?*

Smokey Robinson a leading singer, songwriter, and producer for more than five decades, remains active as a solo performer and recording artist. His most recent album is *Time Flies When You're Having Fun* (Robso Records). An original member of the Miracles, he also served as vice president of Motown Records from 1961 to 1988, writing and producing thirty-seven Top 40 hits during that period. Among his most famous songs are such R & B and soul classics as "My Guy," "Shop Around," "The Way You Do the Things You Do," "The Tracks of My Tears," and "My Girl."

Greg Tate is a writer and musician who lives in Harlem and leads the twenty-first-century big band Burnt Sugar. He is currently writing a critical biography about the Godfather of Soul, James Brown, for Riverhead Press (forthcoming).

Christopher Washburne is associate professor of ethnomusicology at Columbia University and the founding director of Columbia's Louis Armstrong Jazz Performance Program. He has published numerous articles on jazz, Latin jazz, and salsa. His newest book, *Sounding Salsa: Performing Latin Music in New York* was published in 2008 by Temple University Press. He coedited the volume *Bad Music* for Routledge Press (2004) and is currently working on a book on Latin jazz that will be published by Oxford University Press.

Mel Watkins, a former editor and writer for the *New York Times Sunday Book Review*, is the author of *On the Real Side: A History of African American Comedy* (1999), *African American Humor: The Best Black Comedy from Slavery to Today* (2002), and *Stepin Fetchit: The Life and Times of Lincoln Perry* (2005), a biography of the stage and screen comic. He participated both as a consultant and commentator for the 2009 PBS six-part comedy documentary *Make 'Em Laugh*. Currently he is the NEH Professor of Humanities at Colgate University.

Photography Credits

Independent Photographers

Shahar Azran, Shahar Azran Photography, 209BR, 217B, 228LC, 229C; **Kwame Brathwaite**, 11, 179R, 206, 215T, 241BL, 244; **Joe Conzo**, 235C; **Adger Cowans**, 106; **Michel Daniel**, 228R; **William P. Gottlieb**, 110; **Chester Higgins**, 140R, 177L; **C. Bay Milin**, 4-5; **Courtesy of Omer Pardillo-Cid**, 227BL; **Courtesy of Leslie Uggams**, 59BR; **Jennifer Warren**, 108; **Lloyd Yearwood**, 71LC and 101, 102, 139L, 139LC and 150, 155TR, 156T, 158, 159B, 160B, 163, 177R, 195TR

Agencies and Collections

Anthony Barboza Collection: 124, 198RC, 235TC, 236TR; Blum's, 61T; Eddie Elcha, 49, 56, 70LC

AP Images: 136, 180R; ©Ebony Collection, Howard Morehead, 187; Bebeto Matthews, 233

Courtesy of the Apollo Theater Foundation, Inc.: 241TR; ©Chuck Stewart, Kwame Brathwaite, 182

Artists Rights Society: ©Emory Douglas, 179L

Beverly Richards Collection: ©Frank Driggs Collection, 116

Corbis: ©Bob Adelman, 154, 165, 166; ©Bettman, 41L and 58, 53, 57T, 66, 67, 178L, 178R, 180L, 225C; ©Condé Nast Archive, 118; ©Terry Cryer, 157; ©Leonard de Selva, 67T; EPA, ©Justin Lane, 36-7; ©Lynn Goldsmith, 30, 236B; ©John Springer Collection, 40C; ©Library of Congress, Marion Trikosko, 176R; ©Michael Ochs Archives, 21; ©Mosaic Images, Francis Wolff, 195TL; ©Mark Peterson, 249; Marion Post Wolcott, 129BC; ©Neal Preston, 217T; ©Retna Digital/Retna Ltd., Leon, 107; Reuters, ©Eric Thayer, 38; ©Alan Schein Photography, 181; Roger Smith, 135; *Star Ledger*, ©Aristide Economopoulos, 39; ©Randy Sulgan, 12, 229; Sygma, ©Christian Simonpietri, 33; ©Underwood & Underwood, 40L

CTSIMAGES: ©Herman Leonard Photography, LLC/ CTSIMAGES.COM, 196BL

Everett Collection: 16, 41RC, 117, 149, 190; ©Paramount Pictures, 214; ©Sony Pictures Classics, 226

Exxtra Foxx Music, LLC: Linda Lou McCall, 202

Frank Driggs Collection: 26, 41LC, 70L and 250, 74, 82, 83, 97, 105, 138L

Frank Schiffman Apollo Theatre Collection, Archives Center, National Museum of American History, Smithsonian Institution: 78, 87T, 87B, 89T, 91T, 92, 95T, 103, 111TR, 122T, 156B, 159T, 160T, 167, 171T, 173, 191R, 192, 197, 213T, 216R, 224B

Getty Images: 195BR, 199L and 219, 199LC, 199R, 228L, 236TL; Brad Barket, 229R and 246-7, 242-3; Janette Beckman, 235TL, 235TR; Buyenlarge, 129BR, 132; CBS Photo Archive, 141R; Frank Driggs Collection, 138C, 221T, 222B; National Geographic Collection, Stephen Alvarez, 6-7, 40-1, 70-1, 138-41, 198-9, 228-9; Pix Inc./Time & Life Pictures, Claude Huston, 40R; Sony BMG Music Entertainment, 198R; Amy Sussman, 231; Ray Tamarra, 217C; **Getty/AFP:** Timothy A. Clary, 31; Lucy Nicholson, 227TR; **Getty/Redferns:** Charlie Gillett Collection, 138R; Echoes, 154BL; GAB Archive, 153; Brian Hamill, 198LC; David Corio, 200, 239BL; William Gottlieb, 100; Herman Leonard, 71RC; Jan Persson, 161, 215C; Gilles Petard, 20, 88, 131, 155TL, 215B; R.B., 185B; David Redfern, 34, 95B, 109B, 196TL, 196C, 196BR, 239T; Max Redfern, 210-1; Stephen Wright, 235BR; **Getty/Hulton Archive**:113; Bob Parent, 224T; Keystone, 140L; Lipnitzki/Roger-Viollet, 174L; **Getty/ Michael Ochs Archives**: 18, 57B, 77 and 140, 89B, 109TR, 128BL, 129T, 130, 139RC, 139R and 162, 141C, 147BL, 147BR, 147T, 148, 151, 154TL, 175L, 183, 184, 193, 198L, 213BR, 225B; Tom Copi, 225T; David Corio, 109TL; **Getty/ Time & Life Pictures:** Eliot Elisofon, 143; Herbert Gehr, 71R, 104; Allan Grant, 122B; Bernard Hoffman, 170; Gjon Mili, 93; Francis Miller, 172; Ralph Morse, 52; Bill Ray, 152; Paul Schutzer, 176L, 185T; **Getty/WireImage:** Duffy-Marie Arnoult, 240; Jemal Countess, 230, 235BL; Johnny Nunez, 239BR; Bennett Raglin, 228RC

The Granger Collection, New York: 61B; R.E. Mercer, 64T; Rue des Archives, 208, 209TL; Carl Van Vechten, 60

Howard University: 48

Howard Theater Restoration, Inc.: 128

Institute of Jazz Studies, Rutgers, The State University of New Jersey: 90

Jack Shainman Gallery: Adger Cowans, 84

Collection of Robert Langmuir: 91B, 120, 123, 144, 154TR, 186, 221B, 222T

Library of Congress – Prints and Photographs: 47, 70R and 94

Magnum Photos: Eve Arnold, 25, 29 and 141L; ©Bruce Davidson, 155B; Guy Le Querrec, 223

Maryland Historical Society: Eubie Blake Collection, 63

Reprinted by permission of the Museum of the City of New York: 44, 75T, 75C, 75B; Byron Collection, 174R; Gift of the Federal Art Project, Works Projects Administration, Sid Grossman, 43, 40

Courtesy of the National Archives and Records Administration, Records of the War Department: 165-WW-127, 62; Ryan, 111-SC-196106, 71L

Courtesy of the National Museum of African American History and Culture, Smithsonian Institution: 27, 218; Collection of Brenda and Robert Strong, 125, 126; Collection of Brenda and Robert Strong: Harry Rossner, 59TL

Courtesy of the National Portrait Gallery, Smithsonian Institution: ©The Estate of Diane Arbus LLC, Diane Arbus, 23; ©Van Vechten Trust, Carl Van Vechten, 41R, 70RC; ©Bob Willoughby, 98

New York Public Library: 'STEPIN FETCHIT STARHEAD' ©1934 Twentieth Century Fox, All rights reserved, 112; **New York Public Library/New York Public Library for the Performing Arts:** 55B, 55TR, 69T, 80; **New York Public Library/Schomburg Center for Research in Black Culture**: 42, 45, 51, 54BL, 55TL, 64B, 65, 69B, 73, 76, 114, 175R; Gordon "Doc" Anderson, 169, 199RC, 216L, 221C; ©Culver Pictures, 54TR; Dummett, 195TC; Milton Meltzer, 121; Harry Rossner, 127B

Philadelphia Folklore Project: Courtesy of Edith Edwards Hunt and the Philadelphia Folklore Project, 111BL

Pittsburgh Courier: Used with permission from the *New Pittsburgh Courier*, 134

Photofest: 72, 81, 115, 119, 140RC, 146, 188, 191L, 203, 207; BBC/Photofest, 212

Prairie View A&M University, Texas: 79

Redux/The New York Times Photo Archives: 15; G. Paul Burnett, 232

Courtesy of the Robert W. Woodruff Library of the Atlanta University Center: Trezzvant Anderson Papers, artwork drawn by William Kiser Jr., designed by Trezzvant Anderson: 133T

Toots Crackin Productions/Amsterdam News: 127T

The U.S. Army Military History Institute: 133B

U.S. Daily News: ©*New York Daily News*, Bill Turnbull, 204

Yale Collection of American Literature, Beinecke Rare Book and Manuscript Library, Yale University: ©Langston Hughes Estate, 171B

Jacket Photography Credits

Front cover, marquee: Corbis, ©Randy Sulgan

Front cover, background: Getty

Back cover, top row (left to right): William P. Gottlieb; Corbis, ©Lynn Goldsmith; Corbis, ©Lynn Goldsmith; Photofest; Getty/WireImage, Bennett Raglin

Back cover, bottom row (left to right): Getty/AFP, Lucy Nicholson; Courtesy of the Apollo Theater Foundation, Inc., ©Chuck Stewart, Kwame Brathwaite; AP Images, ©Ebony Collection, Howard Morehead; Getty/WireImage, Duffy-Marie Arnoult; Courtesy of the National Portrait Gallery, Smithsonian Institution, ©Van Vechten Trust, Carl Van Vechten

Index

125th STREET APOLLO
AMERICA'S SMARTEST COLORED SHOWS!!
THEATRE 125th STREET NEAR 8th AV · TELEPHONE UN 4-4490

1937

ONE WEEK ONLY BEGINNING FRIDAY, APRIL 9th

CLARENCE ROBINSON
Producer of the New COTTON CLUB REVUE Presents

CHICK WEBB AND HIS BAND

with the greatest of all Sepia crooners and Swing Singers **ELLA FITZGERALD**

AND A FINE SUPPORTING REVUE CAST:

MORTON & MARGO Favorites — COOK & BROWN Eccentric Dancers — WOLFORD'S PETS Sensational Dog Act

"PIGMEAT" — JOHN MASON — JIMMIE BASKETTE
WHITE'S LINDYMANIACS — HILDA PERLENO — 16 DANCING DAMSELS

also "MIDNIGHT COURT" A STIRRING DRAMA OF CROOKS AND THE LAW

| MIDNIGHT SHOW SATURDAY ADDED ACTS Reserved Seats now on Sale | WED. — AMATEUR NIGHT BROADCAST FROM STAGE |

ONE WEEK — BEGINNING FRIDAY, APRIL 16th

| DON REDMAN AND HIS ORCHESTRA with LOUISE McCARROLL | 3 BERRY BROS. | CHUCK & CHUCKLES |

★ WORLD-FAMOUS ★ **APOLLO**
IN THE HEART OF FRIENDLY HARLEM!
125th St. near 8th Ave. • Tel. RI 9-1800

ONE WEEK ONLY BEGINS FRI. OCT. 22nd

The Absolutely Incomparable
PEARL BAILEY
AND HER REVUE FEATURING

BUNNY BRIGGS & **MARTIN BROS.**

PERFORMANCES | WED NIGHT AMATEURS

Blanche **CALLOWAY**

And Her SENSATIONAL **BAND**
with RHYTHM WILLIE · VELMA MIDDLETON · RED & CURLEY
And A Great Leonard Harper Revue Cast of 50

Three KADETS Western Dancing Sensations & PERRY TWINS Sensational Dancing Fighters

5 TOP HATS Singing, Playing Pride of Philadelphia & ALYCE SERF The Year's Acrobatic Marvel

PIGMEAT — JOHN MASON — JIMMIE BASKETTE
And the SIXTEEN LOVELY HARPERETTES

Also The STIRRING ROMANTIC DRAMA "The First Baby"

| MIDNIGHT SHOW SATURDAY ADDED ACTS RESERVED SEATS | WEDNESDAY AMATEUR NITE BROADCAST FROM STAGE |

WEEK ONLY BEGINNING FRI. JUNE 19th CHICK WEBB AND HIS N.B.C. ORCHESTRA

HARLEM'S HIGH SPOT **APOLLO**
WORLD'S GREATEST STAGE SHOWS
125 ST. near 8th Ave. • Tel. University 4-...

ONE WEEK ONLY BEG. FRI., APRIL 11th

WILL MASTIN TRIO
STARRING
SAMMY DAVIS JR.

RECORDING STAR **FRAN WARREN**

COLES & ATKINS - REDD FOXX

| BEAUTIFUL HORTENSE ALLEN'S | DANCING GIRLS CHORUS | Sammy's Own 26 Piece Band |

| Wed. Nite: Amateurs | Sat.: Midnite Show |

125th STREET APOLLO AMERICA'S SMARTEST COLORED SHOWS!!
THEATRE 125th STREET NEAR 8th AV · TELEPHONE UN 4-4409

ONE WEEK ONLY — BEGINNING FRIDAY, APRIL 24th

Great Comedy and Dancing Stars
BUCK AND BUBBLES

W. C. HANDY
(Father of the St. Louis Blues)
and his **St. Louis Blues Band** with BILLIE BUTLER
A New Musical Sensation!

Nat Nazarro's Juvenile Stars
CHUCK & CHUCKLES

| Bessie SMITH Queen of the Blues | EVA JESSYE CHOIR from "PORGY & BESS" | "KALOAH" Sensation of Broadway |

JOHN MASON "PIGMEAT" MONTE HAWLEY "HOT CHA" DREW 16 LOVELY HARPERETTES

ALSO WARNER OLAND in "CHARLIE CHAN AT THE CIRCUS"

| MIDNIGHT SHOW SATURDAY | WED. — AMATEUR NIGHT BROADCAST |

One Week — Beginning Friday, May 1st

| Fletcher HENDERSON and his BAND | 4 INK SPOTS |

Buck & Bubbles · W. C. Handy · Chuck & Chuckles

FEBRUARY FESTIVAL OF SHOWS AT THE **APOLLO**
AMERICA'S FINEST COLORED STAGE SHOWS!
125th ST. NEAR 8th AVE. · TELEPHONE UNIVERSITY 4 4409

IVY ANDERSON · Isabel BROWN · 4 STEP Bros. · "PIG..."

DUKE ELLINGTON
AND HIS FAMOUS ORCHEST...

AIR CONDITIONED ★ WORLD-FAMOUS ★ **APOLLO**
AMERICA'S GREATEST STAGE SHOWS
IN THE HEART OF FRIENDLY HARLEM!
125th ST. near 8th Ave. • Tele. UNiversity 4-4490

One Week, Beginning Friday, June 25

WWRL's "SOUL BROTHERS" — ROCKY "G" · BRUCE BROWN · ENOCH GREGOR... · KING COLEMAN
COMBINED TO PRESENT THEIR IDEAS OF THE GREATEST IN RHYTHM AND BLUES

THE ISLEY BROS.
DIONNE WARWICK

THE FIVE ROYAL...
THE EXCITERS
THE CHARADES
THE CARLETONS

SOME NEW — SOME "OLD" A TREAT FOR ALL AGES

| WED. NITE: AMATEURS | SAT. MIDNIGHT SHOW |

A MONTH OF SUPERLATIVE SHOWS The Greatest Ever—
HARLEM'S HIGH SPOT **APOLLO** 125 ST. near 8th Ave. • Tel. University...

Week Begin. FRIDAY, JAN. 23rd
EARL Hines and His BAND and a Cast of Headliners with RALPH COOPER

Week Only — Beg. FRI., F... LOUIS ARMSTRONG and His BAND
LOUISE BEAVERS IN PERSON

Week Only — Beg. FRI. JAN. 30th
The Loch Lomond Lass **MAXINE SULLIVAN** and the Greatest Array of Stars Yet, with Christopher Columbus and His Great Swing BAND

Week Beg. FRIDAY, FE... THE QUEEN OF SONG **Ella Fitzgerald** and Her BAND and HEADLINE REVUE
AND THEN— FOR ONE GREAT WEEK Beg...

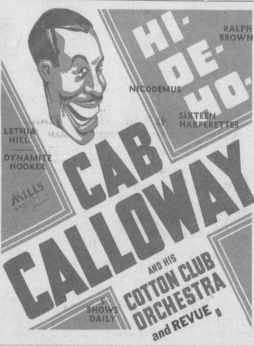